CONSPIRACUS

The Arts Council
An Chomhairle Ealaíon

Published in 1999 by Mercier Press
PO Box 5 5 French Church Street Cork
Tel: (021) 275040; Fax: (021) 274969
e.mail: books@mercier.ie
16 Hume Street Dublin 2
Tel: (01) 661 5299; Fax: (01) 661 8583
e.mail: books@marino.ie

Trade enquiries to CMD Distribution
55A Spruce Avenue
Stillorgan Industrial Park
Blackrock County Dublin
Tel: (01) 294 2556; Fax: (01) 294 2564
e.mail: cmd@columba.ie

© Criostoir O'Flynn

ISBN 1 85635 251 X
10 9 8 7 6 5 4 3 2 1
A CIP record for this title is available
from the British Library

Cover design by
Penhouse Design Group
Printed in Ireland by ColourBooks
Baldoyle Industrial Estate, Dublin 13

Published in the US and Canada by
the Irish American Book Company
6309 Monarch Park Place, Niwot,
Colorado, 80503
Tel: (303) 530-1352, (800) 452-7115
Fax: (303) 530-4488, (800) 401-9705

CONSPLAWKUS

A WRITER'S LIFE

CRIOSTOIR O'FLYNN

MERCIER PRESS

To my wife
Rita Beegan
Without whose love and fortitude
I would not have lived
To tell the tale

FOREWORDS FROM FORERUNNERS

Dante Alighieri (1265–1321):
E como quei che con lena affanata
uscito fuor del pelago alla riva
si volge all'acqua perigliosa e guata . . .
(And just as one who struggles breathless
from the sea to safety on the beach
turns back to view those waters treacherous . . .)
                                    (*Inferno*, Canto I, 22-24)

Alexander Pope (1688–1744):
Why did I write? what sin to me unknown
Dipt me in ink? my parents', or my own?
                                    (*Epistle to Dr Arbuthnot*)

Hermann Hesse (1877–1962):
Conscience provides us with an unerring standard.
Consequently literary conscience is the only law that
a writer must under all circumstances obey and cannot
evade without injury to himself and his work.
                        (*Writings on Literature*, Volume One)

Samuel Johnson (1709–84):
(*reviewing a book*) The only end of writing is to enable
the readers better to enjoy life, or better to endure it.
(*in conversation*) No man but a blockhead ever wrote,
except for money.

Herman Melville (1819–91):
Oh, Time, Strength, Cash, and Patience!

(*Moby Dick*)

Samuel Beckett: (1906–89)
Let me say before I go any further that I forgive
nobody. I wish them all an atrocious life and then the
fires and ice of hell and in the execrable generations
to come an honoured name.

(*Malone Dies*)

Miguel de Cervantes Saavedra (1547–1616):
*La pluma es lengua del alma: cuales fueren los conceptos
que en ella se engendraren, tales serán los escritos.* (The
pen is the tongue of the soul: such as are the thoughts
engendered therein, such will be the writings).

(*Don Quijote de La Mancha*).

Quintus Horatius Flaccus (65–8BC):
Nil desperandum.
(Never despair).

(*Odes*, Book One).

Contents

CONTENTS

1

WHAT YOU ARE GETTING

If you have just picked up this book in a bookshop and are considering whether you should fork out some of your hard-earned cash in exchange for it, I think it only fair to tell you what it is and what it is not.

I have been writing books and plays for about fifty years, in Irish and English, and I have published over fifty books of all kinds; novels, short stories, poetry, essays, plays, adventure stories and books for children. The process of writing, as I am doing just now, involves a period of time spent in hard mental labour and in physical isolation. It is of no interest to anyone but the writer. The end product of that process, if published as a book or produced as a play, may be of interest to readers or to audiences.

In the course of my life as a writer I have had some experiences, more or less connected with my writing, and it is about these that I have written this present book, which takes my story up to about midway through my career; and, *má fhaighimse sláinte*, as the poet Raftery said, there will be a sequel which will round it off. Like most writers, I never had the good fortune to achieve the commercial success with a book or a play that would enable me to devote all my time and energy to creative writing; so, for most of my life as a writer I had to provide the daily bread for self and dependants

11

– my wife and I were entrusted by the Creator with the procreation and rearing of seven children, three girls and four boys – by doing other work that would ensure a regular income, my literary labour being thus confined to evenings, weekends and holiday periods. Fate having directed me into the teaching profession, I spent most of my wage-earning years in the chalk mines (now the computer studios) while doing freelance work in journalism and broadcasting as another source of income. Inevitably, some of my experiences in those other areas are linked with my life as a writer.

To whet the reader's appetite, I here list some of the reasons why I hope this book will, as Dr Johnson puts it in one of the *Forewords from Forerunners* with which I have prefaced this work, 'enable the reader better to enjoy life or better to endure it.' I propose, for instance, to record how I was twice removed from teaching positions by posterior propulsion from a crozier, in short, how I was sacked by two archbishops. But before any irreligious or anti-clerical reader comments cynically on this double strike of episcopal lightning, let me add that I have also been sacked by the Director-General of Bord Fáilte (the Irish Tourist Board). I was even ignominiously sacked after only two days as a salesman (in fancy brushes). All in all, therefore, and whatever my pretensions to any literary fame, at least I may claim to be the most sacked writer in Ireland. And as for those belts of a crozier, I counter them with the claim that I am the only writer in Ireland – maybe in the world – who has worn the parish priest's socks.

I am also, I think, the most censored writer in Ireland, having had my work suppressed or rejected on moral or political grounds by the Abbey Theatre, the Department of Education, the Irish Book Club (*An Club Leabhar*), the Jesuits, and certain newspapers and magazines. I have never seen any reference to this censorship of my work, nor have I even seen my name in any of the books or articles written about literary censorship in Ireland in the twentieth century.

Since such books and articles are usually written by American academics, their authors obviously are guided by Irish sources or advisers who are either unaware of my literary career or choose to ignore it. The thoughtful reader will wonder at this. So do I.

I should mention also that, as far as I am aware – we were cautioned by a good teacher in the primary school to be careful about making sweeping statements – I am the only writer in Ireland who has taught mixed classes in a bedroom. And I am also, I think, the only Irish writer who has jogged at thirty thousand feet above the Himalayas, who has lectured a group of university students in China in the open air and in the dark, and who has caused Éamon de Valera to laugh in public. Obviously, it will not be possible to pack all these stories into one volume, but I hope the second part of this chronicle will be as entertaining as the first.

As I have been writing in our two languages for about fifty years and have done work in all literary genres, including the epistolary style in Letters to the Editor, this account of my life as a writer might also be of interest as part of the history of literature and theatre in Ireland during the second half of the twentieth century.

These then are some of the reasons why I think this book might be worth buying. If you buy it and feel in the end that you did not get value for money, you can always use the book to light the fire or to prop up a bockedy chair or table.

2

'THE CHILD IS FATHER OF THE MAN'
(WORDSWORTH)

When I am asked how or why I became a writer, I sometimes answer facetiously, 'by congenital defect'. I never made any decision to become a writer. When I was about ten years old I began to write poems, stories and plays. I have given an account of this early manifestation of the affliction in my book *There Is an Isle: A Limerick Boyhood* (Mercier Press, 1998). But at that time I was also much given to playing the flute, having been taught by my father; I was also dabbling in art with a large box of watercolours. Given the appropriate circumstances, I suppose I might have developed into a painter or a musician, but in the Ireland of that time – at least in my part of it, a working-class area of Limerick City in the Thirties – the only kind of art to which we were exposed was in the form of religious or patriotic pictures and statues which, whatever their value in the inculcation and development of religious or patriotic sentiment were, as I now understand, of little artistic merit. As a school subject, art was not even mentioned in the primary school, and at the secondary level it was considered a very minor optional extra more related to mechanical drawing than to anything connected with the Muses.

Music was much more of an influence in our social lives

and as part of our formal school education. Local bands added colour as well as harmony to the public scene as they paraded through the streets on Sundays or ceremonial occasions. In those days when the radio was still a novelty and television unknown, variety concerts were universally popular and people were able to provide their own entertainment, vocal or instrumental, in the home or at social functions. I have told in *There Is an Isle* how in our own street near King John's Castle a cultured elderly brother and sister taught violin and piano, respectively, but the cost of such professional tuition was so prohibitive for us children playing on the street outside that house of music that we got only the smell of it, so to speak. My father, as indicated, taught us to play the flute and to read music, he having acquired those accomplishments in one of the local bands under the tutelage and baton of his older brother, and I bless his memory when I play a few tunes in solitude as an antidote to the stress and strain of writing or of life in general.

Literature, oral or written, was the principal cultural influence on life in the society in which I grew up. In the Irish language, oral literature, in the form of verse and story, had been the only kind available to the Irish people for centuries. The novel and the drama, being urban arts, were confined to the garrisoned cities where the English-speaking colonists regarded England as their cultural home. With the compulsory teaching of English in the National Schools set up in 1831, the consequent deterioration of Irish due to this and other causes and the proliferation of newspapers and books in English, literature in English, in all its forms and at all levels, became available in print to all classes of society. Through the public libraries, the treasures of English literature, building up over those centuries when Irish literature had no access to the printing press, became available to the general public. The learning by rote which was a basic element in the educational system, and the

15

compulsory attendance at school up to the age of fourteen, ensured that pupils had memorised an anthology of poems and stories, as well as a repertoire of songs, hymns and patriotic ballads, by the time they left school. While this carried on the tradition of oral literature, the graded school readers gave all pupils a thorough grounding in the printed forms and enabled those who so desired to make full use of the public libraries.

While we never heard the term 'creative writing' which is so glibly bandied about nowadays when children are urged to scribble 'poems' instead of learning to spell, we were familiar with an exercise called composition. This developed our linguistic powers of description, narration and imagination by compelling us to fill a certain number of pages on such topics as *An Old Penny tells its Story, A Walk in the Country in Autumn, A Dream I Had, My Favourite Incident in History, What I Would Like to Be*, and so on. The professional touring companies which had brought live drama to the towns of Ireland in our parents' time had been largely superseded by drama in the form of the film – the local cinema where we went to the 'pictures' was actually an old theatre where my parents in their young days saw blood-curdling or tearjerking melodramas performed – but we were introduced to live drama in the form of school plays as early as the infant school. From this, and from seeing sketches and plays performed in local halls, came the practice of some of the girls in our street, as in many others, of putting on domestic entertainments, in the house or in a backyard, which consisted of songs, dances, recitations and short plays, the latter often composed by themselves.

Like most children in those days when school was a prison where corporal punishment, often severe and sometimes sadistic, was an accepted part of the daily routine, being dished out liberally for failure at lessons, for inattention or talking, for blotting copybooks or similar crimes, and for being late even by a fraction of a minute, I had a natural dislike of it. But from the time when I first began to hear poems recited or stories told at our own fireside I gulped them in with every breath and when I was given my first reading book in the Infant School it seemed to me that Christmas had come early. So, when it came to writing those essays or 'compositions', or to taking part in a school play, something in my spirit responded in a way that made me feel as if I had been put under a magic spell. Inevitably, I suppose, I began to write my own things, poems, stories and plays. Inevitably, also, the increasing pressure of formal school studies put an end to that first childish impulse towards the creation of literature. By the time I felt it again I was in my late teens and hoping to earn a living as a teacher; but even then I did not consciously plan or wish to become a writer – to quote again from Hermann Hesse, one of those prefatory *Forerunners*, 'You can be a writer, but not become one.' I found myself beginning to write poems, stories, articles, and eventually plays but I had no notion of what was happening to me, and I did not realize that my life would be taken over by that urge to construct something remarkable with words just as a composer does with sounds or an artist with colour, mass, light and shade. So, looking back over half a century since then, I ask with Alexander Pope, why did I write? And I answer, seriously this time, I don't know.

3

APPRENTICE YEARS

Just as I never decided to be a writer when I began to write, first at the age of ten and again a decade later, I never decided what kind of writer I would be, poet, playwright or a writer of fiction. The topics, themes and ideas that gave me the stimulus towards literary activity seemed themselves to make the technical choice of the particular genre that suited them. Similarly, I made no choice of linguistic medium but seemed to drift into being a bilingual writer, writing in English or Irish as the theme or the market dictated. I had begun to write in English, my home language but, added to the basic impetus towards artistic creativity, I felt a very strong spiritual urge to write in Irish also, an urge obviously atavistic and patriotic but which commercial sense, if I had been possessed of any, would have advised me strongly to suppress.

Having been born and reared in Limerick City, I was not a native speaker of Irish although our dialect of Hiberno-English still contained some pure Irish words and many of our idioms were derived from the Irish our ancestors spoke for thousands of years. However, I had been learning Irish formally from the day I entered the infant school at the age of three and a half, and up to the end of primary school all subjects were taught through Irish. While this system ensured that all pupils were given a fairly thorough grounding in

Irish grammar and vocabulary, the corporal punishment associated with learning all subjects seemed to militate especially against Irish, a subject which had little or no relevance to our daily life. At the secondary school level, while Irish was not the medium of instruction in the majority of schools, a pass in Irish was compulsory in order to acquire the Leaving Certificate and honours was a requirement for entry to the civil service and the teacher training colleges. These factors, linked with the obvious fact that almost all the politicians who were urging the nation to revive our ancestral language did not practise what they preached – you could even become a government minister or *taoiseach* without knowing a word of Irish – and that Irish was not necessary, might even be a hindrance, in the affairs of daily life, caused a natural resentment and antipathy towards the language, especially among those who failed in the subject through their own inability or through inadequate instruction.

In the latter stages of my academic career Irish had become one of my favourite subjects and as a teacher I was now using the language daily. My studies in history and in Irish literature combined to make me feel it a patriotic duty for any young writer who could do so to write in Irish. I felt a spiritual bond with the Irish poets of former centuries that was a very different emotion from that experienced when reading the much more abundant treasures of English literature. Publishing in Irish was subsidised by the government as part of the general policy of bilingualism but the market for a writer in Irish was limited to a small fraction of the population. Fifty years on, as I write, the readership in Irish has been even further depleted by the influence of the mass media, the increasingly materialistic outlook on life generated by Ireland's economic prosperity and the emphasis on the learning of foreign languages resulting from Ireland's membership of the European Community as well as from the increase in foreign travel. It should be noted, however, that both in English and Irish the opportunities for publication open to new writers in Ireland were much more numerous in the middle of the twentieth century than they are now as we near its end. In a society where radio and the cinema were the only entertainments competing with reading and the theatre – and where radio itself, unlike its equivalent today, was a large market for stories, drama and literary talks – magazines of all kinds were popular, and unlike their glossy counterparts today, those magazines, both religious and secular, contained more print than pictures and their contents usually included some prose and verse, albeit of widely varying standards.

I suppose writers remember their first published work as fondly as a mother remembers the birth of her first child. I recall reading an essay entitled *My First Article*, by the English author, J. B. Priestley, in which he described the thrill of buying the magazine, his elation at observing a woman on the bus actually turning the pages of her copy and the deflation as she paused only momentarily to glance at the title of his piece before turning the page in search of something more interesting. Writers like myself who learned the real value of a shilling early in life will also have a clear recollection of the first cheque, that document more precious than its face value since it is the tangible proof that some professional literary judge has objectively considered a piece of work to be of such merit that it is worth paying for. I should mention that, long before I received my own first cheque, I had momentarily become a professional writer on the day when, at the age of ten, I was rewarded with a big brown penny by a genial schools inspector (certainly an exception to the rule in those days) who, having chatted to us about the figures of poetic diction, offered that prize to the first pupil who would compose a sentence as an example of alliteration. Of more lasting value than the financial reward was the comment of the decent man himself. 'I think we have the makings of a poet here,' he said to our teacher, who made it unanimous by replying, 'I think so too.'

In spite of that early introduction to professionalism and to the market value of literature, I wrote my first poems in English and Irish without any thought of payment. My first published poem in English was one of the minor results of a decision taken in the Vatican. The Pope having declared 1950 a Holy Year, one of the resultant events in my native city of Limerick was an exhibition of historic and contemporary religious art and sculpture in the Holy Rosary church on the Ennis Road. This exhibition was organized by the parish priest, Monsignor Molony, who was noted for his involvement in archaeology, music and cultural affairs generally (like the aforementioned schools inspector, this made him an exception to the rule in his own profession). After visiting the exhibition, I wrote a poem about it, which I now forget except that it began with the line: 'A chalice raised amid the secret hills'.

My only personal dealings with our cultured monsignorial parish priest up to that point consisted of occasionally serving his Mass when we lived in St Mary's parish and I was an altar boy in the Convent of Mercy. He was at that time the bishop's secretary, and I suppose he sometimes stood in for the local clergy at times of illness or holidays. However, I assumed that he would like to see the poem inspired by his Holy Year exhibition; so, I sent it to him. It was not acknowledged (in his delightful essay, *The Two Races of Men*, Charles Lamb divided the human race into the borrowers and the lenders; experience inclines me to follow the distinction made by our Divine Lord himself, and in much the same proportion, between those who say thanks and those who do not). When I opened the *Limerick Leader* at the weekend, there was my poem in print. I have related this episode in some detail not only because that was my first published poem but also because, as the reader will learn in due course, both the cultured monsignor and the editor who published the poem at his suggestion were destined to figure in a very different light in later episodes of my literary career.

My first letter to the editor, and my first article, were also published in the *Limerick Leader*, the latter earning me my first journeyman guinea when, after some delay, I wrote a personal letter to the editor pointing out that I had not been paid. I never met that editor but I made formal contact with Monsignor Molony two years later when I stood at the altar rails in St Munchin's church, side by side with a lovely Limerick girl of nineteen, Rita Beegan (to whom, as you have no doubt observed, this book is dedicated) and we promised to be husband and wife, 'for better, for worse, etc. till death do us part', and the monsignor, as the Church's official witness, gave us God's blessing on our sacramental contract. If that lovely girl could have foreseen all the 'worse' that was to come her way because she was marrying a young writer who would have to earn the daily bread largely as a teacher, she might have heeded the cautionary whispering of her guardian angel (provided that celestial spirit was doing its job and not distracted by the pleasant nature of the proceedings in this most important of all human events).

My first poems in Irish were a lyrical effusion describing the changing colours of the evening sky over the Clare hills and one entitled 'Jeanne d'Arc', written after I had seen the film in which the Swedish actress, Ingrid Bergman, tried to portray the ebullient eighteen-year-old peasant girl who, early in the fifteenth century, took over leadership of the dispirited French army in the war against the English, gained spectacular victories for the weakling dauphin and ended up being burnt as a witch when captured by her political enemies and tried by her ecclesiastical ones. Unlike my Holy Year poem in English, my first poems in Irish brought me financial as well as spiritual reward when, along with my first short story in Irish, they were published in Dublin in the Gaelic League magazine, *Feasta*. The editor, Seosamh Ó Duibhginn, wrote to me in very encouraging terms and asked me to submit further items for consideration. At the same time that I first submitted some poems and a story to the magazine, *Feasta*, I sent a similar batch to another Irish magazine, *Comhar*, which was of academic origin and therefore of somewhat higher literary pretensions. It would appear, however, that the literary efforts of a young and unknown writer in Limerick City were apparently not of sufficient merit or interest to warrant either acknowledgement or return. It will be seen that in addition to serving a diligent apprenticeship in the craft of writing and the art of literature, I was also learning some of the aspects of life for the professional writer connected with the more mundane business of marketing the literary product.

Since there were no courses in writing available to the beginner in those times, no events such as Listowel Writers' Week and no writer-in-residence schemes sponsored by the Arts Council and other academic or local authority patrons, I had nothing to guide my neophyte efforts but my experience of the literature I had studied academically or in private. I had been an avid reader since childhood, and one of the reasons why I regret having become a professional writer is that the time and energy I have had to spend in creating my own work has left me very little leisure to devote to reading. Actually, I sometimes wonder whether all these new systems of encouraging writing talent breed more disappointment and frustration than occasional beneficient results. So, like the Little Red Hen in the fable, I had to adopt the DIY method when seeking instruction in the techniques of the various literary genres. This meant reading everything and anything I could find in the Limerick City Library on any kind of writing.

In these days when the computer is as much a part of the classroom furniture as the blackboard was in former times, it is hardly necessary to advise the would-be writer to acquire the skill of typing. In my schooldays, typing was taught only to girls, and then only in technical or secretarial schools, to prepare them to earn their bread typing documents in an office. I taught myself to type after two articles in Irish, written in longhand, which I sent off to the Irish weekly newspaper, *Inniú*, (now, like the *Irish Press*, to be read only in the archives of the National Library) were returned to me by the editor, Ciarán Ó Nualláin, a brother of Brian O'Nolan (aka Flann O'Brien or Myles na Gopaleen) and himself the author of a few thrillers in Irish as well as of a book about Myles entitled *Óige an Dearthár* (*The Brother's Youth*). I was to become indebted to another brother when my first novel in Irish, *Lá Dá Bhfaca Thú*, appeared in 1955 in a cover designed by Mícheál Ó Nualláin. In returning my longhand efforts, Ciarán praised my talent, encouraged me to continue writing – and strongly advised me to learn to type.

So, on a rickety machine bought for two pounds in a pawnshop and with a manual from the crafts section of the library, I began to tap out *a,s,d,f,g*. Being a natural *ciotóg* who, as was then the pedagogic practice, had been forced to write with the right hand, and being also a flautist from the age of five, I had the advantage of ambidexterity to ease the pain. Nevertheless, watching me as I sat at the kitchen table, my mother worried that I would do serious damage to my fingers and my eyes, and I was glad of her frequent resort to the traditional 'cup that cheers' as a respite from our respective hard labour. With the money from my first book in Irish I bought a brand-new Underwood Portable in a solid case. I wrote many millions of words on that machine, and when, about ten years ago, I somewhat apprehensively transferred my now more skilful fingers to my first computer keyboard, I did not have the heart to throw it out. It rests in honoured retirement in a press only a few yards from where I am typing these words on my second and even more user-friendly computer. And who knows? It may come to my aid yet once more some day when the screen of this new-fangled gadget goes blankety-blank on me and I in the middle of my latest effort to put the best words together in the best order.

4

A PLAY LOST AND A PLAY UNSEEN

If the Irish people were deprived of the art of drama during the centuries while it developed in England and other European countries, when they abandoned their own language in favour of English their natural gift of the gab caused them to take to the stage like ducks to water. Apart from the contribution of Irish dramatists like Goldsmith, Sheridan, Boucicault, Shaw, Synge, O'Casey and Beckett to the art of drama in English, the theatre had already become a feature of social life in the cities long before touring companies from England brought the melodramas of the Victorian and Edwardian eras to every town in Ireland. My mother often enthused about such gripping classics as *The Bells* and *The Dumb Man of Manchester* which she had seen in her youth. With the so-called Literary Revival and the complicated birth of the Abbey Theatre at the end of the nineteenth century, the amateur drama group soon became as common as the various other clubs in every city and town. The advent of radio in the Twenties and its proliferation in the ensuing decades caused drama in a new art form to become available even in the smallest villages and the most remote households. When the Sunday Night Play established itself as one of the most popular items on Radio Éireann, people in any part of Ireland who could never hope to sit in the Abbey Theatre in Dublin were able to imagine themselves there as they visualised the play adapted from its original stage version.

I had twice sat in the 'gods' at the Gaiety Theatre in Dublin during my days as a student in the teachers training college in Drumcondra with a fellow-student, Tom Hurley from Dungarvan. I queued for an hour and paid a shilling I could ill afford to enjoy Verdi's *Il Trovatore* and *Rigoletto* while peering down at the tops of the heads of the visiting artists and the chorus of the Dublin Grand Opera Society. I had, however, never visited the Abbey Theatre, which was within walking distance of the College, nor was I aware of any of my fellow-students having done so. I cannot remember even having heard any mention of it from our lecturers. In those post-war years institutions like the training college were still being run on Victorian lines, much like prisons and orphanages, and cultural activities like theatre, art and music were generally regarded as interests of the dilettante which had better be avoided until the serious business of getting a job for life had been successfully accomplished.

Modern students will find it hard to believe that we were allowed out from our all-male college only three nights a week, having to ask special permission of the dean to stay out till 11 pm. After that hour any latecomers found themselves in exterior darkness for a while, later in hot water and grounded for a fortnight afterwards. This system, of course, was in no way attributable to the harassed Vincentian priests whose order had been saddled with running the place by an Archbishop of Dublin in the previous century. My friend and I were gladly given special permission to be as late as was necessary on the nights we went across the city to see the operas in the Gaiety and on our return around midnight we found the Boss himself waiting to let us in and wish us goodnight after he had asked how we liked the show. Even if we had been urged by the archbishop himself to visit the Abbey Theatre we were much more naturally inclined to spend our meagre pocket-money by going to the céilí and old-time dances at the Teachers Club in Parnell Square. There, as student teachers, we had a half-price concession and were sure of meeting what Brendan Behan called 'female members of the opposite sex'.

It was through the medium of the other famous Dublin theatre, the Gate, that I was enabled to see a wide range of live drama before I eventually sat down to tap out the first words of my own first play on my Underwood Portable. Not that I visited the Gate any more than the Abbey in those impecunious and rule-bound student days in Dublin. In fact, it was the Gate that kindly visited me – in Limerick. The partners in the Gate, Lord Longford and the English-born theatrical duo, Hilton Edwards and Mícheál MacLiammóir, having followed the ancient Irish tradition of civil war, signed a treaty allocating the theatre to each side for six months. While the flamboyant thespian pair were in occupation, Longford Productions toured in the Land of the Culchies beyond the Pale. And so, in addition to the Abbey plays put on by the local amateur group, the College Players, I saw plays by Shaw, Sheridan and Wilde produced by the portly earl himself.

A further stimulus to my second birth as a dramatist (remember my initial efforts as playwright, actor and director at the age of ten, what I call my Woodrow's Backyard period – see *There Is an Isle*) was provided by another touring company, that of Anew McMaster, brother-in-law of MacLiammóir, who brought Shakespeare to every town in Ireland on a financial shoestring. In later years I would hear theatrical people in Dublin making disparaging remarks about McMaster's flamboyant style of acting and sympathising with the tribulations of the aspiring actors who learned their trade in such companies as his. (One such was Milo O'Shea, whom I saw playing a goggle-eyed Lancelot Gobbo to McMaster's Shylock, and who went on to play Friar Laurence in Zeffirelli's film of *Romeo and Juliet*.) Yet

27

to this day I can recall the exhilaration of seeing McMaster play the four great roles of *Hamlet, King Lear, Othello* and *The Merchant of Venice* during a three-week season at the City Theatre in Limerick.

All these plays I had studied academically as printed texts but it was only when I saw them live on stage that I realised something of what Shakespeare's audiences experienced. I also came to the conclusion that plays should be seen and not read and that the prescribing of Shakespeare as a text for written examinations is inimical to the inculcation of an understanding and a love of drama. In spite of this personal belief, as a teacher of English at secondary school level in my latter years in the chalk mines I had no choice but to grind teenage students line by line through the mere words of several of Shakespeare's theatrical masterpieces, plays which the man himself intended not only never to be read but to be seen only by sophisticated adults. The academic pundits who prescribe *Romeo and Juliet* as a text for fourteen-year-olds whose daily reading, if any, consists largely of magazines about pop stars, never have to suffer the spiritual and intellectual agony of translating each line into modern English or waffling through the *double entendres* which apparently titillated Elizabethan audiences.

Having been singled out at birth by the Muses to suffer the lifelong and unceasing torment of literary creativity, it was inevitable that, unlike the more fortunate mortals who witnessed and enjoyed along with me those plays put on by the College Players, Longford Productions and McMaster's Shakespearean Company, I began to conceive a new play in my soul. I wrote a three-act play, of which I remember nothing but that it featured the common thematic triangle of a corrupt politician, his unsuspecting daughter and the upright young hero who loves her and unmasks and unseats her father. This effort was entitled *The Crooked Hill*, whatever that means. I was still so naïve in the ways of the literary world that it never occurred to me to start at the top by sending the play to the Abbey Theatre in Dublin. If anyone had suggested such a procedure to me, I would have replied, in all honesty as well as in blissful ignorance, that the directors of that famous institution were surely eminent literary people who would never condescend to read the first play of an unknown young writer. So, I started at the bottom by submitting my play to the local amateur group, the College Players. By the time I left Limerick with my young bride about a year later to take up a teaching post in Dublin I had heard nothing about *The Crooked Hill*. Subsequent enquiries went unacknowledged, and as I had not yet learned the essential practical lesson of making copies of all scripts, I never laid eyes again on the text of my first stage play.

My first radio play was written because I heard a voice on Radio Éireann announcing a competition for a forty-five minute play in Irish, the prize on offer being fifty pounds. All I knew about the technique of writing a radio play was that it is like an ordinary stage play except that everyone in the audience is blind; everything depends on words and sound effects and the scene can switch at the behest of the imagination. Also, being at the time between temporary jobs as a teacher – I eventually left my native city because I could not get a permanent position there or thereabouts and was offered one in Dublin – that prize of fifty pounds (my last salary cheque was a little less than five pounds per week) was a very tempting carrot to any donkey of a dramatist, even a beginner. My effort, entitled *Na Cimí* (*The Prisoners*) was about the death of an Irish priest in the Korean war – several missionary priests had been murdered by the North Koreans – and the best I hoped for was that the experts in Radio Éireann would tell me that it was a good effort and that I should try again. What they eventually told me was that my play did not qualify for the competition because it was not long enough – it would fill only thirty minutes instead of the stipulated forty-five. They also told me was that they were so impressed with my play that they were accepting it for broadcasting, contract enclosed!

It would be another ten years before Radio Éireann became Radio Teilifís Éireann, and so the fact that a young local writer was to have his first radio play broadcast to the nation was given generous publicity in the *Limerick Leader*. I gratefully record that ever since then all my literary efforts, except one, have resulted in similar recognition and encouragement in that journal. (The exception was the poem I wrote on the death of my friend and one-time classmate, Seán South, in 1957, during an IRA attack on a police barracks in the Six Counties, and as will be narrated in a later chapter, that piece was to cause more trouble for me than the cold shoulder from a local editor). Along with the news about the forthcoming radio play, the *Leader* published a photo of the 'young Limerick writer'. While my mother was pleased to see it, she thought I looked far too serious. 'Why didn't you smile?' she complained. To which 'young Limerick writer' replied, with all the wisdom of a sprat who couldn't teach his grandmother to suck eggs, 'But, Ma, writers aren't *supposed* to smile.'

As the fateful night approached, my mother had another complaint. My parents were both born in 1894 and so they had not been taught Irish in school, a loss which they both regretted. They encouraged us to learn Irish, as did also our maternal grandmother Connolly, and they used to pause in their own work to listen to us chanting the Irish poems we had to learn off by heart as part of our homework. Now, however, my mother complained that she would not be able to understand my play on the radio; not only that, but neighbours, relations and friends farther afield were asking her what the play was about and she could only tell them the essential fact that it was about the death of an Irish priest in the Korean war. So, her maternal pride at war with her lifelong patriotic sentiments, she said, 'Why didn't you write it in English so that everybody could understand it?' I reminded her that I had written it as an entry in a competition for a radio play in Irish, but I typed out several copies of a synopsis of the plot in English which were passed around before the night of the broadcast.

Before that night my father came home one night a somewhat disgruntled man, his paternal pride in my literary achievement having received a severe dint. A man with whom he had played in the Sarsfield Fife and Drum Band in the halcyon days when my Uncle Dan led them to victory in the Tailteann Games of 1924 had told him of a conversation this man had with an old resident of Watergate, my father's native quarter in the Irishtown. (For Irishtown and English-town as the two parts of the hourglass-shaped old walled city of Limerick, see *There Is an Isle*.) It went like this:

'Did you see in the *Leader* about a son of Richie Flynn that used to live near you?'

'What about him?'

'He's going to have a play he wrote done on Radio Éireann.'

'Ah, I wouldn't be surprised,' says the old Watergate man. 'Them Flynns were all a bit strange.'

In his philosophic musings on life, my father often recalled that conversation as an example of the strange ways of human nature.

Some time after the broadcast, I received a letter from St Patrick's Seminary in Maynooth, then a flourishing institution whose episcopal owners would have been horrified if the Lord above had sent them some wild-eyed prophet announcing that before the end of the century the seminary would have only a handful of candidates for the priesthood and be only a small part of a mixed university campus. Apparently it was the custom in Maynooth in those years of approved patriotism that the students who were members of the Irish language society would put on a concert in Irish for St Patrick's Day. A standard item in the concert being a one-act play in Irish, the student committee were asking my permission to put on a stage adaptation of my radio play, *Na*

Cimí. They had heard it on radio and had obtained a copy of the script from Radio Éireann and they were willing to pay me a suitable fee. I was so astonished that I not only wrote back granting permission but, with still vivid memories of my recent hungry days in the training college, I waived . the fee on condition that their boss allow the students involved in the play to spend it on 'lemonade and biscuits' or something similar. A grateful reply informed me that this condition would be graciously complied with by the competent authority. The Maynooth students also courteously invited me to attend the performance of my play but logistically and financially this was not possible. No wonder then that in subsequent impecunious weeks, coming down from the cloud of elation to which I had been wafted by two unseen performances of my play, on radio and on stage, I resorted to the local idiom to ask the once again unemployed young teacher who was the alter ego of 'young Limerick writer': 'Are you a fool or an eejit or what, to be turning down a fee from any source?'

Although, as I have said, I would not have dreamed of submitting my first effort at a stage play to the Abbey Theatre in Dublin, by a strange quirk of fate my first contact with that institution was made through my first radio play. The guest director of that play, Tomás Mac Anna, was employed at the Abbey Theatre as director of the one-act plays in Irish which were occasionally produced as a tailpiece to the current English play. The guest director of the Maynooth stage version of my play was a young actor from the Abbey named Ray McAnally, who had himself spent some time there as a seminarian. This double linking of my play with the Abbey caused me to consider that it would be suitable for production there. I submitted it and it was rejected, no reason given. Subsequently, it was staged by some amateur companies in Irish drama festivals and in some schools and colleges. I was destined to make the acquaintance of both Mac Anna and Ray McAnally when I moved to Dublin in the following year. In the meantime, on 18 July 1951, the old theatre that had taken its name from a street named after an ancient abbey in Dublin burnt down and the company moved to the old Queen's Theatre in Pearse Street on the other side of the Liffey. It would remain there until the new Abbey Theatre opened on the old site in 1966.

5

A JACK OF ALL TRADES

Although I became a writer without ever deciding to do so, as soon as I realised that I was one I knew that this was what I wanted to be for the rest of my life. Not that the Muses of Art and Music let me go willingly. If at the age of ten, in addition to writing poems, plays and stories, I was also playing the flute and spending hours drawing and painting, at the age of twenty I was taking a sketch-book and a box of watercolours when I cycled out alone to the Clare hills or when we went camping for a weekend at Doonass, at Doon Lake near Broadford or in the picturesque Clare Glens near Newport. And after my first year's labour in the chalk mines I bought a secondhand piano and began to teach myself, making sufficient progress to realize that I was starting ten years too late.

Within two years of slowly tapping out that first *a,s,d,f,g,* on a battered old typewriter, I had tapped out efforts at every possible kind of creative writing – and in two languages. I had written poems and short stories in Irish and English, articles in both languages for magazines and newspapers, a full-length stage play, a radio play in Irish and another in English; for the latter I was spared the extra chore of making out a synopsis for parents and neighbours. I had also written three novels in Irish for young readers. Finally, I had written my first Letter to the Editor (of the *Limerick Leader*) and as I have noted earlier the public epistolary style is a distinct if now little-practised form of literary work. In my experience, most writers are too prudent or cautious to express a controversial opinion in the public press where it might result in unfavourable repercussions with the political, literary or media establishments.

Most writers also seem to have a natural talent for practising the art of literature in one genre only, be it fiction, drama or poetry. Whether the writer who practises all of them is a more complete literary artist or, as the adage puts it, is 'jack of all trades and a master of none' is a question for literary criticism; but it is a matter of literary history that fiction writers as diverse as the Spanish author of one of the world's greatest novels, Miguel Cervantes, and the American, Henry James (1843-1916), considered by many to be the finest novelist in English, tried to write plays and failed, as did that magnificent prose writer, Samuel Johnson. James Joyce's efforts in poetry and drama give little indication of literary talent, while some attempts at plays by Irish novelists and poets of our own time, put on at the Abbey or the Gate with much blowing of publicity trumpets while plays by proven or unknown dramatists were being summarily rejected, only proved the truth of another adage which advises the cobbler to stick to his last.

Poetry is obviously the easiest literary genre to practise, anyone can scribble a few lines and call them a poem, especially since metre and rhyme have been conveniently discarded; but even in the sixteenth century the aristocratic French essayist, Michel de Montaigne (1533–92), was expressing the fervent wish 'that this warning would be seen above the doors of all printers' shops, to forbid the entry of so many versifiers (what numbers we have of that tribe!): *verum nil securius est malo poeta (truly there is no one more confident than a bad poet).*' And the line he quotes comes from Martial, writing in Rome in the latter half of the first century. That phlegmatic German genius, Hermann Hesse, some of whose severe dicta I have already borrowed, observes that there is more pleasure in writing bad poems than in reading the best. Indeed it is a moot point whether a poet should be called a writer at all unless, like Homer, Virgil, Milton and Dante, he/she constructs an epic, in which case the poem takes on more of the nature of the novel and the drama. In fact, Dante called his epic poem simply a *commedia*, which in Italian means a play, and an American critic, Francis Fergusson, in a book on the art of theatre, described *La Divina Commedia*, as it is now known, as the greatest *dramatic* work in the world's literature.

When I wrote plays as a boy of ten, my motivation was probably histrionic as well as creative. Having taken part in plays in the infant school and in the primary school, I felt the inclination to act as much as to write. So, although we are told Shakespeare played only minor roles in his plays – maybe he just couldn't act; or was there some physical, political or other impediment that kept him from playing Hamlet, Lear, Othello and Shylock as I had seen Anew McMaster do on the stage in Limerick? – I unwittingly followed the example of Molière and many other playwright-managers by writing, directing and acting in those juvenile experiments in the art of drama. As with the urge to write, this other creative impulse also returned with adulthood and it found an outlet when I became associated with the Gaelic League.

Although in architectural terms it is only one in a long terrace of Georgian houses, many of which, in Limerick as in Dublin and other cities, became tenements in the post-Famine period, the house at 18 Thomas Street which has been the local centre of the Gaelic League since early in the twentieth century is a historic building. Many of the founders of the League, including Douglas Hyde himself, and many of the leaders of the 1916 Rising, spoke at meetings there and probably even danced at the *céilí* in the hall. As a teenage factory girl, my mother went to classes there with her friends in the early days of Sinn Féin. She remembered only some odd words and garbled phrases in Irish from the few lessons they had from Seoirse Mac Fhlannchadha (Geroge Clancy), the close friend of James Joyce at university who was later to become Mayor of Limerick and be murdered by the Black-and-Tans in front of his wife in the hallway of his own home beside the Shannon. The practical lessons in using a sewing-machine and other domestic crafts taught by ladies of the 'quality' proved of more lasting benefit to the daughters of the working classes.

Founded in 1893 as a non-political organization for the promotion of Irish as a spoken language (not, as some hostile revisionists maintain, with the ludicrous and impossible aim of eliminating English) the Gaelic League inevitably became linked in its membership with the physical force tradition in Irish politics, and already by 1915 Pádraig Pearse (1879–1916), who had been one of its most enthusiastic organisers and editor of its official paper, described the League as 'a dead letter'. The further years of military struggle in the Black-and-Tan war of 1919–21, and the internecine bitterness caused by the even more tragic Civil War after the signing of the Anglo-Irish Treaty, left a cultural movement like the Gaelic League only a poor shadow of its youthful self. Still, in every city and town where it had established a centre, a handful of faithful enthusiasts kept the ideals of the League alive and tried to maintain the annual Feis, Irish classes, and the occasional *céilí*, even if the latter was reduced to the single annual occasion of Lá 'le Phádraig.

It was through my older brother, Dick, who had added the skills of drumming to his other musical accomplishments and was currently the percussion part of the three-piece *céilí* band, that I began to frequent the League premises. In addition to enjoying the dances at the *céilí* – how much more social and civilized those traditional dances of every nation were than the formless individualistic gyrations in a cacophonous milieu that pass for dancing today – I soon became involved in helping out with the Irish classes, adding a fireside song session on winter nights. Oddly enough, in spite of this involvement, and my own enjoyment of the dances, I never actually joined the Gaelic League. Perhaps the writer I had become was instinctively aware that the artist *qua* artist must not only be a loner but must also be wary of expending time and energy on activities, however worthwhile in themselves, which are a distraction from the purpose of the artist in life, which is simply to create art in one form or another.

I was not yet wary, or aware, enough however to refuse the invitation to be coopted to the committee of the Gaelic League in a cultural capacity. This was made to me by one of a new and younger faction who were trying to take over power from the old-timers whom they considered to be too set in their ways. The young man who proffered that flattering invitation had sat beside me when we were about twelve years old and in our first year in the Christian Brothers secondary school in Sexton Street and enduring the extra hours entailed in grinding for the corporation scholarship designed to help students through the secondary school. He was known to us then as Jack South, and he was no more enthusiastic about learning Irish or anything else than the rest of us, apart from the natural swots who are to be found in every class. My boyhood impression of him was that of a friendly and pleasant lad who was big and strong for his age, with distinctive sandy hair, a quiet but impressive speech; he was inclined to smile expressively rather than to guffaw and wore heavy boots that should be avoided when we played soccer with a tennis-ball in the school yard – not that he was ever guilty of foul play in that or any other of our games.

By the time he came asking me to join him on the Gaelic League committee as a cultural officer he was working as a clerk in the office of a timber company, and he had become known all over Limerick as Seán Sabhat, an idealistic and self-sacrificing enthusiast for the Irish language. He was also a member of *An Réalt*, the Irish language section of the Legion of Mary, a Catholic lay organization founded in Dublin in the twenties by a civil servant, Frank Duff, to put Catholic social teaching into practice. As a lieutenant in the FCA (*Fórsa Cosanta Áitiúil* – Local Defence Force, a part-time auxiliary section of the army) Seán cut a fine figure as he marched at the head of his company in public parades. This was the young man who was destined to die a violent death on New Year's Eve in 1957 after an IRA attack on a police barracks in the Six Counties, and whose name, along with that of a Monaghan youth, Fergal O'Hanlon, would become known all over Ireland through the ballad 'Seán South of Garryowen'. His funeral in Limerick would be the biggest since that of George Clancy, the mayor murdered in 1920 by the Black-and-Tans, and he was buried in the Republican plot along with the men who died in the Anglo-Irish conflict or in the subsequent Civil War.

The revisionist view of all aspects of Ireland's long struggle for freedom has meant inevitably that Seán South is now denigrated by some academic and media commentators as a political and religious fanatic – in a recent RTÉ documentary he was dismissed as 'a fanatical idealist who wanted to drive the English out of Ireland'. In my opinion the same could be said of Pádraig Pearse and James Connolly and all those others down through the centuries who sacrificed their lives in the cause of Irish freedom. Pearse himself adverted to the fact that in the eyes of the world he was a fool. Idealists are always thus belittled by the worldly wise, just as that evangelising idealist, Paul, was mocked as a nitwit by the philosophers of Athens and as a lunatic by Festus, the Roman procurator of Judea. Since the public in general derive their opinions from the mass media, it would be beneficial to the intellectual welfare of the human race if all journalists and commentators were obliged to study John Henry Newman (1801–90) on prejudice before being allowed to put finger to keyboard, and if all would-be historians wrote on the first page of their first note-book the cautionary words of the great Roman historian, Livy (59BC–AD17), as he began his monumental history of what, forgetting his own caution as soon as he had written it, he was pleased to call the greatest nation in the world. 'I am aware,' says the bold Titus Livius, 'that for historians to make extravagant claims is, and always has been, all too common: every writer on history tends to look down his nose at his less cultivated predecessors, happily persuaded that he will better them in point of style or bring new facts to light.'

In my brief period as a coopted member of the Gaelic League committee in mid-century, I encountered a committee member who was undoubtedly a religious and political fanatic but it was not my old schoolmate, Seán South. Remembering his boyhood exuberance in play and his normality in academic matters, I was surprised by his adult *gravitas* and impressed when he read papers at committee meetings on economic and social matters, with quotations indicating wide reading; it was the custom for a member to give a short paper which was followed by general discussion. With what true politicians would call amateurish naïveté, South and his friends formed an Irish language political party grandly called *Seadairí na Saoirse* (*Champions of Freedom*) and they held meetings in the city and around the county at which only a handful in their sparse audiences knew what they were talking about. I remember one evening when I happened to be in town on some business of my own, I approached the Crescent in O'Connell Street where the O'Connell monument was the common venue for political meetings and saw a few people on a platform and fewer standing listening to the speaker, whose ginger hair enabled me to identify him at a distance. In sympathy with the cause, I departed from my own objective to go and stand for a while looking up at the sky in order to avoid looking my good friend, Seán, in the eye while I listened to his earnest peroration on the current ills of the Irish nation and the way to cure them. By adding one more to the audience of four, I briefly equated the number of listeners with the panel of speakers.

One of Seán South's practical efforts on behalf of the Irish language was to form a club for boys in which all the activities, including summer picnics to Killaloe and other places, would be conducted in Irish. He wrote and illustrated a small paper for this club, and because I was now known to all readers of the *Limerick Leader* as 'young Limerick writer' it was inevitable that he would rope me in to contribute some stories and sketches, which I was glad to do. The chairman of the committee at this time was Father Athanasius Giblin, OFM, a member of the Franciscan community in the city. He was a big, energetic, sociable son of the County Mayo and it was he who gave me my first marketing guidance as a writer by advising me to send articles to the newspaper *Inniú* (with results aforementioned) and poems and stories to the two magazines, *Feasta* and *Comhar*. But like South, the benevolent Athanasius asked the small favour of a literary contribution to a bilingual paper called *Rosc* which the committee had begun, and I gave him some poems and articles in both languages.

In addition to inviting me to join the Gaelic League Committee as cultural officer, in his capacity as president of the local branch of *An Réalt* it was my old schoolmate who initiated me into the role of public speaker when he asked me to come and give a talk on a topic of my own choice at the monthly meeting. I did not feel competent to address the dedicated members of the Legion of Mary on any religious topic, and so I offered as my subject *An Piarsach mar a chímse é* (Pearse as I see him). Of course, for the branch president and members of *An Réalt*, the life and writings of that noble patriot constituted a theme as close to religious as one could get, and I felt later that Our Blessed Lady herself, whose statue was on display – the meeting began

41

and ended with prayers – must have smiled at the almost religious enthusiasm with which my first effort at public speaking was received. Soon after this I was invited to give a talk in Irish at a club for teenagers which had been formed by an enthusiastic young curate in Limerick who had been present at my talk for *An Réalt*. Like Seán South, this young priest, Eamonn Casey, was destined to leave his name indelibly inscribed in the annals of Ireland in our time when, as a bishop, he would be the cause of scandal for those who have never read the New Testament *Letter to the Hebrews* where we are forewarned that 'the Law makes priests of men and men are weak.'

Two other invitations proffered by my sincere friend and one-time classmate I had no option but to refuse. As my first effort at writing a stage play had shown, my interest in politics was philosophic rather than practical, and so I refused Seán's invitation to join *Seadairí na Saoirse*. But he was a patient and determined young man and as we left the League premises one night, and I stood chatting with Seán on the steps of 18 Thomas Street, he asked me if I would like to join an Irish-speaking company which he had formed in the FCA at Sarsfield Barracks. My lack of interest in practical politics was matched by my total abhorrence of guns and uniforms. In the training college in Dublin we had been invited to join the Pearse Battalion of the FCA, comprising students from university and other third-level colleges. While some of my friends donned the uniform and heavy boots, even if I had felt any inclination to join and do my bit in support of the regular army, the fact that the Sunday morning training sessions coincided with our hurling fixtures in the Dublin league would have made the choice for me. The twin delights at that stage of my life consisted in hurling with Erin's Hope, our college GAA club, and going to the midweek dance at the Teachers' Club in Parnell Square. So, I thought to refuse this latest invitation to shoulder the gun without hurting Seán's feelings for the second time.

I give our exchange in Irish as it occurred.

'Ó, a Sheáin, ní bheadh aon mhaith ionamsa sa chomplacht sin agat – ní bheadh fhios agamsa cén ceann den ghunna a mbéarfainn air!' (Ah, Seán, I wouldn't be of any use in that company of yours – I wouldn't know which end of the gun to catch!)

He was not to be put off that easily. With his characteristic slow smile, he replied, *'Ach, a Chríostóir, a chara, múinfidh mise thú.* (But, Criostoir, my friend, I'll teach you.)

As we walked down Thomas Street I had to present my case in detail: I was now very involved in writing; I did not have a permanent teaching job and so could not tell if I would be living in Limerick and I had a girlfriend with whom I desired to spend as much as possible of my spare time. My explanation and my refusal were accepted with good grace, and if he privately considered that I was too devoted to my literary activity and to social pleasure and not enough to the promotion of the Irish language, to social reform and to the supplementary defence of the national territory, Seán was too courteous to reprimand me.

The tables were turned, even if in a lesser way, when Seán refused my invitation to take part in the concert I was producing in the Gaelic League hall, modestly maintaining that he had no ability in singing or acting. Our concert followed the usual formula of songs and dances, a one-act play, a mime and some recitations, and it proved a great success. However, as had happened with my first radio play, it was my mother, a patriotic but practical woman, who pointed out the facts of linguistic reality to me. Having come to the concert with her friends to support the good cause, she enjoyed the singing and dancing and the mime but at our own fireside she observed that, in fairness to the majority who could not understand Irish, I should have included a one-act play in English on the programme. Having discussed this with my enthusiastic cast, we decided to include Lady Gregory's patriotic one-act play, *The Rising of the Moon*, in

43

our next concert. Rehearsals were going along with gusto until word reached the committee.

At the next meeting I was asked to explain why we were putting on a play in English. When I did so, I was amazed at the reaction of some of the members, not all of them of the old guard. One man in particular almost accused me of high treason and he asserted virulently that no word of English would ever be spoken in the Gaelic League hall. My argument that Lady Gregory's play was not ousting the one-act play in Irish but was additional to it and that this famous play would do more to promote patriotic feeling and a consequent interest in Irish language and culture than the play in Irish which might as well be in double Dutch as far as most of the audience were concerned, met with the same bigoted rebuttal. So, my fellow actors and I had no option but to scratch *The Rising of the Moon* from the programme of our next concert.

It was another proposal made in my capacity as cultural officer that caused me to withdraw from the committee and sever all connection with the Gaelic League. The hall in the premises at Thomas Street was still as it had been in the early years of the century and of the League. With its small stage and wooden benches around the bare walls, it was more like a village dance-hall than an urban ballroom. And the *céilí* dances, sociably enjoyable as they were, were soon deserted by most teenagers in favour of the more glamorous modern dances in the city's commercial ballrooms. It occurred to me that in order to counteract this attraction, which increasingly was causing the Gaelic League hall to be considered a place where parents could safely allow younger teenagers to go until they had enough sense to take care of themselves in the more sophisticated arena of a modern ballroom, it was essential to brighten up the plain old hall. We needed to replace the long-trodden boards with a proper dance floor and to allow dances like the waltz, the quickstep and the tango to figure along with the so-called Irish dances which the scholars tell us are no more a true part of our distinctive Irish cultural heritage than the embroidered costumes worn by Irish step-dancers.

The reaction provoked by my proposal to put on a one-act play in English was only a mild murmur compared with the frothing at the mouth resulting from my suggestions about the hall and the dances. If I thought the previous reaction was an example of cultural bigotry, I was now learning what moral fanaticism could do. And as I have already recorded, the fanatic who shouted at me that the 'foreign' dances I was talking about were 'immoral' was not my good friend, Seán South. It should be noted also that in those days the GAA was still stringently forbidding its members to play the 'foreign' games, soccer, rugby – the most popular sport in Limerick then as now – and hockey.

When I countered, with equal vigour but less virulence, that my girlfriend and I, along with my brothers, our friends, and thousands of young men and women in Limerick, went regularly to the city ballrooms and performed the waltz, the tango, etc., that my father actually played the saxophone in a hall called the Catholic Institute at a weekly dance promoted by the Augustinian Fathers in aid of their foreign missions and that this fanatic was therefore accusing me, my girlfriend, my father, and all those others of practising and promoting immorality, the verbal duel became so heated that the reverend chairman, Fr Athanasius, OFM, intervened to restore order and prevent physical violence. But when, after some professional conciliatory palaver, he put my proposal to a vote and I found myself in a minority of one, having first warned them dramatically that the day would come when the only dancers in the historic old Gaelic League hall would be the mice, I bade them all a fond farewell, *as Gaeilge*, and walked out, never to return.

6

THE SLOUGH OF DESPOND

The publication of a novel or the production of a new play has often been likened to the birth of a baby. Conversely, the rejection of a play or a book might be compared metaphorically to the human tragedy of a miscarriage. I heard the late Bryan MacMahon claim in a television interview that he never received a rejection letter in the whole course of his career. That must mark him out as almost unique among the scribblers of this world. I know some talented writers who have never received anything but a succession of formal rejection slips, of which every publisher keeps a supply in stock. The apprentice writer must learn to accept as a fact of literary life that rejection is much more likely than acceptance. What is more important is that rejection should not be taken as any sort of proof that the work rejected is of little or no literary merit. Many factors operate in the literary market, some of them basically commercial, others consisting of what Graham Greene called 'the human factor', in which the ingredients of taste, fashion, envy, friendship or even malice may be found.

Among the basic commercial facts is the obvious one that even an inferior play, book, story or poem by a successful author is guaranteed to do better in the marketplace than a work of better quality by a writer who is known only a little or not at all. One of my father's fireside adages was that there are some things you can learn only by experience, not from books or teachers. None of the books I found in the Limerick city library could teach me the essential lessons a writer must learn if he or she is to survive 'the slings and arrows of outrageous fortune', which in the literary life means to recover from the despondency and frustration of rejection. Even when work is published or produced, the writer may have to endure being ignored by the media commentators or, if noticed, the folly of critics and reviewers or the lack of popular success. The French, as usual, have a word for it, distinguishing critically between the *succès fou* and the *succès d'estime*, and while the former often has little literary merit the latter butters no bread.

My own apprentice efforts in those early years, in various genres of literature and in two languages, had been accepted so readily that I was already beginning to envisage a career as a full-time successful writer. I had so many ideas and themes bubbling up in my imagination that I remember feeling an artistic empathy with the youthful Keats as I quoted, 'When I have fears that I may cease to be, Before my pen has gleaned my teeming brain.' My recurring periods of unemployment in between spells as a temporary teacher, while continually cutting off my income and increasing my disillusionment with the promises of clerical and other managers of schools, served to increase my productivity as a writer by leaving me with time on my hands and no money in my pockets. In this situation, I learned another fact of life for the artist, namely that hack work can bring in guaranteed payment while a genuine work of artistic creativity may end up rejected or earning insignificant and long-delayed financial reward.

In addition to the occasional article, story or poem in magazines, I discovered a welcoming and profitable market for stories and plays in the children's programmes of Radio Éireann. (I grant, of course, that to write even such stories and plays requires talent and craftsmanship.) It was also from Radio Éireann that my first serious rejection hit me with a bang that caused me to realise that the life of a creative writer, to which I now knew I was ineluctably committed for better or worse, was likely to prove more like Bunyan's *Pilgrim's Progress* than the airy-fairy romantic vision of poor Keats. And just as a tentative effort at writing a radio play had been the first source of elation for me as a writer, it was a more assured and confident essay in the same medium that sent me headlong into Bunyan's Slough of Despond.

I had already experienced rejection when Tomás Mac Anna, having directed my play, *Na Cimí* on radio, declined to stage it in the Abbey in spite of its having been successfully staged in Maynooth by the Abbey actor, Ray McAnally. At least this play had been produced on radio and on stage and it had been highly praised in the papers, which in those pre-television years devoted much critical attention to radio programmes. The blunt and total rejection of a literary work which I was now to experience for the first time is an experience that causes not only a natural disappointment and frustration in the young author but a realisation that between the creative writer and the public there stands the middleman, in one form or another, on whose artistic awareness, intelligence and moral integrity the acceptance or rejection of the literary work may depend.

Having written one radio play in Irish and another in English, both well received by public and critics alike, I decided to write a bilingual play based on one of the most famous poems in Irish, the lament of Eibhlín Dubh Ní Chonaill (an aunt of the great Daniel O'Connell) for her husband, Art Ó Laoghaire, an ex-officer in the Imperial Austrian army, who was murdered by a landlord's redcoats near Millstreet in County Cork on 4 May 1773, at the age of twenty-six. Since I first encountered it, albeit as a compulsory item in an exam syllabus, the poem had been one of my favourite pieces of literature in any language, and it later gave me the title of my first novel in Irish, *Lá Dá Bhfaca Thú*. It is the impromptu caoineadh ('keen') in the formal traditional style uttered by the young widow over the corpse of her husband at the wake, and its opening lines, with their remembered emotion of love at first sight, which will remain forever in the memory of anyone who was privileged to learn them at any time:

> *Mo ghrá go daingean thú!*
> *Lá dá bhfaca thú*
> *Ag ceann tí an mhargaidh,*
> *Thug mo shúil aire dhuit,*
> *Thug mo chroí taitneamh duit,*
> *D'éalaíos ó m'athair leat*
> *I bhfad ó bhaile leat.*

For those who cannot read those lines, I make this version :

> My love went all to you
> That day when I saw you
> At the market-house corner,
> You took my eye's attention,
> You took my heart's affection,
> From father's care I fled
> Far from home with you.

I laboured with great personal love as well as improved, I hoped, professional care over that third radio play. It was returned to me by Radio Éireann with a letter signed by Francis MacManus, a name well known to me as to all readers of literature in Ireland as that of a fine novelist. Having duly praised the play as well-written, etc., etc., MacManus informed me that the reason it was being rejected was that he did not think a bilingual play would succeed on radio; consequently, he advised me to write plays either in English or Irish. I can still recall my total astonishment at this negative verdict and blunt directive, which I considered to be totally mistaken, if not actually nonsense. The fact that it came from a literary man who had himself been a teacher and ought therefore to be even more aware of the bilingual situation in Ireland served only to increase my puzzlement.

As that useful book, Dale Carnegie's *How to Win Friends and Influence People* (1936) was not among those I had found in the Limerick library, and as my good mother had always taught me to speak my mind, I wrote back to Francis MacManus and told him that he was wrong. I pointed out that in the period of my play, the eighteenth century, English was the language of the Protestant landlord class and their lackeys, as well as of the English garrisons in all the cities and towns, and had been so for many centuries. It was also, by then, spoken as a second language by many of the native Irish upper class. And while it might be artistically feasible for Shakespeare in the narrow world of Elizabethan England to have Julius Caesar and Cleopatra spouting high-flown English in his plays, it would sound incongruous in a radio play broadcast in the middle of the twentieth century to have an English landlord of the eighteenth century conversing with his friends and his lackeys in the melodious Irish of west Cork.

Furthermore, it seemed to me that the use of the two languages gave the play a contrapuntal linguistic effect, and – I referred to my mother's comments on my first radio play and on that Irish one-acter in the Gaelic League hall – many people who could not understand a play in Irish alone would be drawn to listen to a bilingual play. Although they would not be able to understand the Irish dialogue and especially the extracts from the poem itself, they would be helped to follow the action by their understanding of the English dialogue. The reply to this cogent artistic argument from 'young Limerick writer' was a curt refusal to discuss the matter further. Since the only other market for a radio play was the BBC, to which market it would be futile for a young Irish writer to offer a bilingual play based on an Irish poetic masterpiece, my play on *Caoineadh Airt Uí Laoghaire* served to light the fire in the kitchen range for several mornings that winter, a fire fuelled by my mother's forthright comments which were such as to draw fire and brimstone down on the head of 'that stupid man in Radio Éireann'.

Truth and integrity compel me to record for posterity the strange fact that in subsequent years I submitted many stories and talks in Irish or English to Radio Éireann, and while those in Irish were all accepted by section heads like Cathal Ó Gríofa and Proinsias Ó Conluain, all my efforts in English, even stories and talks that were later to achieve publication in Ireland, Britain or the US, were summarily rejected by Francis MacManus. No wonder, then, that I was puzzled, perhaps even chagrined, to read now and again in the literary columns of the papers that he was an earnest encourager of young writers. Perhaps he was, but certainly not of the only young writer I knew. Any young writers, or rejected writers of any age, who may be reading this, should note that, before I adapted them for radio, two of those stories rejected by MacManus had won first prize, in their original Irish versions, in the Oireachtas competitions where they had been highly praised by the adjudicator, Bryan MacMahon, a writer of equal status with MacManus, and some of those stories were later broadcast by the BBC. Note also that the talks he found 'unsuitable for broadcasting' were all broadcast by me in *Sunday Miscellany* and similar programmes when accepted by later editors. I think it was Sean O'Casey who advised writers never to throw anything away (that, of course, would not apply to a rejected bilingual play for radio).

I met Francis MacManus only once, one evening in the late Fifties, when we passed on the stairs, the lift being out of order, in the GPO in Henry Street (the Radio Éireann studios were situated on the top floor of that historic building until the move to the new RTÉ location in Donnybrook in the Sixties). I was on my way up to read one of my stories in Irish and he was coming down after another frustrating day away from the writing of novels, the work he and Bryan MacMahon and Benedict Kiely and other writers of their generation might have been doing full-time if Aosdána, the scheme of state patronage for writers and artists established in 1983 by Taoiseach Charles J. Haughey on the advice of his cultural officer, the writer Anthony Cronin, had been thought of in his time. The conversation that passed between us had nothing to do with literature, unless it might be open to a metaphorical interpretation. I said: 'It's harder going up than coming down.' To which MacManus replied: 'True for you.' That brief encounter and the rejection of my bilingual radio play in 1951 came back to my mind when I read in the papers earlier this year, 1998, that the Abbey Theatre had begun a tour of the Gaeltacht areas with a new play, what else but a bilingual play based on the poetic lament by Eibhlín Dubh Ní Chonaill for her murdered husband, Art Ó Laoghaire. Anyone who knows the poem, in which Art's horse is the cause of the tragedy and a participant in the action, and who also knows the respective advantages of radio and stage drama, will appreciate that radio is the better medium for such a play.

7

'IRISH FROM THE CRADLE'

It is a proverbial consolation in adversity, and I have often experienced its truth, that when God closes one door he opens another. On the other hand, fate sometimes likes to dish out a few doses of the rough stuff before restoring the spiritual equilibrium with a dish or two of the smooth. 'When sorrows come,' said Shakespeare, 'they come not single spies, but in battalions.' And so, having taken note of the fact that 'young Limerick writer' had embarked, albeit unintentionally, on the quest for fame and fortune by writing in two languages, fate was now giving me fair warning of the trials and tribulations that lay in store for me on my literary odyssey. Hot on the heels, as they say, of the rejection of what I believed to be a unique and well-constructed radio play, there came another setback, and another instance of pedantry, if not of anything more sinister, that almost put a stop to my gallop altogether, at least as far as writing in Irish was concerned.

In order to enable the reader to understand the full import and potential consequences of this second contretemps or kick in the teeth, I must outline the linguistic circumstances in which I was placed as a bilingual writer in the Ireland of the mid-twentieth century. When Douglas Hyde and others founded the Gaelic League in 1893, with the aim of restoring

Irish as a spoken language throughout Ireland, thus making the whole country bilingual, the situation of Irish was much as English would have been if the Normans, after the Battle of Hastings in 1066, had treated England merely as a valuable colony, their territory in France remaining the mother country. Imagine then, down through the centuries, that there developed an Anglo-French upper class in England, who owned all the land, filled all the positions of administration and the professions, and gradually, by one means or another, imposed their French language on the natives. Supposing the native Anglo-Saxon people (themselves descendants of the Germanic tribes that had conquered Celtic Britain some centuries earlier) to have resisted this conquest and then, in 1893, even before gaining political independence in 1922, that some patriotic enthusiasts had formed a voluntary society whose object was to revive the dying English language, now spoken only in local dialects in a few isolated areas and having no official standard and no printed literature. Suppose further that French meanwhile had become firmly established as the actual everyday language of England, and Paris rather than London being the literary and artistic centre to which English writers, all writing in French, looked for publication and recognition.

That was the situation in which Hyde and his colleagues began to try to save the Irish language, which they regarded as the basic and essential factor in the cultural identity of the Irish race. If they could have foreseen the imminent advent and the tidal anglicising effect of the mass media, the cinema, radio, television, and the computer, coupled with the cultural apathy of the nation as soon as the Irish Free State came into being in 1922, they might have directed their idealism into some more promising cause such as the preservation of fairy raths or the development of the plastic leprechaun market for tourists.

Since the days of Goldsmith and Sheridan in the eighteenth century, Irish writers in English had regarded

London as their literary and cultural centre. Even with the Literary Revival which began in the late 1890s, a poet such as Yeats or a playwright such as Synge would not have achieved much recognition if their audience and market had been confined to Ireland alone, and it was the Abbey Theatre's tours in the US that made the name of O'Casey known worldwide. The establishment of the Irish Free State made no difference to the fact that the Irish writer had to look to London or New York for any sort of commercially meaningful publication – in fact, the introduction of official censorship in 1929, in spite of the protests of W. B. Yeats and other literary figures, lessened even further the possibility of any Irish writer earning the daily bread at home.

Young writers in the new state, such as Sean O'Faolain, Frank O'Connor and Liam O'Flaherty (who began writing in his native Aran Island Irish), like Padraic Colum and James Stephens before them, found that they could survive as writers only by living and working in the US where lecture tours and readings provided a form of profitable hack-work that was at least more congenial for a writer than a job in the civil service or teaching in Ireland. Even today, Irish writers in English are still judged successful, even by Irish commentators and critics, only if their books are published or their plays produced in London or New York; a much-publicised poet recently informed the Irish nation that London is his cultural home. As with all imperialistic powers, the Anglo-Normans portrayed the native Irish as a barbaric and inferior race to whom their benevolent conquerors would bring the blessings of civilization and, as it is the conquerors who write the histories, we find a native Irish historian in the years before Cromwell's renewal of conquest, the priest Seathrún Céitinn (c. 1580–c. 1644) beginning his own version of Ireland's story with a vigorous refutation of the English authors who have written about Ireland, he says, in the manner of the dung beetle who ignores all the fragrant and beautiful flowers and settles on manure.

The stage Irishman of later centuries, like the atavistic caricatures of the Irish peasantry, even of Daniel O'Connell himself, in the London comic magazine *Punch* in the nineteenth century, continued this traducement, seen in its milder forms in books like those of Somerville and Ross.

I have already adverted to the historical fact that in the period when the novel and the drama were developing in English and the continental languages, literature in Irish was confined to poetry and storytelling in oral form, some of it being committed to hazardous survival in manuscript by the poets themselves or by rural scribes. With the advent of the Gaelic League in 1893 and the concomitant Literary Revival in English, creative writing in Irish in all the literary genres became possible. Unfortunately, because the basic aim of the Gaelic League was the restoration of Irish as a spoken language, a contention arose as to the linguistic form this new literature in Irish was to take, whether it should bridge the gap of centuries and be based on the sparse printed Irish texts of the seventeenth century, most of them religious in content and now inevitably archaic in style, or take as its medium the Irish language as it was currently spoken in a few small areas known as the Gaeltacht, largely along the western seaboard, where the language had survived.

The more scholarly protagonists, who favoured linking up with the older literature, lost out in the dispute, being dismissed as pedants by the champions of what came to be known as *caint na ndaoine*, literally 'the speech of the people'. Reverting to the analogy of the Normans and England, this was as ludicrous in literary terms as if English revivalists had decided to accept the common speech in small rural areas in Yorkshire, Lancashire and Devon as a literary medium, each area keeping to its distinct dialect. A few real writers, like Pádraic Ó Conaire from Galway and Pádraig Mac Piarais (the patriot Pearse), who were familiar with European models, began to produce original literary work. Much of what was published, however, was evaluated by the non-literary standard of its fidelity to the spoken language, the most prolific scribe in this category being the west Cork priest, Peadar Ua Laoghaire. He, incidentally, must be classed as one of the first unofficial censors of the new literature, having virulently condemned as immoral the novel *Deoraíocht* by Ó Conaire and forced its removal from the syllabus for the junior certificate of the time, where it was replaced by Pearse's *Íosagán agus Scéalta Eile*.

Since the spoken language consisted of dialects that varied in vocabulary, idiom and grammar from one area to another, the new literature in Irish, instead of evolving into a standard medium of communication like English or French, retained the distinctive characteristics of its origin in disparate local patois. In spite of official efforts since about 1950 to bring about a standard in printing and public communications, this situation remains largely unchanged to this day, so that even announcers on radio and television can still be heard using dialect forms and pronunciation. This acceptance of the various colloquial dialects as a literary medium, added to the fact that since the early days of the Gaelic League down to the present day students of Irish have been going to summer courses in the Gaeltacht areas, resulted in the confusion of colloquial fluency in any one of the dialects with literary talent, so that the standard of criticism focused largely on the linguistic content rather than on the purely literary qualities of the work. And the closer an author kept to the colloquial dialect, the better his work was considered, so that the words *Tá Gaeilge bhreá sa leabhar seo* (There is excellent Irish in this book) became almost a critical cliché. This inevitably meant that a book written by a native speaker of any of the dialects was hailed as a likely masterpiece. It had the negative effect, as I was about to discover so early in my literary career, that a writer who was not born in the Gaeltacht, no matter what dedicated study he might have made of the language, and notwithstanding his proven literary talent, was always going to be classified as naturally inferior when it came to writing in Irish because he did not have 'Irish from the cradle', *Gaeilge ón chliabhán*, as the popular phrase put it.

So entrenched did this mistaken and unliterary evaluation become even among educated people that – if I may jump to a later stage in my career – in 1968 I heard a journalist and author who was a native of the Aran Islands and therefore was fluent in the 'Irish from the cradle' (in his own dialect, *naturally*) assert in a radio interview that no writer could write a play in Irish unless he had been born in the Gaeltacht. Like the Greek philosopher who refuted an opponent's theory that motion was a fallacy simply by getting up and walking, I pointed out in a subsequent interview that in that same year I had three plays in Irish produced in Dublin and Galway. I also appealed to the 'native speakers' to consider the fact that Samuel Beckett, an Irishman, and Eugene Ionesco, a Romanian, were both highly regarded in France as writers of *French* literature, while the English novels of a man named Teodor Josef Konrad Korzeniowski, who was born in the Ukraine of Polish parents and began to learn English only when he went to sea as a youth, were now listed among the masterpieces of English literature and prescribed on university courses, his English *nom-de-plume*, Joseph Conrad, being derived from two of his original Christian names.

With regard to the spoken language, this bigoted attitude did untold harm to the revival of Irish because it discouraged many earnest learners of Irish who, despite achieving fluency in the language, were still regarded as inferior simply because they spoke Irish with their own accent – I recall reading in a report in *The Irish Times* a slighting reference to a speech in Irish in the Dáil by a Government minister, Mr. Jim Tunney, TD, a fluent speaker of Irish and an ex-teacher, because he spoke Irish, as he spoke English, with his native Dublin accent. A ludicrous aspect of the whole matter was that the inhabitants of the Gaeltacht areas refused to accept any word or expression in Irish that had not been part of their local vocabulary, with the result that they rejected all new terminology in Irish, e.g. *rothar* (bicycle), mocking this as *Gaeilge Bhaile Átha Cliath* (Dublin Irish) and preferring to use the English terms instead. Sadly, with the continuing encroachment of English through the mass media and travel, not only has the genuine Gaeltacht territory diminished in area but its inhabitants are speaking diluted versions of the vigorous dialects of the pre-television era. Even these are peppered with so many English words, including inevitably the most common Anglo-Saxon four-letter vulgarism, that the worries of the French about *franglais* are as nothing to the concern for the survival of Irish as the rich language heard in those isolated areas by the idealistic enthusiasts in those early years of the Gaelic League.

I proceed now to chronicle the dilemma in which I found myself as a young writer and how my subsequent career as a writer was affected because I happened to be placed in this historical linguistic situation. There would have been nothing to relate, of course, if, like most Irish writers, I had decided to ignore Irish altogether and concentrate on writing only in English. But we are all children of our time and circumstances and I have already stated that I felt a very strong urge to write in Irish as well as English. Apart from any literary consideration, it seemed to me a patriotic duty to write in the language of my own nation. In this aspect of my literary life, as in others, there are memories that serve to renew personal pain and frustration but as my purpose in this book is to give a true account of my career, I must record things as they happened even if it involves remembering what Wordsworth called 'old unhappy, far-off things, and battles long ago.'

With the establishment of the Irish Free State, the Irish language was made compulsory both as a subject and as the medium of instruction in all other subjects, except English and Religious Knowledge, in the infant and primary schools in the state system, but only as an essential subject for Leaving Certificate in the Secondary schools or in the private schools. In order to provide textbooks for the schools, and suitable reading matter for the adults who would have learned to read Irish in school, the government established in 1925 an Irish-language publishing section, known as An Gúm, in the state publications office, itself a section of the Department of Education. The name means *plan* or *scheme*, although in later years the most famous Irish language writer of the period, Máirtín Ó Cadhain, having suffered like others from its bureaucratic delays and officious pedantry, would claim sardonically that the name was derived from that of a large department store in Moscow where cheap goods were sold to the masses.

In addition to publishing original works in Irish at low prices, the pragmatic founder of An Gúm, Minister of Finance Ernest Blythe (whom I was soon to meet in his post-political career as managing director of the Abbey Theatre) decreed that popular novels should be translated into Irish from English and other languages. For this purpose, native speakers with some talent in writing were recruited from the various dialect areas. The books translated from English had already been read in that language by most people, and the Irish versions were destined to be sold by the ton as wastepaper many years later. The books translated from other languages were obviously translated from English versions, and their fate was a similar one. In a radio programme some time in the Seventies, I heard one of those 'native speaker' translators telling how he and his colleagues used to relieve the tedium of their daily labour by betting on who would translate a thousand words in the shortest time. Again with his characteristic pragmatism, Ernest Blythe, adverting to the fact that the potential readership for an author in Irish was only a very small fraction of the population, and that the cheaply-priced productions of An Gúm would mean little in the way of author's royalties, decided to offer an acceptance fee at a rate per one thousand words. This, as any author or critic could have told him, would inevitably tend to increase the quantity rather than the quality of work submitted to An Gúm. It could also lead, as any such scheme might, to more nefarious consequences.

Just as I had become a writer without making a Miltonic decision to devote my life to the creation of literature, I wrote my first long prose work for a reason that was not basically literary or artistic. As a teacher, I was encouraging my pupils to read Irish books in their spare time but when I tried to provide them with suitable material I found that this was in short supply. Most of the Irish books in the public libraries were written in one or other of the three main dialects, as were the school readers, and by native speakers who had as little literary talent as their predecessors in the early years of the Gaelic League. The only non-dialect books available were detective stories by a young Dublin writer, Cathal Ó Sandair, whose indigenous equivalent of Sherlock Holmes or Sexton Blake was called Reics Carló. These books were already gratefully known to many students of Irish, including myself, whose struggles with the tedious and very non-literary books in dialect by native speakers of Irish, which were the prescribed texts for all exam courses even up to recent years, had been alleviated to some degree by these lively and contemporary stories in a straightforward style, uncluttered by dialect idiom and vocabulary or allusions to an outdated rural way of life. It was in emulation of Cathal Ó Sandair that I decided to write a novel in Irish that would be attractive for that same audience. And, although I don't think I was conscious of the influence at the time, it was in emulation of the English adventure novelist, P. C. Wren (1885–1941), whose famous novel *Beau Geste* (1924) about the French Foreign Legion had been meat and drink to my boyhood imagination – I enjoyed the film when it came – that I concocted my first plot and wrote a story called *Faoi Bhrat na Fraince* (*Under the French Flag*).

Being still an innocent abroad as far as the marketing of writing was concerned, I noted that the books of Cathal Ó Sandair were published by An Gúm. If I had known then the frustrations Ó Sandair was suffering from the pedants in the Department of Education – his problems came to light some years later when a question was asked in the Dáil, eliciting the typical evasive reply – or if I could have foreseen what I myself was to suffer from my dealings with the anonymous inhabitants of that official factory for the production of literature in Irish, I would have overcome my patriotic sentiments and used my first (and last) novel in Irish to light the fire as had been done with the script of my bilingual radio play. But I did not know, and so I optimistically sent off my book to An Gúm in Dublin. Whether they were preoccupied with those betting games on translating a thousand words or spending their paid office hours in trying to be writers themselves, it took six months for the official promoters of Irish literature in An Gúm to deliver a verdict on my first novel in Irish. When they did so, it was with a paradoxical verdict that could truly be described as 'the rough with the smooth.' They offered to accept my book, to pay me an acceptance fee at their standard rate per one thousand words (that unit of diction seems to have been much on their minds) but they were not satisfied with the standard of Irish in my book and they would have to deduct from my payment a fee to be paid to a person who would correct the text before publication. If I agreed to these conditions, a contract form would be forthcoming.

Eschewing false modesty, I replied to this offer informing the anonymous Gúm pedants that I had been learning Irish from the age of three and a half, beginning in the infant school with a great Sister of Mercy named Felicitas, that I had taken first place in every examination during my schooldays, including first place in Ireland in the Honours Irish exam in Leaving Certificate (a test in which 'native speaker' pupils from all the Gaeltacht areas would have been competing), that in order to qualify as a national teacher I had pursued a course which involved two years' study of Irish as well as the study through Irish of general and pedagogic subjects, that I had continued since then to study Irish privately with intense application, that I had already published poems, stories and articles in Irish and that no other editor had found any fault with my Irish before publishing my work. Finally, I asked them to furnish me with examples of the alleged faulty Irish in my book.

That letter from a young Irish author who had the audacity to write a book in Irish although he did not have 'Irish from the cradle' – in years to come I often asked my patient mother, in serio-comic vein, why she had not had the foresight to board a bus for some place, any place, in the Gaeltacht, a week before I was born so that I could be counted all my life among those eloquent infants who had gurgled through the medium of Irish in the cradle – must have taken the minds of the native speakers in An Gúm off their translation games for some time at least. When they recovered from the shock, with true civil service delayed action and rectitude, they sent me a brief note enclosing a typed list of what they said were some of the alleged errors for which they were proposing to deduct a corrector's fee from my payment as author of *Faoi Bhrat na Fraince*.

Having studied it, I returned it, pointing out that I was trying to write Irish in a literary standard style in emulation of authors like Pearse and Ó Conaire, that most of the so-called errors were actually words or idioms I had myself assiduously learnt from the books of authors like Tomás Ó Criomhthain, the Blasket Islander author of *An tOileánach*, and An tAthair Peadar Ua Laoghaire of west Cork – that these were being listed as errors in Irish astonished me, but it also made me suspect that somebody up there in An Gúm was either not conversant with or not greatly enamoured of the Munster dialects of Irish. Some of the other words listed were actually translations from English made by myself of modern terms for which there was no Irish equivalent available. The English-Irish dictionary edited by Tomás de Bhaldraithe did not appear until almost a decade later, in 1959, and the Irish-English dictionary edited by Niall Ó Domhnaill came almost twenty years later again in 1977. The only dictionary available to any writer was the one compiled by that magpie lexicographer, Father Dineen, first published in 1904 and in its enlarged edition in 1927, the year I was born. This was the massive conglomeration of words and idioms that was a stand-by source of ready-made material for that brilliant writer, Myles na Gopaleen (Flann O'Brien), when he needed to pad his column in *The Irish Times* with ridicule of the Irish language. But since Father Dineen did not provide 'young Limerick writer' in 1951 with any Irish equivalent for words like *lipstick, dustbin, machine-gun*, etc. or for any English or American neologisms since 1927, I had perforce to choose between using the English term – which any 'native speaker' would do – or concocting what I thought was an equally valid one in Irish. Finally, I found that a few of the phrases listed contained grammatical points for which dialect variations existed and one or two which, having consulted various grammars, I knew were in dispute even among the academic authorities as was the case with their likes in any language.

Having put my case to An Gúm – it begins to sound like some menacing unidentified monster – with detailed references in support of my argument, I waited, not in idleness as will be seen. After suitable civil service delay, a final offer came from the literary section of the Department of Education. I was told, in formal civil service terms, that my letter had been noted, but that it was still necessary to have the text of my book prepared for publication by a third party, whose fee would be deducted from my payment. A contract form was enclosed, which I was to sign, have witnessed and return if I agreed to these conditions; if not, my book would be returned to me. Finally – the sting in the tail – I was advised that I should write in one dialect and not in a 'mixture' as I had done in this book.

One of the Irish proverbs I had learnt in the course of my lifelong studies told me, *Is fearr leathbhulóg ná an gorta* – the English equivalent says 'half a loaf is better than no bread' – and as my alter ego, the young teacher, was now coming to the end of another temporary period of employment and facing into a penniless summer, I had to pocket my pride in order to have anything else to put in my pocket. I signed the contract and returned it with another letter of protest. With the payment I received, a sum of nearly thirty-five pounds (the equivalent of seven weeks' wages for a temporary teacher at the time) I bought the beautiful Underwood Portable typewriter, already mentioned with affection in this chronicle, for which I paid thirty-one pounds and ten shillings. And as crazy young writers do, I forgot about the long penniless summer looming, bought my long-suffering mother a box of chocolates and blew the rest on going to dances and films with my beloved, to whom I was hoping to become engaged as soon as some school manager would actually keep his promise and give me a permanent job after I had taken him out of a fix by filling a temporary post.

8

THE OTHER DOOR OPENS

It was our Divine Lord himself who quoted a maxim that must have been already ages old in his time, that a prophet is without honour in his own country; but I have already chronicled the fact that, as far as our local newspaper, the *Limerick Leader*, was concerned, from the very first acceptance of my apprentice efforts by Radio Éireann or in literary magazines up to the publication of my most recent book, *There Is an Isle*, in which I recorded the life and times of my boyhood in the Island Parish of St Mary's in Limerick, successive editors and journalists have given my work generous and appreciative publicity in news items and reviews. I have told how my first poem in English achieved publication in the *Leader*. My first literary award was also gained through our local paper.

While still a student, and before I began to write myself, I had been an avid reader of the weekly Irish column in the *Leader* written by 'An Mangaire Súgach' (the Merry Pedlar), the pen-name of Mainchín Seoighe, a native of Kilmallock in County Limerick, who worked in the County Council offices and was involved in the Gaelic League and in everything to do with the promotion of the Irish language. If Ireland had an honours list, this man would certainly be knighted by now for his lifelong work for the language, as well as in local history and folklore. Fittingly, his achievement has been recognized recently by Galway University where he was awarded an honorary doctorate. He was the main force behind the annual cultural festival, Féile na Máighe, in the seventies, honouring the eighteenth-century poets of the River Maigue area in County Limerick (it was from the soubriquet of one of those poets, the rakish Aindrias Mac Craith, that Mainchín borrowed his own pen-name).

In recent years he has initiated a similar annual event, Féile na Seoigheach (the Joyce Brothers Festival), to honour the academic, cultural and literary achievements of the County Limerick brothers, Patrick Weston Joyce (1827-1914) and Robert Dwyer Joyce (1830-1883), men deservedly famous in their day but little known in the Ireland of today. (When I told some friends in a Dublin pub a few years ago that I was going to the Joyce Brothers Festival in Kilmallock in County Limerick, I was asked by one Bloomsday enthusiast what connection James and Stanislaus had with County Limerick.) A bilingual writer like myself, Mainchín Seoighe (Mannix Joyce) has published many books and articles in both languages (his *Portrait of Limerick*, published in a series by Robert Hale of London in 1982, is an encyclopaedic guide to the history, topography, folklore and culture of the city and county) but like many another of his kind, down through the years he has also expended time and energy unceasingly on cultural activities of all kinds, including the generous encouragement and promotion of other writers, including myself. And early in my career, it was through Mainchín Seoighe, then a young man himself, and the *Limerick Leader*, that God opened that other door for a young writer who had suddenly found a door slamming in his face.

When Mainchín announced one week in his column that he was offering a prize for a poem in Irish about the Easter Rising, the prize to consist of one pound (good money around mid-century, when you could still get into the Savoy cinema in Limerick for a shilling) and a year's membership in An Club Leabhar (the Irish language book club founded in 1948 which offered five selected books a year for a subscription of five pounds) I set to work on a theme that was congenial to my spirit. The adjudicator for the competition was the Aran Islands poet, Máirtín Ó Direáin (1910-1988), then a civil servant in his early forties who, in the coming years, was to be linked by commentators with two other poets, Seán Ó Ríordáin and Máire Mhac an tSaoi, to form a poetic blessed trinity in modern Irish poetry. To his laudatory remarks on my prize-winning poem, which was prominently published in the *Limerick Leader*, the Aran poet generously added: '*Mura bhfuil aithne go forleathan ar an bhfile seo go dtí seo, ní fada go mbeidh.*' (If this poet is not widely known already, it won't be long.) This encomium-prophecy was worth much more to me than the cheque for a pound from the *Leader* and the five brand-new books in Irish that came from An Club Leabhar over the next year.

In the six months while I waited for An Gúm to give a verdict on my first book in Irish, I had written two more books for teenage readers. One of these was a historical novel set in Limerick and Clare after Sarsfield, having signed the ill-fated Treaty of Limerick in 1691, had gone to France with the bulk of his army in the hope that they would return with French aid to drive the English out of Ireland. The other book also had a military connection but in the modern era, being an espionage story in which two young army officers were the heroes. Some of the Irish school readers in use at that time were published by the Dublin firm of Browne and Nolan. I decided to try them with one of my books; so, I sent them the historical novel, *An tIolar Dubh* (The Black Eagle), together with a letter about my previous efforts in writing. The book was returned to me promptly with a courteous letter from the Irish editor, Máiréad Ní Ghráda, in which she informed me regretfully that they did not publish Irish fiction. However, she praised my book, hoped that it would find a publisher, and urged me to continue writing.

I did not know then that Máiréad Ní Ghráda (1899-1971) was herself an author who had written short stories, plays, and even a science-fiction novel in Irish while I was still a schoolboy. She had also been a member of Cumann na mBan, secretary to Ernest Blythe during the first Dáil, and an announcer with Radio Éireann for some years from its birth in 1926, in which latter capacity she neglected to inform the nation of my own birth a week before Christmas Day the following year. Her name was to become widely known when her *An Triail* was one of the outstanding plays of the Dublin Theatre Festival in 1964. That was the play in which the late Caitlín Maude, folk singer and poet, made her name as an actress, her performance and the play itself being fulsomely praised by the theatre critic of the London *Sunday Times*, Harold Hobson, who didn't understand a word of the dialogue. It was later shown on television and translated into English. I was to meet Máiréad Ní Ghráda very soon, when the finger of fate pushed me from my native Limerick to Dublin in 1952, and I would be indebted to her in the late Sixties when the book of my controversial play, *Cóta Bán Chríost*, was in danger of being suppressed by unofficial censorship on the part of yahoos in her own firm.

When An Gúm finally accepted my initial effort, I felt that their pedantic antics about errors in my Irish were at an end and since they paid cash down on acceptance, and I was in need of cash down, I sent them my book about the two young army officers, *An Claíomh Geal* (The Bright Sword), thinking that this would be likely to find favour with the publications branch of the Department of Education. The book was returned to me after a month with a formal letter stating that it had been considered but was found to be 'unsuitable for publication by An Gúm.' No reason given.

Now this was the sort of carry-on that no citizen should be subjected to by anonymous civil servants. And as a consequence of the excellent training I had received in street fighting and in rugby while growing up near King John's Castle in Limerick – we did not believe in 'an eye for an eye, a tooth for a tooth,' etc, but in *two* eyes for an eye and *two* teeth for a tooth, the basic maxim in rugby being, 'if a fella kicks you once, kick him back twice, then he'll know what to expect before he kicks you again' – I was not the type of tentative scribbler who would humbly tip his cap to those rejecting pedantic peasants just in case they might put me on a blacklist and reject everything else I wrote. Obviously I could not very well travel to Dublin and kick the person or persons unknown who had given my book the thumbs down without even offering a reason. I knew my book was better than the one they had recently accepted and better than most of the boring and outdated stuff they were publishing. So I sent the book back to them and told them that. And as with my bilingual radio play my book was returned in a few weeks with another brief letter which added insult to injury by telling me that it had been considered again and was still judged to be 'unsuitable for publication by An Gúm'.

While this was going on in my life as a writer, things were looking up in the pedagogic field in which I was trying to earn the daily bread. While most schools were under the control of the parish priest or of religious orders, the Model Schools which had been established in many cities and towns in the previous century were under the direct control of the Department of Education, with the local schools inspector acting as manager *in situ*. When the local inspector called to my parents' house one night, I didn't even know who this pleasant gentleman was. When he told me that he had seen my Irish stories and poems here and there, and offered me a three-month temporary job in the Model School (an all-Irish school) with the promise that he would recommend me to the department as his approved candidate for the permanent job that would be coming on line, I felt that

Christmas had come three months early. My beloved and I decided to become engaged at Christmas and to marry in the New Year.

Although I had severed my connection with the Gaelic League, I was still in touch socially with most of the people I had known there, including my Franciscan friend and counseller, the genial giant from Mayo, An tAthair Athanáis, as he was known to us. When I told him of the double rejection of my book by An Gúm and the more courteous but still negative response from Browne and Nolan, and that I was considering burning the two books, he all but threw me into the Shannon. (He would have risked his own life to haul me out again.) He asked me to give him the books to read. Having read them, he gave them high praise and urged me strongly to enter them for one of the literary competitions in the Oireachtas.

As I have already intimated, when the Holy Spirit entrusted me with the talent of literary creativity, that did not include any marketing awareness or business sense, any desire to form literary connections or friendships or any of the craftiness with which some writers and artists seem to be endowed at birth. So, the patient Fr Pádraig Athanasius Giblin had to treat me like one of the birds or animals the poetic St Francis himself talked to. He informed me that the Gaelic League, in its early days, had decided to hold an annual cultural festival on the model of the Welsh *eisteddfod* and the Scottish *mod*. This national feis which included literary, dramatic and music competitions, had lapsed in the doldrum period after the Civil War but had been revived in 1939 and was now held every year in October. In his capacity as president of the local branch of the Gaelic League, my mentor had a programme of the events and competitions for the next Oireachtas. Entries for the literary competitions, under a pen-name, had to be received before July and the prizes were awarded at a ceremony in the Mansion House in Dublin on the opening night of the Oireachtas in October.

The competition to which my attention was directed offered a prize of fifty pounds, the equivalent of about ten weeks' worth of my current salary, for a work of fiction suitable for teenage readers. When I asked Athanasius which of my two books I should enter, with true Franciscan generosity he said, '*Cuir isteach an dá cheann acu – is fearr dhá chapall agat sa rás ná ceann amháin!*' (Enter the two of them – better to have two horses in the race than one!) Which I (or we) did before the next closing date. And went on with our respective lives until the results would be announced in September.

Our two horses came first and second. Unfortunately, there was no prize for second but I still got much more than the cheque for fifty pounds which I collected at the ceremony in Dublin. Two academic literary adjudicators, one male, one female, wrote very nice things about both books, not knowing that the different pen-names represented the same author. My hearty Franciscan mentor and I laughed ironically when, having praised the literary qualities of the stories, both adjudicators went on to praise the correctness and quality of the Irish in each book. And the truth of the old adage about God as a sort of divine doorkeeper was again exemplified in a letter that came to me from a publisher in Dublin, Sáirséal agus Dill, telling me that they wished to read my prize-winning book with a view to publication. This independent Irish language publishing house was a family venture started in 1945 by Seán Ó hÉigeartaigh (a civil servant by profession, son of the historian, P. S. O'Hegarty) and his wife, Bríd Ní Mhaoileoin, in order to provide writers in Irish with an alternative to the labyrinthine bureaucracy of An Gúm. In spite of recurring financial troubles due to the niggardly and unpredictable nature of state subsidy for private publishers in Irish, Sáirséal agus Dill published books of all kinds by many authors and their books were not only far superior to the deplorable productions of An Gúm but comparable in print and format to anything in English. Sadly for the subsequent fate of literature in Irish, Seán Ó hÉigeartaigh died suddenly in 1967 when he was only fifty years old, and if ever a man could be said to have worn himself out with overwork it was that patriotic cultural enthusiast.

When I replied to that initial letter from Seán, I did so with such enthusiasm – probably giving him a graphic account of my dealings with An Gúm, and of their double rejection of my prizewinning book – that when he replied he began his letter with the statement, '*Aithním ó do litir go bhfuil scríbhneoir agam!*' (I recognize from your letter that I've got a writer!) We met when I came to Dublin to collect my prize, and my book was in print two years before An Gúm brought out that first book of mine which they had accepted a year before. Sáirséal agus Dill subsequently published many of my books and plays. However, because of their limited resources and the uncertainty of the official subsidy for private publishers in Irish, they were sometimes unable even to consider works for publication. The result was that in spite of the treatment I had received from An Gúm, in the years to come, with my increasing responsibilities as a breadwinner, I had no option but to try that mysterious institution now and again with some item that would bring in a down payment if accepted.

Reverting to my pedagogic alter ego, I regret to say that Santa Claus, who had sometimes disappointed me in childhood by not bringing what I had asked for in my letter, let me down again and I a full-grown man. After I had taught for three months in a temporary capacity in the Model School, in the week before Christmas the bad news was broken to me by the school principal – I never saw the local inspector again! Not only one, but two permanent jobs were being created in the school but someone in the Department of Education in Dublin had rejected the inspector's recommendation of 'young Limerick writer', with the sad result that my connection with the Model School would come to an end at Christmas. I wondered then, I have often wondered

73

since then, and I wonder even now many years later, what connection there might have been between my literary conflicts with the bureaucrats of the department through An Gúm and the refusal of other officials to endorse the recommendation of the manager of their own Model School in Limerick. And what about that engagement ring which was to be symbolic of the happy Christmas of a young couple? Well, if young couples were to allow their happiness to depend on the machinations of faceless bureaucrats, there would be a lot more misery in the world. 'Sweet are the uses of adversity,' says Shakespeare in *As You Like It*. Anyone who has survived such adversity with love and with trust in God will know that it is a part of our pilgrimage through life and that it truly is beneficial to the soul, perhaps through the ways of the Lord that are a mystery to us. A few days before Christmas Day we bought a nice ring and we went into the Franciscan Church in Limerick and I put the ring on my beloved's finger and we promised in the presence of God to marry as soon as the ups and downs of life made it possible for us to do so. We enjoyed our Christmas, and when the New Year came I found another temporary job, a six-month stint in the Christian Brothers' primary school in Sexton Street.

In my own years in the Brothers' secondary school, which was just across the yard from the primary, I had taken part in a production of Wallace's *Maritana*. When the headmaster of the primary school, Brother O'Flaherty, told me one day that the secondary school were preparing a production of that opera, he added that the brother superior, a noted Irish language enthusiast named Ó Tatháin, had suggested that the primary school should be involved in the event and that I, being already known as a writer, might like to write and direct a one-act curtain-raiser in Irish for my own class, a fourth standard who were aged about ten or eleven. Setting lyrics to a wide range of popular, traditional and operatic airs, I wrote a musical play called *An Cnámh Draíochta* (The

74

Magic Bone), envisaging a comic cultural clash between a returning Fionn Mac Cumhaill and his Fianna and the Hollywood ethos of modern Ireland. Apart from the fact that the audience seemed to enjoy the enthusiastic and very talented acting of my cast more than the outdated and ridiculous plot of *Maritana*, my musical play had resonances long after the curtain came down on the final performance.

One of the pupils in that class of mine in the Christian Brothers School in Limerick was a pleasant young lad named Alfie McCourt. He was well-dressed and well-fed – 'a credit to the mother that reared him' as we say in Limerick – showing no sign at all of the daily starvation and deprivation in which, according to the harrowing account given in *Angela's Ashes* over forty years later by his older brother, Frank, the family allegedly grew up in Limerick. If anything, young Alfie McCourt looked the best beefy prospect in the class as a future rugby forward for Young Munster. I cast him in my musical play as a stalwart warrior in the army of Fionn mac Cumhaill and he acquitted himself very well.

There are two other reasons why those youthful voices singing in *An Cnámh Draíochta* reverberate in my memory to this day. General satisfaction having been expressed at the play's success, and no fault having been found with my daily labour in the classroom, Brother O'Flaherty told me that he would urge his boss, Brother Ó Tatháin, to retain me in a permanent capacity on the staff. This could be done, apparently, by taking in a few more pupils or by re-arranging numbers in the existing classes. But in spite of our mutual enthusiasm for the Irish language, Brother Ó Tatháin refused the request of his colleague and at the end of June and my six-month stint, I found myself once more facing a long summer in which literary hack-work would be my uncertain and delayed source of income. In addition to settling down to writing stories and plays for Radio Éireann's children and adult programmes, and articles for magazines and news-papers, I had also to drag out the sheaf of references and begin yet once more to consult the Teachers section in the Situations Vacant columns of the daily papers.

Defying this latest setback to our hopes, my beloved and I decided to marry in the autumn, even if, like many other people in those years, we would have to emigrate to John Bull's home island to find employment. Younger readers, accustomed to the booming economic conditions and lavish lifestyle of these latter decades, might not be aware that in the depressed conditions of the mid-century about fifty thousand people a year were emigrating to Britain and America, many of them with little education and no professional qualifications. I had a sister living in England who was continually assuring me that, due to the post-war shortage in the teaching as in other professions, I would have no difficulty in finding a good teaching post there. And having now acquired some proficiency and experience in writing, I might also hope to find some success in the literary markets and with the BBC. Actually, a fickle fate did have it in store for me to do some teaching in England but not just yet.

At the end of the summer holidays I got a post as a temporary principal in a two-teacher school in Patrickswell, a village six miles from Limerick. The man who gave me the job, a great GAA man named Canon Punch, assured me that the job would probably last for a year, and maybe, God knows, become permanent, because the man I was replacing was very ill with tuberculosis in a Dublin hospital. That man must have gone to Lourdes on a stretcher, because after five weeks the sporty canon breezed into the school one day to inform me that, thanks be to God and his Blessed Mother, he was coming back, hale and hearty, to his (my) job in Patrickswell. On the strength of that canonical 'one year at least, and maybe for good', my fiancée and I had arranged to be married in October. We were by now so inured to the 'slings and arrows of outrageous fortune' that we decided to go ahead and 'join our hands in wedlock bands', even if, as now seemed likely, we would then be following some of our friends on the emigrant ship.

It was then that God opened, not another door, but a double gateway. Along with a few negative replies from school managers to whose advertisements I had responded, the postman brought me one day a letter from the president of the teachers' training college in Dublin, who was also the manager of the primary school attached to the college. The school was regarded in official circles as the most prestigious in Ireland because the student teachers did their practical training there under the supervision of the teaching staff and the college lecturers. In this letter, I was being offered a teaching post in that special school, a job I had never applied for. It was a job many teachers would have licked the reverend manager's shoes to get but in fact, it was a job I would never dream of applying for if I had any hope of a job in my own Shannonside territory. It involved being part of a red-tape system that I had found uncongenial even as a student and knew would be more so to me now as a writer earning the daily bread by posing as a teacher. It is said that beggars can't be choosers; although I had not begged, I still had no choice. So, I wrote back and gratefully accepted the offer – I was never told why the offer was made – and I informed the reverend manager that as I was being married in a week's time and going to Dublin for a week's honeymoon, I would call to see him to discuss the matter.

The final echo of my musical play constitutes a literary bridge between my early years as a writer in Limerick and what might be called my Dublin period, which has lasted far longer than I expected when I came to the capital in October 1952 to take up that offer of a job. (My young bride and I were quite confident that we would be back in Limerick in a year or two; we have since reared a family of seven in Dublin and are at present rejoicing in the recent birth of our eleventh grandchild.) By now I had learnt some of the practical lessons of authorship, such as: keep a copy of everything and never throw anything away. Since, as will be seen, things did not quite turn out as expected in Dublin, I was compelled for some time to earn money with hackwork of various kinds.

One of the items that put food on the table for my young bride and myself was a radio adaptation, for a mixed adult cast, of *An Cnámh Draíochta*, which, when originally written for ten-year-old schoolboys as a stage play, earned me nothing but profuse thanks in Irish and a summer of unemployment. It was accepted by Radio Éireann, and the broadcast version was directed by that same guest director from the Abbey Theatre, Tomás Mac Anna, who had directed my first radio play, *Na Cimí* and subsequently found it unsuitable for production at the Abbey. The leading male role in this adult version of *An Cnámh Draíochta* was played by a fine singer named Liam Devally, who has in recent years become a District Justice in Dublin, a development which causes me to hope that if ever I should appear before him on a charge of murdering a theatre director or a literary critic, all I need do to gain acquittal is to begin to sing, to the air of 'Comin' through the Rye', these opening lines from the first song in a certain musical play:

> *Tá gach éinín ina nidín ina chodladh sámh,*
> *i bhfad ó bhaile tá an bheirt againn, caillte ag cnámh,*
> *glórtha daonna, radharc ar éinne, níl sa choill seo ar fáil,*
> *ach gaoth na hoích' ag caoineadh léi, is uaigneas ar gach*
> *áit.'*

Before leaving Limerick, however, I must tell the thrilling tale of how I came to wear the parish priest's socks.

My first job as a teacher was a temporary post for a year in the town of Roscommon, where I was shocked at Mass one Sunday by hearing, for the first time ever – the practice was not in use in my native Limerick – a list of the dues received being read out from the pulpit by the priest, names and sums, beginning with the highest and ending with the lowly equivalent of the widow's mite. Surely, I thought, Jesus Christ would not approve of that blatant blackmail of the rich and shaming of the poor. My homesickness was soon overcome by the friendliness of the people but the experience of playing as a light wing-forward in the county senior hurling final and not being able to hold the chalk in the classroom the day after, caused me to hang up my hurley forever in order to ensure that my writer's fingers would be able to work the typewriter.

I was unemployed for the summer, and among the advertisements I answered, while still hoping and praying that I would get a job in Limerick, was one for a teacher in Barefield, Ennis, County Clare. The reverend manager replied to my letter and invited me to come for an interview. I went by train on the day appointed and arrived at the station in Ennis in pouring rain. When I asked a railway porter whereabouts in Ennis I would find Barefield, he said it was not in Ennis at all. I produced my letter and showed him the heading: *Barefield, Ennis, Co. Clare.* I assumed that this was a district in the town, like Garryowen or Thomondgate in Limerick.

'But sure I'm from Barefield myself,' the man assured me, 'and it's about five miles out the Gort road.'

I told him what was bringing me to Barefield, and I must have looked so despondent that he decided to play the role of Good Samaritan.

'I'll tell you what you'll do,' he said. 'I cycled in this morning; so, I'll give you my bike and you can leave it at Fr Smyth's house. I'll get a lift home from a man I know, and I'll collect the bike tonight.'

Wishing him God's blessing with many thanks, I tucked my trouser legs into my socks and set off in the rain. I arrived at the PP's house looking the very picture of the proverbial drowned rat. When the housekeeper ushered me in, the elderly PP took one look at me and shook his head. 'Oh, my

God, you poor man! You're destroyed with the rain. Sit down here by the fire and we'll get you a cup o' tea.' And as the housekeeper began to do so, he called to her. 'Mary, would you get the poor boy a pair of dry socks to put on him, he'll get his death with the way he is.' The housekeeper gave me a fine tea, and the PP gave me the job. He also drove me to the station. When I told my mother the story and the good news, her thanks to God and Our Blessed Lady were mingled with concern for the reverend socks of that decent Clare priest. Those black socks were washed with as much care as if the Lord himself had worn them and I was instructed to post them back with a note of thanks. They became a symbol of sacerdotal goodness that helped me to retain my spiritual equilibrium years later when I felt the metaphorical weight of a parish priest's boot in my posterior.

9

A POUND A PIECE

Fadó, fadó, as the fireside seanchaí used to start his tales, there was a poor Irish peasant who, having heard impressive tales of the big city, decided to go and seek fame and fortune in its bright lights. Returning to his native heath in disillusionment, he summed up his impressions for his enquirers in the pithy saying, '*Níor chathair mar a tuairisc í* (It wasn't a city like its reputation). Knowing Dublin from my student days, when I moved there with my young bride in 1952 it was not a voyage of discovery but like the peasant in the story we were to be disappointed in our rosy expectations.

Not that the move to Dublin was anything like the culture shock experienced by many of our contemporaries who were being forced by economic circumstances to go and start a new life in the big cities of Britain or the US. In that pre-television era, Dublin was a smaller, safer, quieter and much more pleasant city than it is today, a big town where many of the citizens could still walk to work and most of the others used the bicycle or the bus, where pubs were still just pubs – in which a pint of Guinness cost one shilling and three pence (the equivalent of 6p in decimal coinage), and window-shopping was a free entertainment of an evening with no menace of syringe-wielding muggers.

The prospect of living in Dublin for a year or two, until I could find a permanent job in Limerick, did not seem too bad for that young couple who settled happily into a small semi-furnished two-room flat (really the two bedrooms) in an old red-brick terrace in Drumcondra, within a few minutes' walk of the training college near Tolka Bridge and within smelling distance of Lemon's, the fragrant sweet factory that then stood on the bank of the river. The two rooms on the ground floor were occupied by the owners of the house, a huge garda inspector from the midlands named John Finlay, and his wife, Margaret, who was a forelady in Fuller's sweet factory. They were a very pleasant middle-aged couple who had married only recently and who treated us, we felt, less like tenants than like the grown-up son and daughter they might have had if they had married 'young and foolish' as they probably thought we had done. Half-way up the stairs, a bathroom and toilet were communal, the major problem being that the ancient bath was dys-functional and that the Victorian builders had not foreseen that running water in the front bedroom might one day be needed by a young couple making it into a living-room.

We were offered the use of the poky kitchen downstairs but opted instead for the independence provided by a new gas-cooker which the Dublin Gas Company installed, on the instalment system, in a corner of our livingroom. Along with a bedroom suite from Cavendish and Co. of Grafton Street, pioneers in the hire purchase system, that shiny gas-cooker, and the light provided by the ESB, and the coal for what was really only a bedroom grate, constituted a hefty addition to the weekly rent of two pounds, and this before food and clothes were added to the expenditure. So, my teacher's salary of about six pounds a week would have to be very finely stretched. That is, if I had any teacher's salary. In fact, it was to be nearly five months before I had any.

Although the Rev President of the training college had assured me that the appointment was about to be made, and had advised me to find living accommodation while enjoying my week's honeymoon in Dublin, some mysterious bureaucratic problems kept postponing my appointment week by week, until I began to suspect neurotically that whoever in the Department of Education had rejected the local inspector's recommendation with regard to my appointment to the Model School in Limerick was now doing the same dirty trick to keep me from earning my crust as a teacher in the training school. The plot thickened in the fertile imagination of the writer to link all this with the rejection of my work by those pedants in An Gúm. The long finger of fate pushed and prodded from week to week, all the way from October to January, when the promised job finally became a reality. But since the monthly salary was not paid until the middle of the following month, it was mid-February before the postman brought us our first cheque from the Department of Education.

Somebody wrote a play (or was it a book?) called *Love on the Dole* (1933) about social inequality in Britain during the bad times between the wars, and a Tin Pan Alley songwriter made himself a pile of dollars by tootling, 'There ain't no livin' on love alone, but sure I'm going to try.' Even our Divine Lord, Jesus Christ, if I may say so with all due reverence, counsels us not to worry about tomorrow but to 'consider the lilies of the field,' and also 'the birds of the air.' Although this lovely passage proves that if Jesus in his divine nature had not been preoccupied with redeeming the human race, in his human nature he could have become one of the greatest poets of all time, I have found during several periods of crisis in my career that the lilies of the field do not provide sustenance for hungry mouths, and if you do nothing but consider them you are likely to find yourself and dependants living in the field along with the lilies.

So, what did my young wife and I live on for the first five months of wedded bliss? Well, things were not altogether desperate, because in the same month of October in which we married I had collected my Oireachtas prize of fifty pounds for that book which had been twice rejected by An Gúm, plus a few small cheques for stories and plays on the children's programmes of Radio Éireann and for some articles. This fund gave us breathing space while I daily hammered out new hack-work on my Underwood Portable – if my brave young wife had not been so gentle and loving, she might sometimes have been inclined to hit me with one of the saucepans while she waited to put the dinner on the small table at which I was banging out the last lines in a bout of dialogue or the last sentences in a paragraph. Sáirséal agus Dill had also accepted the book that had been placed second in the Oireachtas competition, but unlike An Gúm they did not have the resources to pay an acceptance fee or even a token advance.

Since the items I was now writing, even if accepted by Radio Éireann or some magazine, would not bring in payment for several months, we began to consider the alternatives of seeking a job somewhere else in Ireland or giving in to fate and heading for the emigrant ship at Dún Laoghaire. An unusual item of literary hack-work came my way when Seán Ó hÉigeartaigh of Sáirséal agus Dill offered me a fee to prepare the Irish short stories of Liam O'Flaherty for the press. As the rusty paper clips and the pages themselves showed, most of these had been written in the 1920s, with some later additions, and my task was to bring the script into conformity with the simplified spelling and the standard grammar which had been recently devised by a committee of scholars set up by the government. The stories appeared in 1953 under the title *Dúil*.

In November a letter from the Abbey Theatre came as a surprise and also as what seemed to be a good omen, something in the nature of the silver lining in a dark cloud. (It should be noted that the household phone, like central heating or the car, had not yet become common.) It was from Tomás Mac Anna, who had just directed yet another of my radio plays, this one a retelling, with original rhymes and songs, of the Cinderella story. His letter mentioned this and asked if I would be interested in writing lyrics for the Abbey's Irish pantomime at a fee of a pound per lyric (I have mentioned that the rent of our two-roomed semi-furnished was two pounds per week). If so, I was to call and see him at the Abbey on a forthcoming evening. The theatre had been so damaged by a disastrous fire in the previous year (1951) that the plays were now being put on in the Queen's Theatre across the Liffey; but the upstairs office of the managing director, Ernest Blythe, was still in use, and the foyer of the old theatre was being used for rehearsals. Lyrics at a pound a piece might remind some literary readers of James Joyce's attempts at being a poet in *Pomes Penyeach* which even his admirer, Ezra Pound (no pun intended) advised him not to publish. To me, the offer represented not only the promise of hard cash, but something even more, an entrée, however tentative, to the literary world of Dublin as represented by the Abbey Theatre.

Although I had by now had some success in various genres of literature, in Irish and English, and even won a few prizes in the anonymous competitions of the Oireachtas, I was still an innocent abroad as far as the literary world was concerned. I had never met another writer and in spite of some rebuffs from the nameless pedants in An Gúm and from the novelist, Francis MacManus in Radio Eireann my attitude to writing and writers was idealistic to the point of naïveté. As for an institution like the Abbey Theatre, which like many people I mistakenly believed to be the National Theatre of Ireland, my impression, based on what I had read about Yeats and Lady Gregory, Synge and O'Casey, was that it was a world-famous theatre and that all the people associated with it must be the most talented theatrical people in Ireland. To be actually invited to do any work for the Abbey, even at the level of writing lyrics for the Christmas pantomime, almost, but not quite, put me off my grub with excitement on the day I received that letter. The Abbey and its directors would be the cause of really putting me off my grub, and not with excitement, on many an occasion in the years to come.

It might be of interest to give a brief account of the context in which I, as an aspiring but naïve young writer, was about to make my first contact with the literary world.

The Abbey's Christmas pantomime in Irish had in recent years become a regular feature of Dublin theatre. It was initiated by Ernest Blythe, with the backing of Comhdháil Náisiúnta na Gaeilge, a state-sponsored umbrella body for the coordination of the work of the various Irish language groups and societies. Blythe was a Northern Presbyterian who in his youth had become as fervently nationalistic as those Ulster Presbyterians who formed the United Irishmen and fought gallantly for Irish independence from England in 1798. He learned Irish the hard way, by going to work for a farmer in the Kerry Gaeltacht, and he took part in the Anglo-Irish War of 1919-21. With the signing of the Treaty, he became Minister for Finance in the first government of the Irish Free State, and earned the opprobrium of every pensioner in the country, no matter what their political views, when he cut the old-age pension by a shilling in 1924.

As a minister in that first government Ernest Blythe was responsible for the granting of an annual subsidy to the Abbey Theatre in 1924, and, as I have already noted, for the setting up of An Gúm in 1925. When de Valera's Fianna Fáil party came to power in 1932, Blythe's political career went into decline but his official generosity to the Abbey was rewarded when the board appointed him managing director in 1941. I was not the only playwright to discover to my cost that whatever God intended this zealous and forthright man to be, it certainly was not anything to do with the arts and especially with theatre. In a bitter moment many years later I opined that he would have made an excellent manager of a yard producing concrete blocks. Still I do not hold at all with those who condemn him totally.

This is the attitude exemplified in the entries on the Abbey Theatre and on Ernest Blythe himself in the *Oxford Companion to Irish Literature* (1996), where we are told that he 'served as managing director 1941–67, presiding over a succession of dreary kitchen-comedies during a stagnant period of Irish drama. His policy of employing Irish-speaking actors only in order to advance the cause of drama in Irish led to a loss of some major talents and to the promotion of pantomimes of notorious banality.' This account is inaccurate and biased, nor does it name any of the 'major talents' allegedly lost to Irish theatre because they did not know Irish. From time to time, actors feeling the frustrations and restrictions inevitable in any permanent company left the Abbey to seek fame and fortune in London but they would have done so even if no word of Irish was ever spoken in the Abbey. How many of those who left, for whatever reason, achieved fame and fortune? Two actors who could truly be called major talents of Irish theatre, Mícheál MacLiammóir and Cyril Cusack, both acquired fluency in Irish, and I saw Siobhán McKenna play Shaw's *Saint Joan* in English and in her own Irish translation of the play.

The article on Blythe is also a grossly misleading account of the plays presented in that period – how could even the most biased commentator describe Frank Carney's *The Righteous are Bold* (1946), M. J. Molloy's *The King of Friday's Men* (1948) or Walter Macken's *Home is the Hero* (1952) as 'kitchen-comedies'? My own play, *In Dublin's Fair City* (1959), set in a tenement and telling of an unemployed young man standing as an independent in a general election, was a study of the social and political conditions of the time.

In view of the fact that the Irish Free State had decided in 1922 on reviving Irish and making the country bilingual, Ernest Blythe was being perfectly logical, as well as patriotic, in believing that young actors anywhere in Ireland a generation later, and especially actors in the prestigious and subsidised National Theatre Company, should be able to put on plays in Irish as well as English. The older actors spoke no Irish and were not expected to learn it but with the younger actors, all of whom were supposed to have been taught Irish from infant school upwards, Blythe hoped eventually to form a bilingual company. Unfortunately, although he encouraged the young actors by paying for holiday periods in the Gaeltacht he was over-zealous in ordering that their names should always appear in Irish in the cast list of a play, even when that play was in English as all the Abbey plays were apart from the occasional tailpiece one-acter in Irish.

The Abbey's Irish pantomimes, one of which was about to provide me, in 1952, with my very lowly entrée to that famous institution as a writer of some lyrics, were cast from the younger members of the company, supplemented by amateur actors from the many drama groups associated with the Gaelic League and other Irish societies. They were as entertaining and as popular as the English pantomimes in the other Dublin theatres. The plot, like those in the traditional English pantomime, might not have satisfied Aristotle's theory of the unities or complied with the views of Longinus on the sublime but the standard ingredients of romance, comedy and spectacle, embellished with a mixture of popular, operatic and traditional songs set to appropriate lyrics, with incidental original music by Gerard Victory (later to become Head of Music in RTÉ) and the colourful production in which Tomás Mac Anna was able to display his forte for spectacular effects, made the Irish pantomime a regular outing for many families at the festive season. Many parents were glad to find their rusty school Irish being revived and the children discovered that Irish could be a means of fun and entertainment instead of a mere school subject. Unlike those in other Dublin theatres, the Abbey pantomimes were based on Irish legends instead of being imitations of the British product based on English folktales.

Before leaving the comprehensive *Oxford Companion to*

Irish Literature (1996) – to which the more concise *Mercier Companion to Irish Literature* (1998) is a valuable complement – and as I am trying to give a true account of my life as a writer, I must advert to the brief paragraph entry which summarises my fifty years' hard labour in two languages and in all genres and which bluntly informs the reader that I was 'educated at Trinity College'. As will be seen in due course, I am indebted to Trinity College and particularly to Professor J. V. Rice and his colleagues in the Education Department, for providing me with a meal ticket, in the form of the Higher Diploma in Education, at a time in my life when an archbishop's crozier was prodding me on to the emigrant ship for the second time. To say that I was actually educated there is a solecism which constitutes a grave injustice to the Sisters of Mercy, the lay teachers, and the Christian Brothers, to all of whom I owe my formal schooling. My education in the broad sense, which is ongoing, draws on sources ranging from my grandparents to my grandchildren, with inputs from the hard school of experience and from the few good books I have found time and leisure to read often enough to remember something from them.

And now, where was I? as my mother used to say when, while telling us our bedtime story, the poor woman fell asleep herself and had to be roused by the unsatisfied wideawake audience.

(Patient Reader: 'You were on your way in to meet Tomás Mac Anna in what was left of the Abbey Theatre in order to discuss the writing of lyrics for the Christmas pantomime in Irish'). Ah yes! Well –

When I walked into the spacious foyer of the old theatre where the new one now stands, Mac Anna was rehearsing a scene with a few actors. Others were sitting or standing around. I went quietly over to an empty chair and sat down beside a young actor to watch Mac Anna in action. After a while, the young man beside me whispered to me.

'Are you Críostóir Ó Floinn?'

I had no wish to deny it, wondering only how he knew. He told me.

'I recognized you from your photo in the papers.' (The Oireachtas results were given a good deal of publicity in those days).

He went on: 'I directed a play of yours in Maynooth on St Patrick's Day.'

Only then did I realize that I was talking to Ray McAnally, who was to play the leading role of the prince in the pantomime. He asked me what I was doing there. When I told him, he asked me one of the most shocking questions I had ever been asked in my life up to then.

'Have you a contract?'

'A contract? But they only want me to write lyrics at a pound a piece.'

'Don't do anything until you get a contract from Mr Blythe,' Ray advised.

We were interrupted by Mac Anna, of whom my first and lasting impression was that he was some years older than me, big, ebullient and loquacious. While the cast were enjoying a break, he gave me my first assignment, which was to write suitable lyrics for the popular song, 'Walkin' My Baby Back Home' – he gave me a brief outline of the context – and deliver it to him as soon as possible, tomorrow at the latest, when he would give me more of the same. I walked home to Drumcondra in a very muddled state. Here I was, a young writer actually being asked to write lyrics by a young director at the world-famous Abbey Theatre. My writer's imagination conjured up visions of a future play of mine being accepted. At the same time a young actor in the Abbey company, the man who had directed my play in Maynooth and who had just been speaking very highly of it, was practically telling me that – well, what was Ray McAnally telling me? Whatever it was, I felt it would be very foolish of me to refuse the opportunity to work for the

Abbey Theatre but neither could I regard it as anything but audacious for a young and practically unknown writer to approach the managing director of the Abbey and demand a contract merely for the writing of a few lyrics for the Christmas pantomime.

My experience in writing lyrics for my own musical play, *An Cnámh Draíochta* and for several children's radio plays, made concocting Irish lyrics for 'Walkin' My Baby Back Home' an easy task. As Christmas drew nearer, however, and we learned that payment for the Abbey lyrics would not be made until the New Year, I began to fear that the title might turn out to be prophetic if we did not have the train fare to Limerick. (We had neither the money nor the inclination to provide a Christmas for ourselves in Dublin.) I wrote ten lyrics in all, the most difficult being words to the famous Figaro comic aria in Rossini's *Il Barbiere di Sevilla*. This was to be performed by a Cork actor named Joe Lynch, widely known in recent years as one of the stars of the television series, *Glenroe*, but then a young member of the Abbey company (I remember his impressive Christy Mahon in Synge's *Playboy*) in a scene in which he portrayed a zany post office counter clerk. In addition to the *Figaro* lyrics – for which my proficiency on the flute proved an essential aid – I was asked by Mac Anna, who had himself profited by my dramatic ability as a guest director in RTÉ, to write the actual scene, which was subsequently noted by the critics as one of the most successful in the pantomime. In our domestic calculations, my wife and I figured that we were now owed ten pounds by the Abbey Theatre, plus a few more – maybe even a fiver! – for that post office scene.

After purchasing two return rail tickets to Limerick in the city office a few days before Christmas, we had one pound left in the world. (The common citizen didn't have a bank account in those days of cash-in-hand). I had by now begun to make a more down-to-earth appraisal of the Abbey Theatre and all connected with it, and I decided that on our way to Kingsbridge (as Heuston Station was called up to 1966 when the principal railway stations were renamed in honour of the men of 1916) I would call to the Abbey and politely request payment for my contribution to the Christmas pantomime. While my young wife shivered outside in the cold of midwinter – and probably wondered what was to become of us after Christmas – I went up the stairs from the door in the side lane and knocked at the office door. It was opened by a woman who, when I told her that I wanted to see Mr Blythe, demanded to know my business in a manner such as a dramatist might imagine if he wanted to put a female prison warder in a play. I was to learn later that this was the managing director's secretary, whose duties included keeping people like me from bothering him.

'Wait there and I'll ask Mr Blythe,' she ordered, and closed the door.

After some sounds within, the door reopened sufficiently for her to hand me a brown envelope. 'There it is for you,' she observed.

I thanked her and went happily down the stairs, to learn that you should never be happy until you open the envelope and examine the contents. The Abbey envelope contained a cheque for *five* pounds. Leaving my wife to endure the cold for another while, I went back up the stairs and knocked again (I wonder if Seán O'Casey used to knock at that door when he wanted to talk to Lady Gregory or Yeats?) To the female guardian, I explained the mistake – I had written ten lyrics at an agreed fee of a pound a piece, plus an entire scene for which I expected a fee of five pounds, total fifteen pounds.

'Wait there and I'll ask Mr Blythe,' and the door shuts again in the honest face of 'young Limerick writer' who is getting older and wiser by the day.

The door reopens slightly and the same envelope is handed back to me.

'Mr Blythe said there's no mistake. They don't ever use all the stuff in the pantomime, they always have to cut out a lot; you're being paid for what they're using.'

And the door closes much like the gates of Hell in Dante's *Inferno*.

In the New Year, when I had put in my first week's work as a teacher in the Training School in Drumcondra, my wife and I went to see the pantomime in the Queen's Theatre. We enjoyed the show as did all the audience and I had the added pleasure of seeing and hearing a little bit of my work in a theatre for the first time. When we met some of the cast afterwards, I took the opportunity to tell Ray McAnally about the deficiency in my payment.

'I warned you,' he said quietly, 'but now you know.' And as he had just been giving living proof on the stage that Mr Blythe's Irish language policy was not all in vain, at least with the more nationalistic members of the Abbey company, he added, '*Ciall cheannaigh, a Chríostóir, sin an chiall is fearr.*' (Sense that is bought is the best).

I was well armed with that *ciall cheannaigh* when, a few weeks after the pantomime season ended, I was invited to attend a meeting in the offices of Comhdháil Náisiúnta na Gaeilge (they were in the building beside Clery's in O'Connell Street) where representatives of all the bodies connected with the production of the pantomime were to discuss the one just ended. Among them were Ernest Blythe himself and my enthusiastic publisher, Seán Ó hÉigeartaigh, as well as the director of the pantomime, Tomás Mac Anna. I was surprised to be introduced to them all by Donncha Ó Laoghaire, the genial and overworked secretary of the Comhdháil, as a young writer who had written some of the lyrics for the recent pantomime and who, he understood, would be asked to write the entire script for the next pantomime. I sat and listened to the ensuing discussion. I was told that a fee of one hundred pounds would be forthcoming for writing the script. Mac Anna added that of course I would be paid also for any lyrics I might contribute. I told them that I would consider the proposition. When the meeting ended, Mac Anna took me aside and advised me to submit a script to him as soon as possible, the story to be based as usual on some old Irish tale or legend, and that he himself would work on it with me throughout the year.

Having discussed the proposition with my wife, we were unanimous in our decision, based on our recollection of standing in the laneway outside the Abbey on a bitterly cold day a few days before Christmas, looking at a cheque for five pounds. We did not need an angel from heaven to tell us that the fee of one hundred pounds would pay the rent of our flat for a year or that a refusal of the offer might blacken my name not only with the Abbey but with the Irish language establishment. I wrote to the Secretary of Comhdháil Náisiúnta na Gaeilge and told him that I did not wish to write the script for the next pantomime; but being my mother's son, I told him why. And I also told him the story about another Limerick playwright, a man named Andrew Cherry. Born in 1762, he became a renowned comic actor in London's Covent Garden, although now known, if at all, only as the author of *The Dear Little Shamrock*. In our fireside tales, my father told us how, having put on a season of plays for some theatre manager and not been paid, Andrew replied to a request from the same manager to do another season with the following:

Sir,
You have bitten me once, and I am resolved that you shall not make two bites of
A. Cherry.

10

THE BEST OF THE WORST

Since coming to live in Dublin I had begun to read my own stories and talks in Irish on Radio Éireann, having been invited to do so by Cathal Ó Gríofa. (My stories in English were still being returned by MacManus as *unsuitable for broadcasting'*.) The first story I broadcast on the adult programme was one about Matt Talbot's metamorphosis from habitual drunkard to total abstainer on the night when, penniless because of a period of unemployment, he stood near his local pub and was ignored by the boozing companions on whom he used to squander much of his hard-earned wages. I practised this story so assiduously, with my patient young wife as audience and critic, that she almost had it off by heart before the fateful night – and then she listened to it on our new radio (which, like the gas-cooker, worked on the HP system) in order to tell me how it sounded to the people of Ireland. Among the plays I wrote was a four-part serial on Joseph in Egypt for the children's programme; this was long before Andrew Lloyd Webber was to make a fortune with his musical version but I was happy to get six pounds a part for my dramatic rehash of one of the most fascinating stories in the Bible and in all literature. I owe a lot to those people in Radio Éireann and RTÉ who accepted my work down through the years. They gave me the recognition that is the essential factor in a writer's survival, as well as the occasional cheque which helped me to survive when the actions of others put me in what the cliché calls 'straitened financial circumstances'.

My troubles with the nameless rejecters in An Gúm who, alone among all the editors to whom I had submitted work, had found fault with my Irish, were put into a broader context when a quarrel erupted in the Irish language literary world just as I was settling into my new job in the Training School in Drumcondra in the spring of 1953. *Eireaball Spideoige*, the first collection of poems by the Cork poet, Seán Ó Ríordáin (1916-1977), which some critics hailed as the best thing in Irish poetry since Brian Merriman (died 1805) a farmer cum schoolmaster in Feakle, County Clare, composed *Cúirt an Mheán Oíche* (The Midnight Court) – was denigrated in reviews in the Gaelic League magazine, *Feasta*, and the weekly newspaper *Inniú*. In *Feasta* Máire Mhac an tSaoi found fault with the poet's Irish and with his metrical structures. She advised him to go and listen to the 'native speakers' and to study the folk poetry in the Kerry Gaeltacht (where, incidentally, she herself had been privileged to spend many holidays and even attend the local school in Dún Chaoin, because her uncle, Monsignor Pádraig de Brún, of UCG, had a holiday home there). The review in *Inniú* was written by the editor, Ciarán Ó Nualláin (a brother of Myles na Gopaleen, as I have noted earlier) who mocked the poet's philosophical introductory essay and also deplored his Irish because it contained expressions that were more like translations of English idiom than genuine Irish. Such usages were called *béarlachas* (anglicism) by the pedantic purists and the accusation was a common one against any writer who dared to be innovative by using any phrase or expression that had not been heard in the spoken language (James Joyce would have got short shrift from the Irish language pedants if he had tried to write in Irish). Seán Ó Ríordáin was born and reared in the west Cork Gaeltacht, moving to live near

Cork City at the age of fifteen when his father died. If his attempts to write in Irish were being denigrated, writers like myself who had been born and reared in an English ambience in a city had little hope of being accepted by the narrow-minded pedants who demanded that all modern writing in Irish must read exactly, in vocabulary and idiom, like one or other of the dialects being spoken by uneducated peasants in the Gaeltacht areas. The Cork poet was fortunate in having able defenders. His critics were replied to by several competent literary people, including his friend, Seán Ó Tuama of UCC, but most notably and generously by the Aran poet, Máirtín Ó Direáin (1910-1988), a writer whose own work was not given due recognition for many years to come.

I met Ó Direáin and other writers when I joined *Cumann na Scríbhneoirí* (Society of Writers), a sort of Irish language version of the international PEN Club (which I also joined). In spite of my chastening experience as a coopted member of the Gaelic League committee in Limerick, I found myself appointed to the committee of Cumann na Scríbhneoirí when Donncha Ó Laoghaire, the versatile, ubiquitous and continually over-worked secretary of Comhdháil Náisiúnta na Gaeilge, asked me to represent the younger generation of Irish writers. The president of the committee was the 1916 veteran, Piaras Béaslaí (1883-1965), poet and dramatist, and the other members were Máiréad Ní Ghráda (1899-1971), the Irish editor at Browne and Nolan Ltd. to whom I had submitted one of my books from Limerick, Máirtín Ó Direáin and Donncha Ó Céileachair (1918-1960) from west Cork who had been a teacher and was now one of the editorial team working on the English-Irish dictionary of Tomás de Bhaldraithe which was published in 1959.

The committee met once a month in the Comhdháil offices in O'Connell Street. As we had little or no practical business to discuss, the sessions were in effect a general discussion on literary matters, with digressions to affairs of current interest in Irish language circles and in the country or the world at large. Whatever apprehensions I might have had at sitting on a literary committee with persons older and of much greater reputation than a beginner like myself were quickly put to rest. In the long years since then I have had dealings with people of all kinds in the literary world, but I have never met such a blend of courtesy, friendliness, intellectual modesty and genuine erudition, as in that group. When the meeting ended and the senior members, Piaras and Máiréad, departed, Máirtín, Donncha and the *garsún* Críostóir would adjourn to a nearby pub to continue our chat. At our first pub adjournment, when Máirtín asked me if I would like a pint of Guinness, I told him that I did not drink stout because I was a member of the Pioneer Total Abstinence Society since my schooldays (I had lost my Sacred Heart lapel badge some time previously) but I would have a glass of cider, my favourite drink. I was amazed to learn from two heads older than mine that cider, which I believed to be merely a fruit drink because it was made from apples, was even more intoxicating than stout. What they thought of the naïve *garsún* from Limerick they were too courteous to say. It would be a few years more before I faced up to my first pint of Guinness, purely in the cause of literature as will be seen.

At my first meeting of Cumann na Scríbhneoirí, I had thanked Máirtín Ó Direáin for his remarks about my prize-winning poem in Mainchín Seoighe's *Limerick Leader* competition, and Máiréad Ní Ghráda for her encouraging letter when returning my book from Browne and Nolan. But my clearest memory of that little group and of those literary chats is of the shock I got at one of our meetings when Donncha Ó Céileachair, a native speaker of Irish whose reputation as a writer was built on his short stories, congratulated me sincerely on winning, among other items, the short story prize in the Oireachtas competitions of that year. 'You beat my own effort!' he added. I would never have known this if he had not told me. How many other writers would have done so? And when my story was eventually published in the Gaelic League magazine, *Feasta*, Donncha commented on it at our next committee meeting, telling me that it deserved the prize. His death in 1960, at the age of forty-one, deprived modern Irish literature of a talented writer who was also one of nature's gentlemen and a true scholar.

While I was still adjusting my perspective on the literary world because of my first personal involvement with the management and personnel of the Abbey Theatre, a notice appeared in the papers to the effect that the same Abbey Theatre was offering a prize of three hundred pounds for a new play, the winning entry to be guaranteed an Abbey production. Just as I had been stimulated into writing a radio play by a Radio Éireann competition, I now began to envisage Mr Ernest Blythe, in person, presenting me with a cheque for three hundred smackers *and* signing a contract for the production of my prizewinning play. (I now realized the paradoxical truth of Sam Goldwyn's shrewd dictum, 'a verbal contract ain't worth the paper it's written on'.) But, as Mrs Beeton is supposed to have said, 'First catch your hare.'

From my studies of those books in Limerick City Library in my apprentice days, I had picked up the practical advice to keep a notebook or several notebooks, in which ideas for plays, stories, novels, plays and articles would be written down. Just like sowing cabbage or any other seed, the author said, some will grow better than others; some might even lie dormant for years and suddenly begin to sprout. One such idea that I had noted and that was already sprouting strongly in my imagination, was the story of the blind man in the ninth chapter St John's Gospel. This is a drama in itself, even as recorded in the New Testament. This blind man is more alive than most of the characters in modern novels and plays; in fact, he is so alive that any unprejudiced writer of fiction will instinctively feel, as I do, that this man and the things related about him are not fiction but history. Like other incidents and characters in the New Testament – I'll be recording my debt to the mother of James and John in a later chapter of this book – this unnamed blind man has helped me to keep my faith in Jesus Christ and the Catholic Church when the unChristian actions of some Church officials were tending to blind my own intellect and allow emotion rather than reason to influence my conscience. I had *The Blind Man* (St John: 9) down in my notebook as the raw material for a novel. Now I decided that it was so dramatic already that it could be filled out into a three-act play by adding some more characters and background, and by complicating the plot.

In the Central Catholic Library in Merrion Square – an excellent library to which I still resort, and which is sadly under-used – I spent many hours researching the period and getting to know all about the Pharisees and other types. I called my play *The Light of the World*. It did not win the prize, which was divided between two entries (both were eventually given a production and made neither fame nor fortune for their authors). But the letter from Mr Blythe which accompanied my returned play was interesting: 'This play,' it said, 'is not being awarded a prize; nor is it one of the few others that might be considered for production later on; but it is certainly the best of the rest.' So, my effort was not in vain after all; being the best of the worst is an accolade of some kind.

Some time later I read an article in which a priest in Maynooth referred to the blind man in St John in much the same terms as I have been doing here. I wrote to him and told him about my play; he replied asking to read the script with a view to showing it to some people who might stage the play. No need now to tell what was the end of that correspondence. I have already stressed that one of the first lessons for the apprentice writer is to keep a copy of everything, but, as that wise lady, Portia, says in *The Merchant of Venice*, 'It is a good divine that follows his own instructions: I can easier teach twenty what were good to be done, than be one of the twenty to follow mine own teaching.' The reader might recall that another maxim I had been taught by my forerunners in the business was never to throw anything away. I had my notes from those hours of research in the Central Catholic Library. Years later I wrote a shorter version of the Blind Man play in Irish, with the same title, *Solas an tSaoil*. It won an Oireachtas prize, was broadcast twice, published in book form by An Gúm (it took them only seven years from the date of acceptance) and duly rejected by the Abbey Theatre.

I was only settling into the permanent teaching job I had been so long waiting for when I was offered the opportunity to leave it for a while. The man I have already mentioned a few times, Donncha Ó Laoghaire, an ex-teacher from County Cork, whose job as secretary of Comhdháil Náisiúnta na Gaeilge involved the unenviable task of coping with many disparate and sometimes contentious groups and bodies promoting the Irish language – the latest addition to his chores was the Irish Book Club, An Club Leabhar – invited me to come and see him in his office. He told me that the Comhdháil had initiated a new scholarship scheme under which Irish language writers who had not been born in the Gaeltacht would be given the chance to live for six months in any Gaeltacht area in order to experience a linguistic milieu that was totally Irish. It was hoped that this would both encourage them to continue writing in Irish and also improve their own knowledge of the language. Two writers per year would be chosen for this offer. The conditions were that the six-month period must be in the non-tourist or winter period, the writer would neither lose nor profit financially; the equivalent of six months' current salary, plus essential expenses if any, would be paid. The writer would not be required to do anything except reside permanently in the Gaeltacht for the six-month period; if married, author's spouse could accompany author only if they were habitually using Irish as their domestic language.

Currently availing of this scheme, Donncha told me, was the Cork poet, Seán Ó Ríordáin, whose normal occupation was that of clerk in the motor tax office of Cork Corporation but who was at present domiciled in Dún Chaoin (a development which probably caused Máire Mhac an tSaoi much satisfaction). Donncha did not tell me, but I heard unofficially later, that a promising Dublin writer named Brendan Behan, who had written a few poems and articles in Irish, had been offered the scholarship and had gone to the Aran Islands, where he settled down to boisterous sessions of drinking and singing until the supply of money from the Comhdháil in Dublin was abruptly cut off and the Dublin jackeen returned to his native heath to become one of the most successful and notorious English-language writers of his time.

When Donncha told me that the committee of the Comhdháil, the same people who had invited me to write the script of the next pantomime, had decided to offer the scholarship for next winter to myself and another young writer named Risteard de Paor, I was impressed by the fact that the committee, which included Ernest Blythe and my publisher, Seán Ó hÉigeartaigh, did not bear me any grudge for my refusal of that other offer. I pointed out, however, that I would have to discuss the offer with my wife. We had decided shortly after our marriage that we would speak Irish as much as possible but I had reservations about asking the girl to come and spend the darkest and bleakest six months of the year in Dún Chaoin at the tip of the Dingle Peninsula. I would also have to obtain permission from the Department of Education and from the reverend manager of the school (the Vincentian priest who was president of the training college) and I would have to employ a substitute teacher for the six-month period.

My wife's attitude to the offer was totally positive. I think we both felt that it would be the kind of change that is said to be as good as a holiday; if we had known anything about the primitive living conditions in the Dingle Peninsula at that time and what a winter in Dún Chaoin was like, we might have rejected the offer and confined our further study of Irish to our books and the radio. The pleasant couple downstairs who were our landlords agreed to hold the flat for us at half-rent and the Vincentian president of the college, Fr Kilian Kehoe CM, surprised me by his supportive and encouraging reaction to my request to be absent for six months from a job in which he had just installed me after much trouble with the department. He merely urged me to write a novel in Irish that would be easier to read than the ones written in dialect by 'native speakers'. (He was currently struggling, he told me, with *Cré na Cille* by Máirtín Ó Cadhain). I discovered also that the officials of the Department of Education were not bureaucratic clones whose automatic response to any request would be in the negative. The officials I encountered then and in similar situations later in my career seemed to be a different breed from the people with whom I had been dealing in An Gúm. I was readily given permission to avail of the scholarship offer – provided, of course, that a suitable substitute was approved by the reverend manager of the school – and I was wished good luck with the hope that I would benefit by the offer.

So, as the year went by, we made the necessary arrangements, opting on the advice of our mentor, Donncha of the Comhdháil, to stay in the same house in Dún Chaoin in which Seán Ó Ríordáin had spent his six months Gaeltacht season. And everything was going along so well that we should have known fate does not let life go on like that, not for long anyway. While we were staying with my wife's family in Limerick during the summer holidays, her first pregnancy ended in a miscarriage, and when the time came for taking up the scholarship the doctor, perhaps knowing more about conditions in Dún Chaoin than we did, ordered her to stay in her father's house until further notice. So, at her insistence, I set off on my own.

I had spent a month in the west Cork Gaeltacht when I was nine years old, on a Gaelic League scholarship, but apart from learning some songs, I had acquired more knowledge of rabbits and birds than of Irish. In spite of my antipathy to dialect and colloquial speech as the medium of literature, I hoped that my writing in Irish would benefit from this golden opportunity to live in a society where Irish was the language of daily life.

11

'LEANANN TRIOBLÓID LEABHAR'

I got my first taste of the colloquial living Irish of the Gaeltacht before I arrived there. On the bus from Tralee to Dingle, two women behind me were chatting volubly in Irish just as their counterparts would be in English on a bus in Dublin. As I said earlier about writing in Irish as compared with writing in English, there is some spiritual link with our ancestors in the Irish language. It is something that cannot be explained to those who have not experienced it, and people who are hostile to the Irish language are in blissful ignorance of their own deprivation. I can still remember the tingling in my spirit when I heard those two women chatting behind me and the subsequent feeling of regret that I was never likely to hear two ordinary citizens on a bus in Dublin conversing in our own language. That was in 1953, in the pre-television days in Ireland. If I could have foreseen the accelerating deleterious effect of the mass media and the pop culture on Irish through the second half of the century – their effect even on English, as well as on society in general, is not my concern here – I would probably have turned back at Dingle and asked my wife to consider emigrating with me to New York or Australia.

A shock of a different kind awaited me in the town of Dingle, then a very different place from the cosmopolitan tourist town of today. There was no bus service around the peninsula but in a small pub, where a woman poured the stout into the glasses from an enamel jug, I got directions to the house of a man who had a taxi and who would, maybe, be available to drive me the fifteen miles or so to Dún Chaoin. The parish of Dún Chaoin – there was no village as such – consisted of scattered houses facing the Great Blasket Island three miles out in the Atlantic. There was a small church and an adjoining graveyard, a school, a post office with a phone, a small shop and guesthouse but no resident priest, no doctor, no pub, no electricity and no running water. From the village of Ballyferriter about five miles to the north, the parish priest or his curate came to say Mass on Sunday. To Ballyferriter, on foot or bicycle, the man who needed a drink had to go unless he was satisfied with the bottle of stout available under the counter in the shop.

It was during that winter of 1953 that the Great Blasket island was abandoned by the last of its inhabitants; the population had dwindled to about twenty, including one small boy but no youths or girls, from an average of around one hundred and fifty throughout the previous century and up to the establishment of the Irish Free State in 1922. I did not realise when I arrived in Dún Chaoin that I would be one of the last – perhaps the last – outsider to visit the Island while it was still inhabited. My boyhood experience of boats on the placid Shannon in Limerick did not prepare me for the experience of crossing the three-mile stretch of unpredictable Atlantic current between Dún Chaoin and the island in the traditional *naomhóg* rowed by two men using what seemed to me more like long poles for holding up a garden clothesline rather than proper oars. Eventually, having been accepted as a friend rather than a tourist – Seán Ó Ríordáin had paved the way for me by his sojourn during the previous winter – and having got over the shock of learning that none of the local men could swim, I was having a learner's go myself under the guidance of the tolerant experts.

When the new houses on the mainland were ready and the evacuation got under way, everything had to be transported piecemeal by *naomhóg*, and I used to stand on the cliff-top in Dún Chaoin watching those boats coming from the island laden, like the *Queen of Connemara* in the song, 'so that the water laps her gunwale' and marvelling at the casual skill and courage of the boatmen. I could hardly believe my eyes one day when I saw a peculiar shape approaching across the sound which, as the boat drew nearer, turned out to be a huge wooden press or wardrobe lying obliquely in the centre of the boat with much of it extending over the water, the two oarsmen leaning in the opposite direction to maintain the boat's balance as they rowed. As the boats neared the slip at Dún Chaoin, I went down to join the local men in helping to unload furniture or cattle or household goods and bring them to the new residence. One day an old islander arrived holding a ship's compass which he allowed me to hold only while he was getting out of the *naomhóg*; he told me that it had come from a wreck many years ago and it was a gadget that would be very useful if you found yourself away out there on the Atlantic Ocean on a dark night. I owned a small box camera but my 'straitened financial circumstances' made the purchase of a film a luxury, and I regret to this day that I was unable to photograph the islanders while they were still living on the Blasket and those scenes at the slip in Dún Chaoin.

In the course of my academic and private study of Irish, I had read and reread all the books emanating from the Great Blasket especially those by Tomás Ó Criomhthain (1856-1937) whose autobiography, *An tOileánach* (The Islandman) was translated by the English scholar, Robin Flower, known to the islanders by the affectionate nickname, *Bláithín* (little flower). It was with a feeling of emotion and reverence that I stood in the ruins of the islandman's cottage, imagining him labouring at his task by the light of an oil-lamp in the winter nights with the Atlantic wind howling over the island. It was on one of my visits, as I took a stroll alone up the hill, that I encountered a garrulous old man whose battered hat and moustache and walking stick and two rabbits hanging from a snare-wire should have been a subject for a painting rather than a photograph. It was from this old man that I heard the three words that form the title of this chapter. They constitute an epigrammatic and ambiguous utterance that could epitomise the life of a writer and they would have made an appropriate title for this book if it were in Irish. But my conversation with this old Blasket Islander also spoilt my day by reminding me of the whole painful context in which I was writing as a bilingual writer.

From the founding of the Gaelic League in 1893 people had been going to the Gaeltacht areas to learn Irish, either on organized summer courses or on private holidays – foreign scholars were coming too, anxious to study one of the oldest living languages of Europe before it died out altogether, as seemed likely. As I have had reason to point out already, this combination of academic attention and romantic summer-holiday association had inevitably magnified the importance of the 'native speaker', to the detriment of the development of a modern language of communication and literature. But the fact that autobiographical books written or dictated by some native speakers had been published and acclaimed – the acclamation being also affected by a romantic rather than a literary valuation – caused every native speaker to feel that their own life story was of equal interest and could be as profitable as those other books obviously were, especially when prescribed as compulsory texts on school and college courses.

Writers as well as scholars and learners had been visiting the Gaeltacht for many years before I came to Dún Chaoin; J. M. Synge came to the Blaskets in 1905 and found material for his plays and other writing there, although some of his comments did not please the Islanders – and if in my apprentice days I had been described in the *Limerick Leader* as 'young Limerick writer', I was not long in Dún Chaoin before I was known as *'an scríbhneoir óg as Baile Átha Cliath'* (the young writer from Dublin). The last of the summer visitors having long gone, I was also conspicuous as the only stranger in the area. Seán Ó Ríordáin came in his small car from Cork on a few weekend visits during my six-month stay but apart from a few one-day tourists, the only other stranger was a dotty English actress who stayed for a few weeks in the local guesthouse and whose delight it was to walk in her bare feet and talk to the local donkeys. A distinguished visitor who appeared as celebrant of the Mass on a few Sundays was Monsignor Pádraig de Brún from Galway University, uncle of Máire Mhac an tSaoi as already noted. I was told by the locals that he came for weekends and invited certain loquacious old men to visit him in his holiday home in order to improve his Irish. He spoke to me a few times after Mass or when his car met me on the road and, like everyone else, he knew the why and the wherefore of my being in Dún Chaoin. I was never invited to the monsignorial bungalow but we were destined to meet in Dublin in a few years' time and to exchange unfriendly words.

The old Blasket rabbit-snarer knew more about me than I about him. And being a wise and practical old peasant, he got down to business after the usual prologue of God's blessing and the weather. He asked me if I had read the books about the island. He then said that he had the material for as good a book as any of them, all in his head, which he indicated by removing his hat, but that he was unable to write. So, his proposition was that, as he would soon be coming to live on the mainland in Dún Chaoin, where I would be staying for some time to come, we could have regular collaborative sessions, sharing the profits from the resulting book.

'Mar, an dtuigeann tú, a bhuachaill,' (Because you know, Boy,) he concluded, *'leanann trioblóid leabhar.'*

Leanann trioblóid leabhar. It is a poem in itself, a nugget of succinct wisdom that would have delighted that concise English essayist, Bacon ('Some books are to be tasted, others to be swallowed, and some few to be chewed and digested'). And it would almost require an essay to explain and comment on it. For it is ambiguous. The first and obvious meaning is that trouble follows on, or is the consequence of, a book. In the broad context of my own career, this is very true. But the sense in which my would-be collaborator used the words is that writing a book is a troublesome business, a truism to which every true writer might add that *rewriting* a book or a play involves even more trouble than the first version. Anyway, I had enough troubles on my plate already without adding more, and so I commended the islandman's notion without making any commitment, and when the move to the mainland took place, although I met him a few times, he seemed to accept that he would have to wait for some other collaborator. His pithy summing-up of the writer's task, however, remained with me for life, as did another such statement made by a clifftop philosopher with whom I was discussing the romantic notions formed by summer visitors to Dún Chaoin, a place that would seem on a fine summer's day to be an idyllic haven of peace and scenic beauty. He dismissed those airy-fairy sentiments of the tourists and summer students and expressed the hearty wish that he could escape from his grim and hopeless bachelor life to America where, like most people in Dún Chaoin, he had some relatives. 'Mar níl faic anseo,' he said, 'ach carraigeacha, síon agus síor-bháisteach' (Because there's nothing here but rocks, gales and perpetual rain).

Although I waffled my way out of the old islander's invitation to collaborate with him on a book, I came to know an old woman whose conversation and stories fascinated me to the extent that I considered them material for a book that would be at least as good as, if not better than, the much acclaimed autobiography of Peig Sayers. This gentle and courteous lady was a widow who lived with her adult daughter Cáit and son Mícheál in one of a cluster of cottages near the cove called Clochar, on the road from Dún Chaoin to Ballyferriter. Her Irish title would be Bean de hÓra, but she always used her maiden name, Mary Martin. In her schooldays, as she told me, it was all English, even to the names the pupils were forced to use; she could even write English but not Irish. (In his comprehensive and copiously illustrated book, *The Blaskets, a Kerry Island Library*, Muiris Mac Conghail writes of the author of *An tOileánach*:: 'While Tomás signed his name in English on the 1901 census as Thomas Crohan, he signed the 1911 form as Tomás Ó Criomhthain, the only signature in Irish in that census on the Blaskets.')

Mary did not know her age and was so feeble that she could not go out but sat at the fire with her rosary beads at hand; and so she was all the more delighted to have a listener. When my wife came to stay for a while, the old lady took a great liking to her and often told me what a lucky man I was to have such a lovely young girl for my wife, after which she would order me to take good care of that treasure. These people did not have much of this world's goods but like others among the islanders and the mainland people, there was a quality of refinement, civility and hospitality about them that made one recall how the plantations of Cromwell and others had driven many of the Irish aristocracy and educated classes to the infertile areas along the western seaboard. For a long time afterwards I kept the notebooks which I thought might form the genesis of a book for and about that remarkable woman. I burnt them, along with the diary of my six months in Dún Chaoin and many other notebooks and manuscripts, in a bonefire of disillusionment ten years later when the crozier of Cashel signed a deportation order for myself and my family.

In the house where I was a paying-guest for six months there was a battery radio but as card-playing by the fire was the nightly pastime, it was used only to hear the news. In keeping with the general practice in writing and publishing, the news in Irish was broadcast, night by night, in one of the three major dialects, Ulster, Connacht or Munster. But I heard the news only on the nights when it was broadcast in Munster Irish. If the voice on the radio began with an Ulster or Connacht accent, the common reaction from one of the card-players was, '*Múch an t-amadán sin, in ainm Dé!*' (Silence that fool, for God's sake!). I made no comment, of course, but became all the more convinced that Irish would have to develop a standard medium of communication and literature outside the Gaeltacht if it were to survive as a modern language.

Another manifestation of the complicated linguistic situation in which I found myself by making the commitment to writing in Irish, as well as in the universal and more potentially profitable English, came to my attention courtesy of one of the nightly card-players. This was a genial middle-aged man known as 'Pound', about whom Seán Ó Ríordáin wrote a sentimental poem prefaced by a few lines of prose in which he describes him as 'one of the finest and sweetest native speakers of Irish in the country', a statement that would undoubtedly be contested by the poetic champions of eloquent native speakers in every other parish in every other Gaeltacht. 'Pound' lived with his sister in a dilapidated old cottage, existing on the dole and casual work, and they were among the poorest of the local people. (A bottle of milk was filled every night before he arrived and discreetly left where he could slip it into his pocket on the way out.) Except on nights when the rain and wind combined to discourage me, I liked to stretch my legs after the cards with a brisk walk under the stars, beginning with an ambling down the road with 'Pound' and sometimes one or two others. One night as I walked with only the man himself for company, he stopped up and addressed me as follows in Irish that was plain and direct, certainly not of the quality that might even put him in contention for the title of 'the finest and sweetest native speaker in the country'.

'Listen to me now, Críostóir, my friend, and I'll give you advice that will benefit you. You don't get much Irish above at the house there when we're playing cards or when you're walking around during the day. What you should do is get a little car like Seán Ó Ríordáin has. When Seán was here last year, we used to go north to Ballyferriter in his car now and again, and we'd go into a pub, and after a few pints – by God, 'tis then I'd be spoutin' the Irish at him! Now if you had a little car like Seán, we could do the same.' As with the old Blasketman who had put his eye on me as a prospective collaborator, I assured 'Pound' that I would consider his advice but that buying a car was beyond my means at present. There was little point in telling the poor man that buying a bicycle was equally beyond my means; to him, as to most of the local people, a young writer who could come and spend six months idling around in Dún Chaoin must surely be classed with all those other well-off academics and writers who had come and gone in the past. I could not explain to them that for various reasons I was actually much poorer than themselves. His suggestion, however, left me ill at ease with him and with others like him, during the rest of my stay.

Although the house in which I was staying, like the other houses, had neither electricity nor running water, and the cooking was done on the open turf fire – on wet and windy days we choked as the smoke blew back down the chimney, the door being shut tight against the gale and sealed at the bottom with a sack – the family were comparatively well off to the extent of having a few cows and a bank account in Dingle. When the parish priest from Ballyferriter gave a discourse about rural electrification one Sunday, he informed the congregation that a man from the Electricity Supply Board would be visiting the houses during the week to explain the benefits and the cost. My wife and I happened to be eating dinner at our side table in the kitchen – the room used as a guest dining-room during the summer was

113

left unused in winter – on the day when the ESB man arrived. He went through his piece, in English of course, outlining the benefits of electricity and the cost for each use to which it might be put in such a country house. When he asked the family for questions, he got only one – the adult son of the house (there were also two daughters, with an older son in America) piped up and asked, 'Shouldn't the electricity be free for us, because we're living in the Gaeltacht?' Many schemes and grants were devised by hypocritical politicians to encourage native speakers to continue living in the Gaeltacht, with the inevitable result of the 'poor mouth' attitude so savagely satirised by Brian 'Myles na Gopaleen' O'Nolan in his novel *An Béal Bocht* (1941). The face of the unfortunate ESB man was a sight to behold. Back in Dublin and wondering often how to budget for the ESB bill among many others, my wife and I often quoted that question ironically.

In spite of the primitive conditions – the two-storey house was plain and solid, but there were nights when an Atlantic storm resulted in raindrops falling on our bed – we were young enough to regard our stay in Dún Chaoin as an adventure and we were on very friendly terms with our host family and with everyone else; the family sheepdog seemed to think we were lost sheep who needed to be guarded when we went for a stroll and we discovered that the pig is a much-maligned animal when the sow began to follow my wife around wanting to be petted like a kitten. As Ó Ríordáin observed in another poem, there were very few young women in Dún Chaoin in those days, with the result that the prospect of marriage even for the heir to one of the small holdings was not good. The two daughters of the house we stayed in had both spent some years away from home, the elder one as a maid in the house of General Richard Mulcahy in Dublin – some politicians and academics in Dublin employed young girls from the Gaeltacht so that their children would become fluent in Irish – and the other in the

US. My wife and I being forewarned by the girls sat with them in the darkness on the landing at the top of the stairs on a winter's night when three men arrived, armed with a bottle of whiskey, to try to make a match, the two older men acting on behalf of the middle-aged candidate. Little did they know that their discussion with the parents was being overheard by the quartet above, the two daughters sharing a towel to stuff their mouths so that their hilarity would not be audible.

On the few weekends when Seán Ó Ríordáin came from Cork in his car, the card sessions gave way to fireside chat and discussion (the local gossip had it that the elder daughter of the house was in love with the consumptive poet and that a marriage would have been in prospect but for his recurrent ill-health). Although the father told me how much he enjoyed the arguments between Seán and myself, I found the poet to be paradoxically cynical about most things and naïvely sentimental about Dún Chaoin and its inhabitants. I was ten years younger than the Cork poet and had not read as widely – no writer can be widely read in the true sense – but I had read enough to feel that Ó Ríordáin seemed to be spiritually more in communion with Voltaire and Montaigne than with Pascal and Newman.

One weekend stands out because of the coincidence that brought Seán Ó Ríordáin from Cork and Seán Mac Réamoinn from Dublin to stay in the house. Radio Éireann had decided to do a radio documentary on the evacuation of the Great Blasket and Mac Réamoinn, then in his early thirties, arrived in a van with an engineer-driver and the heavy old recording machine. When I saw that he was proposing to go into the island dressed in city clothes and shoes, and bareheaded, I togged him out in my own raincoat, cap and nail boots. Later, the car from Cork and the RÉ van from Dublin made a united trip to Ballyferriter and brought supplies for a céilí in our kitchen, to which the neighbours – some of them islanders already settled in their new homes – came and contributed fine singing. There was also the memorable spectacle of big men in heavy nail boots dancing on a cement floor with a balletic grace that brought to mind their own phrase about a skilful dancer: one who wouldn't break eggs under his feet.

The following night, Ó Ríordáin from Cork, Mac Réamoinn from Dublin and Ó Floinn from Limerick were the guests of the local poet – known in the parish by that title, *an file* (the poet) – Mícheál Ó Guithín, son of Peig Sayers and scribe/editor of her lucrative autobiography, *Peig*, a book which remained a prescribed Leaving Certificate text for many years and was a daily dose of frustration and boredom for teachers and pupils alike. At the poet's fireside, we three wise men from the East were treated to a reading of his poems over a session of a few hours. As we walked back to our guesthouse under a vast canopy of stars that seemed to stretch all the way to Boston, Mac Réamoinn asked Ó Ríordáin what he thought of what we had heard. The Cork poet paused and then uttered a cryptic judgement. '*Hm! Tá an File beagán* derivative' (The Poet is somewhat *derivative*).

Apart from the verdict, the use of the English word was typical of the trend among the local 'native speakers'. Ó Ríordáin was surely quite capable of expressing the idea in Irish, in several ways. When I pointed out to him that the Poet's verses were the kind of folk poetry that Máire Mhac an tSaoi, in her review of *Eireaball Spideoige*, had advised him to study with a view to improving his efforts, he dismissed her comments. I felt, however, then and in further discussion on a later occasion, that the adverse criticism of his first book had affected him more than he cared to admit. He produced only one other collection of any merit, after an interval of twelve years, and although it contained some excellent poems, it was only about one-third the size of *Eireaball Spideoige*. Significantly, it was dedicated to the people of Dún Chaoin and in the final poem we are advised to discard from our intellect 'the straddle of English, Shelley, Keats and Shakespeare' and to go to Dún Chaoin, the door through which, by the medium of the spoken language of the locals, we will enter into the possession of our cultural heritage. It is an attitude with which Pearse, advocate of bilingualism and a collector of Shakespeare editions, would not agree.

The owner of the local shop and its adjoining guesthouse, Muiris Caomhánach (Maurice Kavanagh) was known as 'Kruger'. He was also a loquacious rogue – he was seen and heard on the *Late Late Show* in the Sixties – with many entertaining tales of his years in America, where, he boasted, he had played a leading role as publicity manager for de Valera's fund-raising campaign some years after 1916. Like other stories of his, this one was spoilt for me by a corrective gloss from some of his customers, who were all pleasant chat when we played cards at the fireside in the shop under the overhanging flitches of bacon from which 'Kruger' cut rashers for customers, but cynically critical when I met them anywhere else. Their version was that 'Kruger' had been working as a billposter in Chicago or some other city when Dev went to America and among the posters he pasted up there were some about Dev's visit. From this tenuous connection he built himself into the publicity manager of the story.

The man himself told me confidentially, as he probably told many other people, that he was writing a book that could not be published until after his death because of its revelations concerning politicians, gangsters, corruption, etc. in Ireland and the US. 'Kruger' was also the owner of one of the three seats in the little church, and when the doctor finally allowed my convalescent wife to spend a few weeks in Dún Chaoin, 'Kruger' kindly invited us to join himself and his wife in their pew. We declined with sincere thanks, our ideas of democracy and Christianity being hostile to such a distinction between pew-owners and the common mob. But we attracted sharp glances from the celebrant on Sunday, as well as from the congregation, when we knelt and stood together, ignoring the traditional segregation that allocated one side of the little church to the men, the other to the women.

By his own account, 'Kruger' was a patriotic republican and so it was with some surprise that, as I roved out one Saturday afternoon, I saw a Union Jack waving in the breeze on a high flagpole in the middle of the field beside his guest-house. Curiosity as well as puzzlement led me to investigate. The field had been turned into a campsite, with tents all around the perimeter, and young scouts were to be seen at various tasks. Their uniform of khaki fitted with the Union Jack. A tall scoutmaster was moving among them. I went into the field and engaged him in conversation. They were a scout troop from somewhere in England, planning to spend a fortnight in the area, with their base in this field which had been rented from 'Kruger'. I told the scoutmaster that, while I hoped his troop would enjoy their holiday in Ireland, it was not advisable to fly the Union Jack in Kerry or anywhere in the Twenty-Six Counties, while in the Six Counties still under British control Irish nationalists were being arrested for flying the Irish flag. I had no wish to alarm him or the boys, I said, but there were people who were likely to be so infuriated by the sight of the British flag flying over a field in Kerry that they might come during the night and burn down flag, tents and all. The scoutmaster told me that he was actually a policeman by profession, that they were not breaking any law, that they had flown their flag on camping holidays in other countries, and that 'Kruger' had assured him that it was legal and safe to do so here. I assured him again that it was not safe, whether legal or not I did not know. He offered to compromise by moving the flag-pole to a corner of the field. I warned him that the Union Jack could still be burnt down.

After Mass next day, Sunday, I went for a stroll and

arrived back at the house to be told that the sergeant from Dingle had called while I was strolling. He had received a complaint about my threat to burn the English scouts out of 'Kruger' Kavanagh's field. He left a diplomatic but cautionary message for 'the young lad from Dublin' to the effect that he understood my attitude in the matter but that I would be well advised to take no more notice of the flag – they'll be gone in a few weeks, and sure who'll see it anyway. So, the Union Jack flew over a part of the Gaeltacht and of the Kingdom of Kerry for two weeks. And when I bought a few sweets or a bar of chocolate in his shop, or played cards now and again with the lads, 'Kruger' greeted me with his usual voluble cordiality and made no reference to flags or scouts or policemen, British or Irish.

If our proposed sojourn in Dún Chaoin had suffered something of a setback at the outset because of my wife's illness, fate set us another test half-way through the six-month period. From Donncha Ó Laoghaire, secretary of Comhdháil Náisiúnta na Gaeilge, came the bad news that, because of a shortfall in their budget, they would be unable to continue the monthly funding for the remaining three months; but, he promised, a further three months in the Gaeltacht would be offered at some time in the future. Any such offer from a bureaucratic source containing the phrase 'at some time in the future' is of as much value as that 'verbal contract' decried by Sam Goldwyn. Irish and English both have the proverb, 'Live, horse, and you'll get grass.'

In my circumstances, factors even stronger than this indicated that I should stay in Dún Chaoin and survive by hook or by crook. I had contracted a substitute teacher for six months and could not morally or legally turn up at the school after the Christmas holidays and tell him to look for another job. And after the first three months in Dún Chaoin, I was now fully accepted by the local people as a friend and I had established a routine of visits, reading and writing that was becoming progressively more beneficial both to my knowledge of Irish and to my development of ideas and material for literary work. If I had been totally dependant on the monthly cheque from the Comhdháil, it would have been impossible for me to stay on in Dún Chaoin. Fortunately, in October, just as I was beginning my six-month sojourn, I had been awarded a few prizes in the Oireachtas competitions, just as in the previous year. A book for junior readers again won the fifty pound prize, a one-act play won the prize for a historical tragedy and a short story won first prize of fifteen pounds. I also had a few articles and some radio work bringing in a few cheques, albeit slowly and uncertainly. Although medical bills and incidental expenses had eaten into our resources, I could just about survive a further three months – a combination of weakness and threatening appendicitis had forced my wife to return to her father's house in Limerick – and I could also hammer out more articles and radio stories on the typewriter that might replenish our resources when we returned to Dublin at the end of March. In the meantime, Sáirséal agus Dill accepted my new prize-winning book and Radio Éireann accepted the one-act historical tragedy, which was broadcast twice. I submitted it also to the Abbey Theatre, where it was rejected by Tomás Mac Anna.

The half-year I spent living in that pre-television, totally Irish-speaking society in Dún Chaoin must have been of great benefit to my ability to think and write creatively in Irish but it did not alter my belief that dialect should be left to colloquial speech, where it could be expressive and colourful but also stereotyped in idiom and vocabulary, and that a standard literary language, capable of enrichment and development from every and any source, was essential for the future of modern literature in Irish. The change from the urban life of Limerick and Dublin to the more basic rural milieu of the Dingle peninsula was also of benefit to my spirit and to the broadening of my views on society in Ireland and of the human condition in general. The more

Spartan domestic and culinary circumstances resulted in a succession of colds and bouts of tonsilitis. On my way back to Dublin, I stopped over in Barrington's Hospital in Limerick where I left my tonsils, at a cost of twelve guineas to the surgeon. How we remember such sums when every shilling had to be hard earned and carefully spent!

12

THE PRAM IN THE HALL

Before going to Dún Chaoin I had begun to map out the plot of an Irish novel for adult readers. The scenario of the rugged Dingle peninsula, the Blasket Islands and the Atlantic offered a picturesque and compact setting for my plot, and the fact that Irish was the language I was hearing all day made it easier for me to hear my fictional characters talking in Irish. On my return to Dublin I finished the novel, *Lá Dá Bhfaca Thú*. It was selected by An Club Leabhar (the Irish Book Club) as one of the five books for 1955. The Book Club was at its peak around that time, with a membership of over two thousand. The selected books were published in both hardcover and paperback editions and the fortunate authors were guaranteed a lump sum in royalties. That, of course, was practically the end of the sales; anyone interested in Irish would be a member of An Club Leabhar and people who could not afford the annual fee could get the books free in their local library.

In the office of Comhdháil Náisiúnta na Gaeilge – who eventually, by the way, recouped my expenses for the second half of the six-month scholarship in Dún Chaoin – the secretary, Donncha Ó Laoghaire, showed me the comments of the five directors of the Book Club on my as yet unpublished book. They had each read the typed script without knowing who wrote it, and the chairman, Professor Liam Ó Briain of UCG, began his enthusiastic report with a statement that I would have dearly loved to shove under the noses of the hostile pedants in An Gúm. 'I'm fascinated by this. This is what we are looking for. Who wrote it? I'm sure it must be someone from the Munster Gaeltacht who spent time in the Connacht Gaeltacht or vice versa.' Another director, while praising the story, was critical of a non-literary aspect of the book. 'The author does not give a true picture of life in the Gaeltacht – he actually has cars and radios in the story and one character is planning to build a hotel in the area!' Actually, as I pointed out to Donncha, I had used fictional names for Dún Chaoin and the Blasket and I had made no reference at all to the Gaeltacht – I was merely writing a romantic novel. It was the romantic aspect, in fact, that resulted in the most serious objection – and one which I was told would require some rewriting. This came from a director who said the novel was very good but that it contained elements of 'Hollywood sexiness and violence.' This was my first encounter with censorship, and it puzzled me that an educated person could be so puritanical and narrow-minded. On one page of my book, the young hero of the novel took note of the figure of the heroine as they drove to the local creamery one morning with the milk from the two houses. And at the end of the book he actually kissed her. That was the sum total of the 'Hollywood sexiness'. But the secretary advised me to remove the first and tone down the second. The violence consisted in a fist fight and a foiled plot by one character to stage a shooting accident on the mountain. This was eventually allowed to pass – apparently, fistfights and murderous shooting accidents were not as likely to shock or corrupt the readers as the hero noting that the girl had a shapely bosom and attractive features (I was allowed to retain the kiss on the last page but on a muted level).

The book was a popular success and I got letters, as did

An Club Leabhar, from many readers – a Jesuit wrote to tell me that it was the only book in Irish that had ever kept him out of bed until he finished it. I was told many years later by a woman who had been a student in the preparatory college in Dingle at that time (these colleges were established to give secondary school education, on a scholarship system, to pupils from the Gaeltacht who would then go on to the teacher training colleges) that the girls there were almost fighting to get their hands on one of the copies bought for the library by the nuns. The secretary of An Club Leabhar told me that they hoped I would write more of the same, and he said to me, using a phrase then current in boxing parlance, 'Is tú dóchas bán na Gaeilge' (You're the *white hope* of Irish).

Whatever about being their white hope, two aspects of the matter were significant for me. All the Book Club directors, as well as their anonymous professional readers, praised the excellent standard of Irish in the book, and the lump sum of something over two hundred pounds that came with publication helped to put a deposit on our first house (semi-detached, three-bedroom, with garage, cost in 1955, £1,950). Some years later, however, I got a delayed-action kick in the teeth when an academic who had written to me admiring the novel wrote to me again. He was a member of a committee established by the Department of Education to formulate a new syllabus in Irish for the Leaving Certificate. He enthusiastically proposed my modern novel, a romantic story that would, he believed, appeal to students in secondary schools much more than the outdated texts like *Peig* that were more folklore than literature. His suggestion was rejected – not that any fault was found with the novel, but because the author had not been born in the Gaeltacht and was therefore not a native speaker of Irish. Only books by native speakers were to be considered suitable as texts in the schools. So, *Peig* remained on the course, and in later years, earning the daily bread as a teacher in a girls' secondary school in County Dublin, I shortened my purgatory by grinding reluctant young minds through it, line by line, for seventeen years in succession.

While the publication of my first novel laid most of the foundation for a new house – provided we could get a mortgage, of course – in the same year the birth of our first child initiated us into the real meaning and purpose of human life and creativity. A renowned English literary critic, Cyril Connolly, wrote a book called *Enemies of Promise* (1938) in which he outlined the various obstacles that prevent writers from fulfilling their talent – he lists principally drink, domesticity, journalism, politics, conversation, worldly success. The problem posed by domesticity is symbolised for him by the pram in the hall. Like Oscar Wilde, Connolly had leanings that would eliminate the pram-in-the-hall as an obstacle. As a failed writer himself – he published one novel before becoming a critic – Connolly seems set on discouraging rather than encouraging young writers. Consequently, no young writer should read the book, which contains a mixture of grandiloquent pontification, platitudes and nonsense. I had not read the book when we installed a brand-new pram in the hall of the house in Drumcondra where we had our two-room flat. But I could have told Connolly even then that the pram in the hall was a symbol for me of something greater than all the books and plays that have ever been made.

I must record, however, that my wife's pregnancy drove me to drink, at least in a minor or preliminary way. And this, as the old storytellers used to say, this is how it happened. The gynaecologist in the Rotunda Hospital advised the girl to drink a snipe of stout every day. As we were both teetotallers, we did not know what a snipe of stout meant. Our landlord, the paternal Garda Inspector, explained that it was a small bottle containing one-third of a pint, specially produced by Guinness for expectant mothers. I dutifully procured a half-dozen snipe from a local pub.

The young expectant mother took one sip and nearly fainted. The expectant father tried it and found that it was more bitter than lemonade or fruit drinks but tolerable. So, I drank a snipe a day for six days and my wife eventually had the baby, an excellent example of cooperation and domestic harmony.

I began to learn more about the insidious effects of censorship on literature when my brother, Dick, who had gone to work in London, sent me a copy of *Room at the Top* (1957), a first novel by a young English writer named John Braine. This was a bestseller and was later made into a successful film. My brother thought that I would be interested in it professionally. But when the postman delivered a limp, brown-paper parcel, I noticed a label on it indicating that it had been opened and re-sealed by the Customs, and when I opened it, it contained no book. Along with the note from my brother, there was an official form telling me that the book had been confiscated under the Censorship of Publications Act (1929). I had read in the papers some time before this that Senator Owen Sheehy-Skeffington, a formidable opponent of censorship, had been making yet another protest in the Senate not only on the usual grounds that books by Irish writers were being banned but that writers, critics, and academics were being prevented by censorship from reading books that were necessary for them to keep abreast of developments in other countries. He was assured by the Minister for Justice that professional people who required *any* banned book need only apply to his department and explain why; they would then be given permission to obtain the book.

I applied, referring to the recent exchanges in the Senate and pointing out that as a young Irish writer I wished to read a successful novel by a young English writer which had been sent to me by my brother in London but confiscated by customs officials. The official reply informed me that I was not being granted a licence to import this book. I wrote again, informing the minister and his officials that I had not applied for such a licence, that I was not in the business of *importing* books but of *writing* them, that the copy of the book, which was my property, was already in the country, in the offices of the customs, and was probably being read by customs officials and civil servants; so, would they please send it to me so that I also might read it. In reply I was informed that 'this correspondence is now closed.' A year later, on my first visit to London, I bought another copy of *Room at the Top* and brought it back in my suitcase along with some other banned works of literature. When the customs officer at Dún Laoghaire asked me if I had anything to declare, I replied in the negative, and he chalked a routine mark on my case.

That, of course, was only a minor example of how official censorship hindered the development of literature. What was perhaps even more harmful was the general attitude to literature and drama as somehow being potentially a source of danger to personal and public morality. This attitude was the result of the puritanical teaching on everything to do with sex to which the people were subjected by the clergy and the bishops. And the nefarious effects of official censorship were added to by the unofficial freelance censorship applied by publishers, editors, theatre managers and librarians (in many places the local librarian set up a reading committee of 'respectable' people who vetted books before they were made available to the public). When I had occasion to ask for copies of the scripts of some of my radio plays, I was amazed to find that expressions like *damn it*! and *by God* and *blasted, bloody, etc.* had been deleted by a blue pencil in Radio Éireann before the plays were broadcast.

Just in case the Book Club's listing of my first novel, *Lá Dá Bhfaca Thú*, in 1955 might prove to be too much of that 'worldly success' listed by Cyril Connolly as one of the enemies of promise for the writer, an enemy of promise unknown to that English critic gave me another discouraging push backwards. For the third time, a book of mine for junior readers had been awarded the Oireachtas prize in anonymous competition by two adjudicators. Their independent reports praised everything about this book, *Cuas an Óir*, including the quality of the language, of which one of them wrote: 'and also as far as the standard of Irish is concerned, this is by far the best entry; the language in the book is fluent, clear and correct.' I have indicated elsewhere that this emphasis on language went too far in assessing the quality of a literary work in Irish, but because of my own troubles with the pedants in An Gúm, I was now happy to quote this encomium when I submitted my prize-winning book to that institution. Sáirséal agus Dill, having two other books of mine to publish, were unable to add a third to their list. I thought that since *Cuas an Óir* had won the Oireachtas prize for a book for junior readers and had been highly praised for its Irish as well as for its literary qualities, a contract and an acceptance fee would be forthcoming without further ado – the fee per thousand words being all the more welcome now since the installation of our pram in the hall. My logical optimism turned out to be a delusion. The book was returned to me as being 'unsuitable for publication by An Gúm'. No reason was given.

Since An Gúm was a branch of the Publications Branch of the Government, and directly under the Department of Education, I wrote to the Minister, who happened to be General Richard Mulcahy. I gave him an account of the history of my dealings with An Gúm from the day when I sent them my first book, and I added an outline of my literary career to date. I requested that he order whoever in An Gúm had rejected my book to give a reason for the rejection or else that he arrange to have my book considered by independent literary judges, whose decision I would accept. The minister's secretary informed me that the minister would have the book considered as I requested. Subsequently, he wrote to tell me the good news that the verdict had been in favour of publication and that the Minister had so instructed An Gúm. I got a contract, and an acceptance fee.

It turned out to be a hollow victory. When the book was published, a review appeared in the Irish weekly newspaper, *Inniú*, where the first book of poems by Seán Ó Ríordáin had been disparagingly reviewed by the editor, Ciarán Ó Nualláin, a few years earlier. My book was reviewed by Niall Ó Dónaill, a native of the Donegal Gaeltacht, who had worked as a translator of books in An Gúm and was to begin work in 1959 as head of the editorial team of the Irish-English dictionary which eventually appeared in 1977. Under the banner headline, *Earráidí Gaeilge Gan Cheartú* (errors in Irish uncorrected), the Donegal 'native speaker' informed the readers of *Inniú* that my book was weak in plot and weaker still in Irish. The kind of faulty Irish in it, he said, was undoing the good work being done every day in the schools by teachers. I replied in a letter to the editor, giving the history of the book and quoting the Oireachtas adjudicators' praise for every aspect of the book, including the language. I also pointed out that, as I earned my daily bread in teaching, and wrote at night, according to Ó Dónaill I was undoing each night the good work I had done by teaching Irish in school that day, a literary and linguistic feat comparable to the trick Penelope, the resourceful wife of Odysseus, played on her importunate suitors by unravelling each night the material she had woven on the loom during the day.

It is worth recording in this context that only a few weeks before, a colleague in the Training School in Drumcondra had come into my classroom to show me a letter he had received from the father of one of his pupils. 'What do you think of that?' he asked. It was the standard note explaining the boy's absence from school, so that I was at a loss to know why he was showing it to me. Until he pointed to the signature, *James Green*, and said, 'You know who that is, don't you?' I didn't. 'That's the Irish writer from Donegal,'

he explained, 'the man who uses the pen-name, "Máire".
He's a civil servant here in Dublin. He maintains that school-
teachers like us don't have the correct Irish, and so he always
writes letters like this in English and signs his name in
English.' Now I knew!

This was Séamus Ó Grianna, brother of another author
from the Donegal Gaeltacht, Seosamh Mac Grianna (the
latter insisted on using *Mac* in the surname after a quarrel
with his older brother). They had both trained as national
teachers in St Patrick's, Drumcondra, and they were of that
class of 'native speaker' writer who wrote in dialect and whose
every page was regarded as literature of the highest order by
those, like themselves, who considered the Donegal dialect
to be the best Irish, just as their counterparts in the dialects
of Munster and Connacht were championed by their own
supporters. Like Niall Ó Dónaill, Seosamh Mac Grianna
had worked in An Gúm translating those English novels
which were afterwards sold off by the ton as waste paper.
But what most amused me ironically about that 'note from a
parent' shown me by my colleague was that in his auto-
biography the same Séamus Ó Grianna/James Green relates
how, when he first went to the local school in Donegal in
the early 1890s, the teacher asked him his name, and when
he gave it in Irish, the teacher sternly informed him that
from then on his name was *James Green*.

I concluded my letter to *Inniú* by stating that since the
editor, Ciarán Ó Nualláin and Niall Ó Dónaill were in
agreement with the anonymous pedants of An Gúm in telling
me that I did not know enough Irish to write books in it, I
was now informing all concerned that I was actually a 'native
speaker' of English and that I would henceforth write in
that language only. I began that week to write a play in
English, *In Dublin's Fair City*, that was eventually accepted
by the Abbey and staged at the Queen's in 1959. As well as
the officials of bodies like Comhdháil Náisiúnta na Gaeilge
and my other publisher, Seán Ó hÉigeartaigh, some people,

both known and unknown to me, wrote to ask me to continue writing in Irish. One correspondent urged me not to let the hostility of a Donegal pedant or a narky newspaper editor deprive myself of the spiritual fulfilment of writing in the language of my nation, or the nation of my contribution to its literary riches. After a suitable cooling off period of a few years, during which, as will be seen, I had trouble enough dealing with the Abbey about my play in English, I began to write in Irish again.

13

A PINT FOR A PLAY

Among those enemies of promise for the writer that gave an English critic material for a book, the demon drink is undoubtedly the one that has caused most havoc on the literary scene in Ireland. I grew up in an Ireland where children receiving the sacrament of Confirmation at the age of ten or eleven were given a forearming pledge against intoxicating drink, and where the parish Temperance Hall was still a feature in many towns from the early decades of the century. My father-in-law, Paddy Beegan, was lifelong honorary secretary of one such, St Michael's Temperance Society and of its famous rowing club. A newer movement, the Pioneer Total Abstinence Association, was promoting abstinence from drink as a personal sacrifice of atonement to the Sacred Heart of Jesus for the sins of drunkenness committed by others. Pubs were solely for men, women hardly drank at all, although some might indulge in a celebratory glass of sherry on special occasions and the grannies could enjoy their glass of stout in the privacy of the snug. Wine was unknown among ordinary people, as were the canned beers that have made teenage drinking, with its concomitant evils, so prevalent in the latter decades of this century.

Even if I had not been a teetotaller when I arrived in

Dublin as a young writer, the lack of funds would have been a safeguard against the booze as a menace to my literary career. I was not long in Dublin when a friend whom I encountered on a summer's day in Grafton Street invited me in for a drink. He suggested that we go to McDaid's, a pub nearby which was, he said, reputed to be a 'literary' pub where writers like Brendan Behan drank. A literary pub is a journalistic cliché; if there were such a pub, it would be a very boring hostelry. A good pub is one with a good pint, no television, a good mix of clientele and civilized conversation with intelligent contradiction. My friend knew the head barman in McDaid's, Paddy O'Brien, to whom he introduced me as 'a young writer from Limerick'.

In subsequent years, as an irregular patron, I spent some pleasant sessions, and many a boring one, in McDaid's. I remember a long afternoon alone with Patrick Kavanagh when his main topics were the unrelated ones of barefist boxing and how he had put some smartaleck literati in London back in their box on a recent occasion. I came to regard Paddy O'Brien as the most sensible man in the place. I also realised very soon that we writers are of necessity individualistic and egoistic – some are narcisisstic as well, such as go to a pub not for company but for an audience – and generally not good company for one another. With many others of his clientele, I followed Paddy O'Brien when McDaid's was sold in 1972 and he moved around the corner to Grogan's in South William Street, where the partners, Paddy Kennedy from Tipperary and Tom Smith, a Cavanman, welcomed us into a more spacious premises. 'We followed Paddy here out of loyalty,' one pintman told a newcomer. 'Ye followed me out of effin' debt!' Paddy laughed.

I have told how I was gently apprised by some amused fellow-writers that cider was not a mere fruit drink and how, as an expectant father, I made my first acquaintance with the product brewed on the banks of the Liffey since Arthur Guinness took up in 1759 where the monks of the Abbey of

St Thomas were forced to leave off nearly two hundred years before, when the new religion from England provided an excuse for wholesale robbery of land in the name of reforming the Catholic Church. The half-dozen snipe for expectant mothers which served as my introduction to Guinness left me with little desire to taste more of what seemed a bitter drink in comparison with the minerals I had been used to since childhood. If I were not a writer, I might never have tasted Guinness again. And although I can claim facetiously to be the only writer who has taken to drink in the cause of literature, I am only too well aware of the fact that drink has prevented many Irish writers from fulfilling their potential. I am consequently grateful to my parents, and to good teachers and priests, who taught me that self-discipline is as necessary as talent in any walk of life.

Although in the line of duty the Garda must often be seen as the enemy of those who are devotees of Bacchus, it was a Garda who encouraged me to take to drink. Since the day when he first heard the sound of my typewriter in the bedroom turned living-room over his head, and had interrogated me in a paternal manner to assure himself that it was not a sub-machine gun, our landlord Garda Inspector, John Finlay, had taken a friendly interest in my activities as a writer. He listened to me reading stories in Irish on the radio even though he could not understand them and he invited me on a few occasions to go with him when he did his tour of inspection of various stations in south County Dublin, thinking that this would serve the dual purpose of giving me a rest from the typewriter and perhaps finding material for my writing. On one such trip, he played a practical joke on a fat sergeant from Kerry by introducing me as a visiting detective from Scotland Yard and when he could no longer suppress his hilarity at the sergeant's manner, we were treated to a string of fiery Kerry maledictions, the scene concluding with a conciliatory cup of tea all round.

I was cast in the role of detective again when John asked

me one day how the writing was going. I told him I was writing a play in English which I hoped to submit to the Abbey but that I had run into difficulty. The play was set in a tenement in Dublin and, although I had worked out a plot with interesting characters, I felt that they were not speaking in Dublinese but rather in the English of my native Limerick. John advised me to go into the pubs and talk to the natives. I told him that I had been going into pubs in Summerhill and Parnell Street long before I even started the play but that the Dubliners seemed unfriendly, even hostile. He considered this for a moment, and then surprised me with his verdict.

'Ah, I see what's wrong – they think you're a detective.'

'Me, a detective?' I thought they might possibly have suspected that I was a civil servant or a teacher but hardly a detective!

The professional policeman explained. 'Look at yourself the way they see you when you walk into a pub. You're a young man, six feet tall, dressed in a belted gaberdine, wearing a tie, and the minute you open your mouth they know you're a culchie, up from the bog, as they'd say themselves. And when you walk up to the bar, what do you ask for?'

'Usually a Club Orange,' I admitted.

'O my God!' John groaned. 'A Club Orange! Sure that's a little girl's drink!' And then he put on his question-the-defendant air again. 'Tell me this, when you walk into a pub in Parnell Street or Summerhill, and you walk up to the bar and ask for your Club Orange, do you notice any fellows sneaking out the door?'

Not being a real detective, I had to shake the head. 'I never noticed.'

My avuncular landlord was disappointed in me. 'Ah now, even as a writer, you should be keeping your eyes open. Now, in future, watch for them, I'll guarantee you one or two will slip out as soon as you walk in. If they haven't reason to skedaddle themselves, they'll be darting off to warn their butties in some other pub that there's a lawman snooping around.'

I told him that there didn't seem to be much point in going into the pubs or going on with the play. At this point I had never seen or read O'Casey's Dublin plays, so I couldn't even make a plagiaristic attempt at the colloquial speech. And if I couldn't get the Dublin idiom right, there was no hope that the Abbey would even consider my play.

'Don't say that!' he cautioned me. 'But you'll have to change your tactics. Wear an old jacket and don't wear a tie, don't talk too much for a start; just say something about the weather – in a Dublin accent if you can. And – this is the most important thing – forget about the Club Orange, you'll have to drink a pint.'

'I couldn't, John, honest to God. I could never drink a pint.' I told him about the snipe.

'Well, you'll get used to it,' he advised. 'If you want to finish your play, you'll have to start drinking pints.'

I took his advice, suffering in the cause of literature until, like many a man before me, I acquired the taste for the creamy pint. And a few years later, in 1959, he had the pleasure of seeing his advice vindicated when he sat with his wife among the audience at the first night of my play, *In Dublin's Fair City*.

Having been freed from the daily grind in the chalk mines during the six-month sojourn in Dún Chaoin, I had experienced, albeit in somewhat primitive living conditions, what life would be like for a writer who could devote all his time and energy to creative writing. This, in fact, was why Cyril Connolly listed domesticity among the enemies of promise, and painted a pessimistic picture of the young writer falling in love, starting a family (the pram in the hall) and then finding himself compelled to labour daily at non-literary work, or at some form of literary hack-work. It must have been obvious even to a literary critic that domesticity is the beginning of civilization. If our ancestors ever lived in the trees, which is still a hypothesis, it was only when they came down and began to make houses with the branches that human society began. Even if I had been born with a silver spoon in my mouth or if a leprechaun in the Blasket Island had given me a crock of gold which would enable me to have an assured income for life, I knew that such a life, ideal as it might be in one sense, was not the normal human condition. In another and more basic sense, since literature is based on life, it might be better for a writer to experience life as the common man does, earning the daily bread in the sweat of one's brow, whether literally or metaphorically.

All this being granted, it was obvious to me by now that teaching, however noble it may be when philosophers blather about it, is a job in which the mental and nervous strain is constant and severe. I decided to look for a day job that would be more congenial to my true vocation as a writer. In the meantime like many other primary teachers and civil servants in those years, I enrolled with some of my teacher colleagues in the evening courses at UCD, then located at Earlsfort Terrace in what is now the National Concert Hall. A university degree added about ten shillings a week to a primary teacher's salary but I considered also that it might help me to get a job in publishing or lecturing. I was surprised to find that most of the Irish and English texts for the BA course were ones I had already studied – some, like *An tOileánach* and the prescribed Shakespeare plays, I almost had off by heart – and the lecturers seemed for the most part to be unaware of the basic pedagogic principles which were part of the training course for primary teachers.

The history lectures were even more boring but I enjoyed the lively discussions in a small tutorial group under a young scholar named Brian Farrell who displayed the talent for polemics and communication that would subsequently find larger scope on television. (He has recently been appointed chairman of the Arts Council.) I recall also the fascination of listening to Denis Donoghue, who went on to become a professor of English at Yale, lecturing on such themes as 'Light and Darkness in *Romeo and Juliet*', although some of my more pragmatic student colleagues grumbled that he should come down from such heights and give indirect hints, as other lecturers did, concerning the probable contents of the examination papers. He congratulated me when *Lá Dá Bhfaca Thú* was published in 1955, when I was half-way through the farcical process of acquiring a degree, and he generously gave me a comprehensive list from his own notebooks when I asked him to direct me towards books that would help me as a writer.

When I got to the MA stage, the lack of funds put a stop to my academic gallop. Student loans are a common factor in the banking business today – even the university fees have recently been abolished – but in the less prosperous years of mid-century a bank loan of any kind was not easy to obtain. The only bank I could find that would even consider my application for a loan of fifty pounds (the MA fee was thirty pounds) was the Ulster Bank in College Green where the manager, having weighed my teacher's salary against the mortgage on our new house, and the pram-in-the-hall now occupied for the second time, came to the conclusion that none of the cash of his wealthy investors should be risked on such a bad prospect.

Among the 'literary' jobs I applied for was one in Radio Éireann as a translator of news from English to Irish. After a three-stage process comprising interview, microphone test and written test, I was informed that I had qualified in all three but that I had not obtained the first place. However, if a vacancy should arise in the future, I would be considered for the position. I learned subsequently that the successful candidate was a native speaker from Donegal who had been six months in the job, in a temporary capacity, before it was advertised in the papers. And if any vacancy did arise in after years, I heard nothing about it. I applied also for a position as press officer with organisations as disparate as Aer Lingus and the Irish Pig Breeders Association, none of whom showed any desire to avail of my literary talents. And when I was interviewed for a job as a sub-editor with the *Irish Independent*, an elderly man sniffed at what I thought was my impressive CV and said that he had found people with a university degree to be unreliable and generally incompetent. So, I laboured on in the chalk mines and laboured on with my play for the Abbey. There was always the chance, I dreamed, that a successful Abbey play might make my fame and fortune.

The hope of another period of freedom from the chalk mines was inspired by an advertisement in the papers announcing the establishment of exchange scholarships between Ireland and the US, the scheme to be administered on our side by the Department of Foreign Affairs. One of the scholarships would be in drama and would enable the successful writer to spend a year in an American university. I applied for this three years in succession, was called to interview in Iveagh House each year and received each year a letter telling me that my application had not been successful but that I should apply again next year. It was at one of those interviews that I met again with the man I had first seen on the altar of the little church in Dún Chaoin, Monsignor Pádraig de Brún of University College Galway, uncle of Máire Mhac an tSaoi, the promising Irish poet who was later to marry Conor Cruise O'Brien.

That interview was itself like a scene from a drama and it was a learning experience for me. I was confronted with a triumvirate consisting of the chairman, Dr C. S. (Tod) Andrews, also Chairman of Bord na Móna, the monsignor from UCG and an observer from the American Embassy whose name did not linger long in my memory. Dr Andrews, whose sons, Niall and David, have emulated their father in giving long service to Ireland in public life, greeted me cordially and put me at ease with the offer of a cigarette.

When I told him that I had given them up after my first puff at the age of ten, he laughed and said, 'Ah, you matured early!' The American asked me politely why I wanted to go to an American university. I told him what it said in the advertisement – to study drama. At which point the monsignor opened up.

'You don't seem to know much about it,' says he, in a monsignorial tone.

I told him that all I knew was what it said in the papers.

'But what would you plan to do when you got to the university?'

I got the feeling that this man was not being helpful, to say the least.

'As I told this man,' I said, indicating the quiet American, 'I want to study drama.' I could have told them all that I had been reading up on Eugene O'Neill with a view to writing a thesis for my abortive master's degree, and that one of the quotations I had noted from that famous American dramatist was that he had pulled out of a university drama course after one term because he felt it was a waste of time. That would certainly have put the kibosh on my chance of bringing the wife and two kids across the pond to enjoy a change of scene for a year.

Tod Andrews gave me a chance to blather on safer ground by asking me what I thought of the current state of drama in Ireland. But the monsignor cut my waffle short with another question.

'What do you think of *The Quare Fellow?*'

Do you mean the play or the author?

Of course I didn't ask him that. From my observations of the author in McDaid's, I could have told him in plain Dublinese that Brendan Behan seemed to be a gurrier and a bowsie, or in common English, a man both noisome and noisy. I said that I thought the play had been overpraised, that it had profited by the fact that its theme of capital punishment was one of the most controversial topics of the day. The monsignor didn't seem to like that; but maybe, I thought, he's the one they have chosen to try to upset me with narky questions.

'But don't you think,' says he, 'that the play is a powerful sermon on death?'

'If I wanted to hear a sermon on death,' I countered, 'I'd go to a church, not to a play.' At this stage the fighting spirit of my native island parish came up in me and I proceeded to say goodbye to my vision of a year in America. 'The best sermons on death I ever heard,' I informed the monsignor, 'were delivered from the pulpit in the Redemptorist church in Limerick when, as boy and man, I was a member of the Archconfraternity of the Holy Family.'

Tod Andrews was grinning behind his cigarette smoke. 'Go on, tell us more!' said he.

Well, as the Granny used to say, you might as well be hung for a sheep as for a lamb.

'Well,' says the suicidal eejit, 'I think a play should be judged as a work of dramatic art, not as a sermon or an argument or propaganda. Shakespeare's *King Lear* should not be called a great play because some psychiatrist might consider it to be a revealing study of madness or some sociologist might write about it as a case history of the parent-child relationship.'

'Very true,' says Tod. If only *he* had the giving of the scholarship, I might have been in with a chance. The monsignor came back at me.

'I couldn't agree with that at all; even the Bible is didactic.'

'But the Bible isn't a play,' I threw back. 'It's a collection of books about the history of the Jews and the early years of Christianity.'

The American shook his head when the chairman asked him if he had any questions. He seemed to be wondering what was going on. The monsignor changed his tack.

'Apart from your own writing,' he said – he had made no reference to our meeting in Dún Chaoin but I wondered if he was being sniffy about my novel – 'what else have you done that would prepare you to benefit from this scholarship in America?'

I couldn't say I had academic contacts in the US or even that I was on the invitation list of the US embassy in Dublin as some writers were known to be (a journalist had offered to get me on the list of the Russian embassy but I declined the offer). The only American contact I had was that my Uncle Joe emigrated to New York the year after I was born and was still there. That didn't seem to be the kind of thing de Brún had in mind; but – the basic rule at interviews of any kind – you can't sit there with the gob shut, you have to say something.

'Well, all a writer can do to prepare for anything is read and think. Dr Johnson said a writer should spend a lot of his time reading, that a man will turn over half a library to make one book.' (A weighty man on your side in any discussion, old Sam!)

'So, what do you read?'

Currently I was rereading *Carry On, Jeeves*. But I felt that P. G. Wodehouse himself would caution me not to mention it. I broadened the issue to a perspective that should suit the monsignor.

'I started recently on a course of reading recommended by F. J. Sheed in a booklet called *A Ground Plan for Catholic Reading*.'

'What's that about?'

I explained that Frank Sheed sets out a list of sixty books which he thinks an intellectual Catholic should read – but since *The Holy Bible*, edited by Ronald Knox, *An Introduction to Philosophy* by Jacques Maritain, *The City of God* and the *Confessions* of Saint Augustine, *A History of the Church* by Philip Hughes, *Apologia pro Vita Sua* and *The Idea of a University* by Newman, *The Satin Slipper*, a play by Claudel, *The Religions of Mankind* by Otto Karrer, and *Natural Theology* by a Jesuit Joyce, were only a few of the books on the list, the compiler himself admits that his 'ground plan' covered a lot of ground.

'How much of all that have you read?' de Brún enquired.

'Not much so far, a bit here and there; but I live in hope.'

Tod Andrews chipped in. 'You'll have to live a long time.'

I agreed. 'I don't have much time for reading. I have a full-time job as a teacher. I try to do some writing at night and at weekends.'

The monsignor seemed like a man who was not just pretending to be narky. 'I don't think you should be spending time on stuff like that great reading plan,' he commented. And then he made the statement that really shocked me. 'Anyway, we don't need an Englishman to tell us what we ought to read.'

I had been advised in many books to write down an account of events or impressions, not as a diary but as potential material. I was glad I wrote an account of that interview, because some people who knew Pádraig de Brún were incredulous when I told them that story, while others showed no surprise. Anyway, that about wrapped up that dramatic interview, and the result of it all was that I was again deprived of the chance to see the Statue of Liberty and my Uncle Joe in New York. Many years ago an old gipsy woman in a caravan on Arthur's Quay in Limerick looked at my palm, after I had crossed hers with silver, and told me, among other things, that one day I would go to America and also get a big amount of money. It hasn't happened yet, and here I am, long years after, still picking away at Frank Sheed's *Ground Plan for Catholic Reading*. (How many times does one need to read even a page of Newman, Augustine or Maritain before the mind not only understands but assimilates the thought of such intellects!) And sometimes I pause in reminiscence over this paragraph in Sheed's introduction: 'Facts can be shoved into the mind like books into a bag, and as usefully ... A phenomenon the student will have noticed, at first incredulously but with a growing acceptance as the years pass, is that very learned people are often utter fools. And far from this being a paradox, one sees how it happens; so far from learning and foolishness being incompatible, they are frequently bed-fellows. There is no fool like a learned fool.'

14

ELEGY FOR A FRIEND

On the evening of the second day of January (feast of Mainchín, the patron saint of Limerick) in 1957, my wife and I were sitting down to tea in the kitchen of our new house in Drumcondra. I turned on the radio to hear the news. The voice on the radio said that two members of the IRA had been killed on the previous night in an attack on a police barracks in Brookeborough, County Fermanagh. One of the two was my friend and former schoolmate, Seán South. The other was a youth from Monaghan named Fergal O'Hanlon. Even if I had known that Seán had joined the IRA, hearing of his tragic death would have been a shock. As it was, when we left Limerick nearly five years earlier, Seán South was as I have described him in an earlier chapter, selflessly active in promoting the Irish language and social justice, and displaying his patriotism in another way by his membership of the auxiliary military force in which he had been promoted to the rank of second lieutenant. He was also well known for his membership of the Legion of Mary (in its Irish section, An Réalt) and Maria Duce, a more radical Catholic action movement founded by Fr Denis Fahy of the Holy Ghost Order and destined to fade away after earning the disapproval of the bishops.

I had corresponded with Seán and sent him a copy of

some of my books, and my wife and I had met him on the street in Limerick a few times when we went back at Christmas or in the summer vacation. I learned after his death that only a very few of his closest friends in Limerick were aware of the fact that he had resigned his commission in the FCA and joined the IRA, an organization which had been dormant since the end of the Second World War in 1945 but which became active again ten years later in order to launch a campaign in the Six Counties. By attacking army barracks and police stations, they intended to bring the fact of Partition to world notice – and that the Catholic Nationalist minority found themselves reduced to the status of second-class citizens, all power and privilege to be permanently in the hands of the Unionists. Apparently, Seán South had come conscientiously to the conclusion that the oppression of the Catholic Nationalist people in the Six Counties could go on forever unless the state of affairs in Ireland was brought to international notice. That, of course, is precisely what television has done in the past thirty years, with obvious results in the form of some changes for the better – but sadly only after a savage internecine conflict in which over three thousand lives have been lost.

When we heard of his death, my wife and I knelt to say a prayer for Seán and for his comrade, Fergal O'Hanlon. We went to Limerick for Seán's funeral, attended by fifty thousand people, which made it the biggest expression of public sympathy and national emotion seen since the funerals of the mayor and ex-mayor of Limerick who were murdered by the Black and Tans in 1920. On our return to Dublin a few days later I wrote a poem in Irish entitled 'Maraíodh Seán Sabhat Aréir' (Seán South Was Killed Last Night). I sent it to the *Limerick Leader*. It was returned with a note from the editor. 'We do not publish poetry in our columns,' he said. I wrote back and reminded him that he had published my first poem, the one about the Holy Year Exhibition in Limerick, when it was submitted to him by

Monsignor Molony, and that he had published my Irish poem on 1916 which won the competition organized by his popular columnist, Mainchín Seoighe. I got no reply. The poem was subsequently rejected without comment by the *Irish Independent* and the *Irish Press* (I didn't even try *The Irish Times*, a very different paper then than what it is now). A friend suggested that I try the IRA's own paper, *The United Irishman* (a title later changed to *An Phoblacht*). The editor accepted the poem but made a strange request.

I mentioned in the poem that shortly after O'Hanlon and South were killed, some bishop had stated that anyone who did as they had done was committing a mortal sin. And since all Catholics had been taught from childhood that a person dying in the state of mortal sin was certain to be damned, the implications of the bishop's pronouncement were clear. The worth of his theological fulmination as Christian consolation to the families of the two dead men was also clear. In a later line, I commented that it was a pity the bishop in question had not known Seán South personally. The editor of *The United Irishman* asked me to remove the references to the bishop. 'We're in a lot of trouble already with the government,' he told me over the phone, 'and if the bishops get on to them, they're likely to close us down altogether.' To add force to his argument, he pointed out to me that I myself was earning my living as a teacher and that my clerical manager was directly subject to the Archbishop of Dublin, John Charles McQuaid. The lines about the bishop in my poem could be seen, the worried editor told me, not only as a challenge to an individual bishop, but as a questioning of the Church's teaching on mortal sin and damnation, which would classify me as a heretic and could result in my being found unsuitable to teach in a Catholic school.

I knew that Seán South himself would not wish a poem of mine to be the cause of the suppression of the IRA's paper, and I knew that if the 'pram in the hall' might be a handicap for a writer, the pram in the street would be an injustice to the writer's wife and children. But I could not remove the lines in question without harming the technical structure and the polemical content of the poem, an alteration which I would consider to be a mortal sin against truth and artistic integrity. I offered the editor an alteration to the problem lines; instead of 'some bishop said' I wrote 'people said' and instead of 'It's a great pity that bishop did not know you,' I wrote (poetic tongue in cheek): 'It's a great pity those good people did not know you'. The poem was duly published in *The United Irishman* without repercussions from state or church establishment for the paper. The repercussions for the poet came in the form of delayed action.

Seven years later, in 1964, Sáirséal agus Dill published an Irish biography of Seán South written by our mutual friend, Mainchín Seoighe. Mainchín asked me if he might use my poem as a prologue and its title, *Maraíodh Seán Sabhat Aréir*, as the title of the book. He added as an epilogue, entitled *Bláthfhleasc* (Wreath), a collection of poems and prose tributes by other writers, in Irish and English, including the ballad by Seán Costelloe, 'Seán South of Garryowen', that became part of the national repertoire within weeks of the tragic death of those two young patriots. Before the biography was published I was walking along by the Grand Canal one day when I encountered Liam Ó Briain, the elderly chairman of An Club Leabhar (The Book Club). This veteran of the 1916 Rising (his memoirs, *Cuimhní Cinn*, were on the Book Club list in 1951) had been Professor of Romance Languages in UCG and he was largely responsible for encouraging Mícheál MacLiammóir and Hilton Edwards to start An Taibhdhearc, the Irish language theatre, in Galway in 1928. Ó Briain himself translated plays by Shakespeare, Molière, Synge and others for An Taibhdhearc. He was a well-known figure around Dublin in his retirement, easily picked out by his black overcoat and hat, his silver hair, his walking stick and his little dog. I had known him since my own novel was selected by An Club Leabhar in 1955 (he was the man who had wondered whether my book was written by a native of the Munster Gaeltacht who had spent some time in Connacht, or vice versa). I had always found him to be a vigorous and forthright conversationalist. And it was in that style that he responded to my greeting as we met on the bank of the Grand Canal. We always, of course, conversed *as Gaeilge*.

'I had to censor some of your writing lately,' he told me, with an air that was definitely censorious.

'What was that?' I enquired, truly puzzled.

'That poem you wrote about Seán South, it's in the book by Mainchín Seoighe that we have selected for the Book Club list, but I had to cut out a lot of it.'

'Why?'

'Ah, you said a lot of things that would cause trouble, things about Seán South and the North, and what you said about John A. Costello.'

I could have asked him why he took a gun and went out to fight the British Army in 1916 when he was about the same age as Seán South. But as a man who had taken the Treaty side in the Civil War, and who had been a staunch supporter of the Blueshirts in the Thirties when General O'Duffy was trying to set himself up as an Irish Hitler, the retired academic Ó Briain did not now have the same attitude to attacks on the British Army and their allies in Ireland as the young lecturer who was nicknamed 'O'Brien MA' by the Citizen Army men in Stephen's Green in order to distinguish him from all the other descendants of Brian Boru in their company.

'I didn't mention John A. Costello in my poem,' I said, and with the way the conversation was going, I thought it well to keep an eye on the blackthorn stick and on the dog.

'You mentioned the Taoiseach, and everyone knows who that is. And you said that he doesn't know any Irish. I know John A. Costello well, and I can tell you that he does know Irish.'

Birds of a feather! Of course you know John A. Costello, leader of Fine Gael and a former Blueshirt like yourself...

'I did not say that he doesn't know Irish.'

'You did, it's there in the poem.'

'If you read the poem properly, you'd see that what I said was that the Taoiseach spoke on the radio about the IRA and the attacks in the North, *without using a word of Irish*. And if he does know Irish, why doesn't he use it? Whenever de Valera speaks in public, he begins and ends his speeches in Irish.' (Having been elected President of Ireland in 1959, Éamon de Valera was deservedly sitting pretty in Áras an Uachtaráin above in the Phoenix Park while we were having our argybargy on the canal bank).

The old Blueshirt banged his blackthorn stick on the ground.

'Ah, don't mind de Valera!' he growled, 'he's only codding the people!'

The old Irish storytellers used to describe their characters as parting *go buíoch beannachtach* (with gratitude and blessings). It was not thus that Ó Briain and Ó Floinn parted. I felt like throwing him in the canal – two reasons dissuaded me: my respect for a man who had once risked his life for the freedom of Ireland and the fact that the same man was now armed with a blackthorn stick and guarded by a dog. My elderly antagonist – he was then seventy-six – probably felt that I had a lot to learn about life and politics.

Like sensible men we did not carry a grudge from our canal-bank dispute into our subsequent meetings. And on a summer's day four years later, when I was combining the usual daily grind with the Higher Diploma in Education course in Trinity College in order to earn a more secure meal ticket for self and family, I spotted 'O'Brien MA' sitting on a bench – black hat and overcoat, silvery locks, blackthorn stick and dog – watching a cricket match with great interest. I sat beside him and we enjoyed an amicable chat about writing and other matters. I asked him that day why they had not taken over Trinity College during the Easter Rising of 1916 (Trinity became a British military centre and machine-gun fire from the roof was directed at O'Connell Street and the GPO).

'We hadn't enough men,' Liam explained. 'There was confusion about the Rising, as you know, and many men didn't turn out. I was so confused myself I couldn't get to my own company and that's how I got in with the Citizen Army in Stephen's Green.'

The confusion of Easter Week 1916 was echoed in a minor way when the biography of Seán Sabhat was distributed to the Book Club subscribers in Ireland and abroad. Except for the first four lines, the two preliminary pages that should have contained my poem were blank, with my name at the bottom of the second page. Some of the pieces from the epilogue collection were also omitted. Sáirséal agus Dill had objected to this censorship by the directors of the Book Club and in protest had produced a separate edition with the complete text of my poem and the other censored pieces. Anyone who owns a copy of the two editions is in possession of a unique example of unofficial literary and political censorship.

The reaction to this censorship from people who had paid their annual subscription to the Book Club was a cancellation of so many subscriptions that it was no longer a viable enterprise and it declined rapidly until it was wound up altogether by the umbrella body for Irish organizations, Comhdháil Náisiúnta na Gaeilge. The newspapers picked up the controversy. The *Irish Independent* ran a prominent feature on it, in which Seán Ó hÉigeartaigh (Sáirséal agus Dill) accused the directors of the Book Club of censorship. To this charge Liam Ó Briain, as chairman of the Book Club, replied that the changes they had made in the book were not censorship but 'necessary editing'. I wrote to the *Irish Independent* giving an account of my encounter with Liam Ó Briain on the bank of the canal, where he began the conversation by telling me bluntly that he had recently *censored* some of my literary work. My letter was not published.

My elegy on the death of Seán South was to cause further trouble five years later, even to the extent of being the subject of an altercation in the Dáil of the Irish Republic.

15

THREE BRASS BALLS

Having finished my play, *In Dublin's Fair City*, the writing of which had driven me to drink, I sent it to the Abbey Theatre and tried to forget about it – every writer knows the gnawing of that rat of suspense running caged in the brain, morning, noon and night – while I got on with the daily grind of teaching, doing more writing at night and at weekends. I was learning by experience what that pessimistic English critic had in mind when he listed marriage and a family as a problem for the writer. By now I knew enough about life to appreciate the paramount importance and the positive value of love, marriage and children, and I knew enough about other writers, living and dead, to be aware of the more negative and potentially destructive aspects of the other 'enemies of promise'. But I also knew why, somewhere in that tremendous novel, *Moby Dick*, the creative literary artist, Herman Melville, suddenly seems to stop thinking about the white whale and Captain Ahab, while the common man, Herman Melville, throws down his pen, bows his head in his hands, and groans and sighs in the words I have prefixed to this book: 'Oh, Time, Strength, Cash, and Patience!'

If the hours spent daily in teaching drained some of my *strength*, there is no better profession in which to test and develop *patience*. As for *time*, the proverb tells us: 'The man who made time made plenty of it,' and I always answer queries about how I found time to write so much by suggesting that if you start with the assumption that there are *twenty-five* hours in the day, you're sure to find a spare hour somewhere for what you really want to do. That prolific novelist, Anthony Trollope, who wrote many a page while travelling by train in his pioneering work for the Post Office in Ireland, asserts in his autobiography: 'Three hours a day will produce as much as a man ought to write,' and Dr Johnson weighs in with, 'A man may write at any time, if he will set himself doggedly to it.' Unfortunately, no source that I am aware of, literary or otherwise, tells the writer what to do about the lack of *cash*, without which the other three items in Melville's plaintive list cannot function.

People who have grown up in the world of plastic credit cards and commonplace bank overdrafts will not be able to understand the economic ambience of former times when ordinary people did not have a bank account and when 'ready cash' paid for all purchases, transactions and services. The working classes, as they were called, were paid weekly in cash, the professionals such as civil servants, teachers and gardaí were paid monthly by cheque. In the final days before the next pay packet or the next cheque, people were often desperately counting their shillings and pence, and many families, even of the middle class, found the provision of food, clothes and fuel to be a constant struggle. Life for most people was still ruled by the economic theories of that indomitable optimist, Mr Micawber, which is still valid although obscured nowadays by the alluring rainbow of plastic credit cards. It is a Dickensian gem that deserves to be quoted in full, both for the delectation of the generation who survived the lean years of 'ready cash' and as a warning to those who have grown up in more affluent times that there is no crock of gold at the end of the credit-card rainbow. (The latter will need to understand that in the pre-decimal coinage there were twenty shillings in a pound, and twelve pence in a shilling, so that sixpence was half a shilling.)

> My other piece of advice, Copperfield, . . . you know. Annual income twenty pound, annual expenditure nineteen, nineteen and six, result happiness. Annual income twenty pounds, annual expenditure twenty pounds ought and six, result misery. The blossom is blighted, the leaf is withered, the god of day goes down upon the dreary scene, and – and in short you are for ever floored. As I am!

Having been employed only in temporary posts for several years before marrying and having married on the strength of a promised job that did not materialise until five months later – all of which meant that I was not entered even on the lowest rung of the incremental salary scale until some years after more fortunate colleagues who found a permanent teaching post as soon as they qualified – I would probably have furnished the English critic with a case history for a new edition of his book. He would have been all the more appalled at the folly of a young couple who, enjoying their extended honeymoon in a very basic two-room flat, bought a second-hand car as soon as we had a few hundred pounds in hand from some prizes and other writing. We enjoyed that little car for a few years until we had to sell it and put the proceeds with the money from my first novel to make the deposit on our brand new semi-detached house, a house we were able to furnish, of course, only in the essentials.

A new house bought with a down payment and a mortgage requires an assured income that will cover the monthly repayment as well as all the other costs of living, and we were well aware that my teacher's salary, already lagging behind in the incremental scale, would have to be supplemented by other means. Many teachers even on full salary did this by giving grinds but I was confident that I could earn enough, through various forms of writing in English and Irish, to ensure that the wolf would not even get into our back garden. Confidence is an essential quality in the writer or in any other artist but unfortunately it does not guarantee success in the marketplace. One of my most lucrative sources of income from writing was the children's radio programme but a change of director there resulted in the postman bringing me a string of rejected scripts instead of acceptance cheques. Delays in the publication of some books and rejection of articles submitted to magazines and newspapers added to my experience of literary life and to the need to find money somewhere, anywhere, each month. Even when I imitated my colleagues in the chalk mines and added hours of grinding at night to the classroom toil of the day, the extra income was so little and so uncertain that the wolf was sometimes to be clearly heard growling at the back door.

Came a day when there was nothing in the household funds to pay the mortgage. The only alternative to robbing a bank – being an amateur, I would probably have ended up doing a long stretch in Mountjoy, from which I might have got material for a play; meanwhile my lady wife and our children would have gone to live in a tent – was to visit an establishment outside the door of which there hung the professional sign of the three brass balls, in short, as Mr Micawber would say, to pawn something. In my childhood in Limerick I was well used to the pawnshop (or pawn office as we called it) as an essential factor in the survival of the poor, although my father's labour and my mother's industry had mercifully saved us from that degradation. In my years in Dublin I was aware of the fact that in spite of the heroic efforts of the Society of St Vincent de Paul and other charitable societies, the pawnshop was still a thriving business. Coming out from Mass or Confession in the Jesuit church in Gardiner Street, one could see the three brass balls gleaming invitingly over a doorway on the opposite side of the street.

I knew where to go. What to bring was the question. And the answer posed a dilemma that might fairly be called cruel. The only object that was likely to raise the sum required was my Underwood Portable. Apart from the personal anguish of parting with it – the cliché, 'like cutting off a finger' would be apt – without a typewriter I would be unable to churn out items for the literary market. (I was actually half-way through a new adventure story in Irish.)

I cycled from Drumcondra to Gardiner Street on a day when sleet and rain were making life unpleasant even for people with money in the bank. My typewriter in its black box-case was perched on the handlebars, living up to the manufacturer's claim that it was 'portable' in a way the Underwood company had not intended. I fancied myself as a picture of misery. Until I stood in the pawnshop waiting my turn while the proprietor, a large man who looked as if he had never known a hungry day in his life, rejected a man's suit being offered by a thin woman who looked as if she had known too many such days.

'No use,' the man said, 'I told you, we have too many, and that one isn't worth anything.'

'Ah, please,' the woman pleaded, 'give us somethin' on it, will yiz, I'll take anythin' at all, please, mister.'

He turned from her to consider the large black box I had placed on the counter. She bundled the worthless suit into newspaper wrapping and went out, muttering something that was not a blessing. The big man cast his professional eye over the black box and over me.

'What's this?'

'A typewriter.' I opened it. I really felt as if I were offering him a finger to be chopped off.

'Is it your own?' He moved his pudgy fingers over the keys.

I assured him that I was the lawful owner. He was not assured. I must have looked like a potential dealer in stolen goods.

'Have you a receipt?'

He examined it as if it might well be a forgery. What he was really looking at was the price of the article, thirty-one pounds and ten shillings, and date of purchase.

'How much do you want?'

To keep the roof over our heads, I needed to pay nine pounds into an office in Dublin before closing time tomorrow. As I said already in this book, how we remember such sums exactly forever after.

'Twenty pounds,' I suggested, hoping for fifteen.

The big man made a lugubrious face and shook his head slowly.

'Ten pounds is all I can offer.'

'But it's only a few years old and it's in perfect condition,' the amateur pawnee protested. I was still naïve in many areas of life.

'We get a lot of these,' he said, and pushed my beloved portable away with one hand, much as he had pushed that old suit of clothes back to the poor woman.

'All right.' Beggars can't be choosers.

The trouble with getting money by pawning something is exactly the same as the trouble with using these plastic credit cards, they each add a fee to the sum obtained. As I cycled home through the sleet and rain, I considered that next month's salary was already lessened by the ten pounds I had in my pocket – about a week's wages. And from that salary, or from some other source, another monthly payment would have to be made on the mortgage. When that charitable bishop of Myra, St Nicholas (he would soon undergo his seasonal metamorphosis into the commercial extortioner, Santa Claus) gave three bags of gold to the daughters of a poor man to save them from dishonour, little did he think that he would become the patron saint of pawnbrokers and that his three bags of gold would become a symbol of usury and misery.

I was now a writer without a typewriter, much like a

soldier going into battle without a gun or a cook with no fuel. But every time I looked at my wife and children I thought of that thin woman in the pawnshop, pleading for a few shillings on an old suit. At least I had come home with ten pounds. What was *she* going home to, without the few shillings?

Necessity being the mother of invention – Irish puts it better: *Múineann gá seift* (literally Necessity teaches initiative) – I called into an office supplies shop in Dublin the next day and impressed a salesman by my keen professional interest in the typewriters on display: 'Actually, I'm a writer – *ahem*! – plays on the radio, three books published, a play with the Abbey Theatre at present' – *with, nice word*! My present machine was giving me some trouble, I explained – God's truth! – and I was considering getting rid of it – barefaced lie; it was gone already if I didn't pay back ten quid with interest within three months. When the eager salesman directed me towards an electric typewriter and even suggested a seven-day trial – 'We'll deliver it, and if you don't like it – but I'm sure you will, it's a marvellous job altogether – we'll collect it from you' – I felt that maybe old Saint Nick was still on the job.

It took me a little time to get used to the electric machine, which was indeed, as the man said, a 'marvellous job altogether' but with a price tag that sent shivers through my empty pockets. However, before the seven days were up and I phoned my earnest salesman with the disappointing news that 'for the present, anyway, *blah-blah-blah*, but I'll certainly bear it in mind, *blah-blah-blah*', I had finished my adventure book and written some other bits and pieces that might bring in a cheque at some future date. My education in the world of the pawnshop was not yet complete. In two similar crisis situations during the next few years – while I was still hoping that the play in the Abbey would make my fame and fortune – I brought my Underwood Portable back to the proprietor of the three brass balls in Gardiner Street. Having got ten pounds on my first visit, I knew how much to expect on my second venture. I knew wrong.

'I'll give you eight pounds,' the big man said.

'But you gave me ten a few months ago and it's the same machine.'

'Well, we get a lot of these, very common now.' Hard to imagine that there were lots of other writers in such 'straitened financial circumstances' that they were pawning the very machines they needed for their work.

On the third visit, my typewriter was valued at six pounds. If it went on like that, the day would come when he'd be offering me a shilling for the same machine. A Dublin friend in McDaid's, more experienced in the pawnee ways since childhood, explained the finer points to me. 'When he sees that you're able to come back and redeem it, he knows he won't ever get his hands on it to sell; also, he knows that you only came in the first place because of some crisis, he knows he'll never see you or your typewriter again as soon as the trouble is over.'

Which it was, thank God – and Saint Nicholas – when, like the long-unheard-from ships of Antonio in *The Merchant of Venice*, a few of my submissions here and there began to bring in cheques, and the book I finished on the electric typewriter won first prize in that year's Oireachtas competitions. In justice, I should have sought out that earnest salesman and bought him a few drinks; life is complicated enough without bringing more troubles on ourselves. Many years and many troubles later, I happened to be going into the church in Gardiner Street and I noticed that something was missing on the other side of the street. The three brass balls and the sad business they stood for had disappeared. And here was I with my family reared and done for, and my courageous and loving wife still putting up with me. I had something to thank God for when I went in to kneel and pray where the holy Dublinman, Matt Talbot, often prayed after he gave up the booze. I recalled the story told of his drunkard days that he once pawned a fiddle he stole from a poor street musician who fell asleep in the pub. I remembered too that on one Saturday night in those years when the three brass balls kept a roof over our heads, I was kneeling with a crowd of other sinners and edging slowly along towards the confessional when I recognised that the man beside me was Mícheál O'Hehir, the man with the golden voice that brought the thrills of Croke Park into the homes and hearths of Ireland, and I half expected him to come out with, *'A chairde Gael! Fáilte romhaibh go dtí Páirc an Chrócaigh . . .'*

16

MEETING MR BLYTHE

When I was growing up in Limerick in the 1930s, there was a lovely shop, a grocery-cum-pub, just up the street, at 'McCarney's corner' near St Mary's Cathedral, to which my mother used to send us now and again. It was owned by two sisters named McCarney, the older one thin and very prim, the other stout and more homely in manner. The door separating the shop from the pub was adorned with two advertisements for Bovril. One showed a cheery chap dressed in pyjamas riding the waves in a turbulent sea on a bottle of Bovril, and it carried the slogan: 'Bovril prevents that sinking feeling.' The other showed a more harassed individual turning into a sidestreet as he was being chased by a ferocious bull, and it proclaimed: 'Bovril helps you to turn the corner.' When these examples from the pre-television era of advertising come to my mind, I sometimes think that every writer should keep a bottle of Bovril handy for those days when the postman brings the bulky envelope or parcel containing a literary creation, the result of months or even years of hard labour, that is now in effect only a pile of waste paper.

When the postman brought me such an item, about six months after I had submitted my play, *In Dublin's Fair City*, to the Abbey, I experienced that sinking feeling at first, but subsequently I turned the corner into a more hopeful vista.

The letter in Irish accompanying my script was from Mr Blythe. (We always conversed and corresponded *as Gaeilge*.) He told me that the directors were very impressed with my play but not satisfied that it was ready for production. Enclosed I would find opinions from various people who had read the play. Mr Blythe asked me to consider these opinions, rewrite the play, and submit it again.

Although disappointed that the play as I had conceived and written it had not been accepted, I was more than consoled by the fact that the board of directors of the Abbey Theatre was very impressed with the play. The sinking feeling returned when I read the readers' reports which were supposed to guide me in rewriting the play. These were six in number, and they bore letters, A,B,C,D,E,F, rather than names. And they were so contradictory of each other that it would be impossible to follow their suggestions. The character or scene praised as excellent by one, another thought weak or even superfluous, and so on with dialogue, plot details, ideas and themes. I was reminded of the song in *The Mikado*:

See how the Fates their gifts allot,
For A is happy – B is not.

But I was also left confused and frustrated. I had fondly imagined that when a writer sent a play to the Abbey Theatre, the script was read by the board of directors, including Mr Ernest Blythe as managing director, all of whom, I thought naïvely, must have been appointed to the board because they were experts in the art of drama. Even if the opinions of the four directors were included in the six I had been sent, they were just as ridiculously contradictory as the others. I learned later that the Abbey paid people in various walks of life – some of them actors, some even rejected playwrights – a fee of a few guineas to read a script; if the preliminary opinions were generally favourable, the directors themselves would then read the play and accept or reject it.

I wrote to Mr Blythe and explained my dilemma. I asked for a meeting with the directors. He invited me to come to his office in the old Abbey and discuss the problem. When I did, as I went up the stairs I remembered that day in Christmas week some years before, when my wife waited on the street while I hoped to collect fifteen pounds for writing lyrics and a scene in the Irish pantomime. The same middle-aged lady answered my knock at the office door and again the door was closed in my face while she informed the man himself. When I was admitted, Mr Blythe, a heavily-built, bald man with a smile that was often unkindly likened to a Mongolian leer, greeted me cordially while I took in at a glance the untidy state of his office and the ancient desk, the latter cluttered with documents and what looked like playscripts.

Before we settled down to discuss my play and my problem, he asked me if I had ever been in the Abbey before the disastrous fire of 1951. When I replied in the negative, he invited me to see what was left of the auditorium. We stood together on the famous stage where the plays of Synge and O'Casey had been brought to theatrical life from the playwright's script, the stage where W. B. Yeats had faced the indignant protestors with his aristocratic rebuke, 'You have disgraced yourselves again.' The dark and charred auditorium seemed to rustle with ghostly echoes of those audiences of nights long ago. But perhaps there were voices whispering too that the glory days were gone forever. The man standing beside me on the stage of the ruined theatre was not the poet Yeats, but a prosaic and pragmatic businessman, a veteran of the Anglo-Irish War of 1919–21 and of the bitter Civil War of 1922-23, during which he had been a member of the Free State government that sentenced many of their own old comrades to death. He was appointed manager of the Abbey only because his political career had failed, and although he succeeded in keeping the Abbey going through the difficult years between the disastrous fire of 1951 and the opening of the new theatre in 1966, he was too dictatorial in his manner and too philistinic in temperament to be anything but a hindrance to the artistic development of such an institution.

It should be noted, however, that it was the poet Yeats who rejected *The Silver Tassie* (1928), O'Casey's attempt to break away from the realism of his Dublin trilogy, with disastrous consequences for O'Casey and for Irish theatre, and that plays like Denis Johnston's *The Old Lady Says 'No!'* (1929) were rejected while Lady Gregory was in command. And in this context I have a theory, which I offer for the consideration of all who are interested in philosophical speculation, that the play with which Samuel Beckett became known to the world when it was produced in Paris, *En Attendant Godot* (1952), was rejected by the Abbey when first written in English some time in the 1930s and taken out of a drawer after the war when Beckett, having become more French than the French themselves, decided to write only in French. Beckett, a taciturn as well as a prudent man, never said so, of course, but it was to the Abbey Theatre that any Irish writer would send a play and I feel that it is only a rejection by the Abbey, if not of *Godot* then of some other play, that would have elicited the vitriolic passage in the novel, *Murphy* (1938), where the eponymous hero's last wishes are read out. The passage, like Mr Micawber's economic theory, is worth quoting in full:

> With regard to the disposal of these my body, mind and soul, I desire that they be burnt and placed in a paper bag and brought to the Abbey Theatre, Lr Abbey Street, Dublin, and without pause into what the great and good Lord Chesterfield calls the necessary house, where their happiest hours have been spent, on the right as one goes down into the pit, and

I desire that the chain be there pulled upon them, if possible during the performance of a piece, the whole to be executed without ceremony or show of grief.

On the other hand and in spite of the fact that he rejected what I considered to be my best plays, I remember Ernest Blythe as one of the most honest and forthright people with whom I have had dealings in the course of my literary career. He said what he thought about a play, however mistaken and foolish anyone, including the author, might think his opinions to be. And when he accepted a play, he put the resources of the Abbey, such as they were in finance and in personnel, at the disposal of that play, whether the author was an unknown young writer or a dramatist with many productions to his name. And he adhered faithfully to the purpose for which the Abbey was founded, to produce new plays by Irish authors. All in all, I would much rather have a play of mine mistakenly rejected by a man like Ernest Blythe than mauled and mangled in production by some other people I've come across.

When we returned to his office from our nostalgic tour of the ghostly auditorium of the old Abbey, Mr Blythe sat me down opposite him and treated me to a long talk about the Abbey and its playwrights, and about the present state of theatre in Ireland. He told me that the Abbey could only put on a handful of new plays each year; they actually received about three hundred submissions a year, over 90 per cent of which were rubbish – one recent offering was a brief one, written in longhand on a piece of brown paper (an opened sugar-bag, Blythe surmised) and the author had added a note along these lines: 'Dear Sir, I am thinking of writing a play that would be suitable for the Abbey Theatre. Here is an idea of what the first part would be like. If you think this is good, I will write the whole play and send it to you.'

One of Mr Blythe's remarks indicates that, like the director of the Dublin Theatre Festival with whom I would have to deal a full decade later in the late Sixties, the managing director of the subsidised Abbey was conscious of the fact that the moral standards and social attitudes of the society in which we lived must be taken into account when considering any play for production. Only a few years before, in 1951, the inevitable opposition of the bishops to Dr Noel Browne's mother-and-child health bill had caused the collapse of the coalition government led by John A. Costello and Fine Gael. And all theatre managers were only too well aware of the recent court case in which Alan Simpson, an ex-army officer and co-director with Carolyn Swift of the little Pike Theatre, had been prosecuted under the public obscenity laws for having produced *The Rose Tattoo* (1951) by Tennessee Williams. I was in the audience myself on the last night before that play was taken off, and I observed a man in the back row taking notes; he turned out to be a plain-clothes policeman who later gave evidence in court as to what he had seen on the stage. It was at the Pike that Behan's *The Quare Fellow* (1954), the play that brought him fame and fortune (also misfortune), was put on after it had been rejected by both the Abbey and the Gate. Years later, after its success in London and New York, the Abbey cashed in on it with several productions, as it did with other rejected plays like John B. Keane's popular folk-play, *Sive* (1959). 'We get all sorts of plays here,' Mr Blythe told me, 'and even some good plays can't be done because of the topics they deal with. For instance, we had an interesting play some time ago by a well-known Irish writer but it was about the relationship between two men; of course, we couldn't put on that sort of thing.'

When we discussed the problems of playwriting in a general way, the old politician confided in the young dramatist by relating an event from his own life to illustrate a basic theory of playwriting which I had already assimilated in my apprentice days from those books in the Limerick City library. The suspension of disbelief on the part of the audience, essential to the success of the illusion of drama, cannot be pushed too far. Even Shakespeare pushes it dangerously so in *King Lear*, one of his greatest plays, which cannot be enjoyed unless the audience accepts the opening scene where the ageing king decides to divide his kingdom between his three daughters, but first demands from them a public declaration of how much they love him. People will believe that inexplicable things can happen in real life, they will even believe everything they read in the newspapers but in a realistic play they will demand logical reasons for every development.

'When I lost my seat in the Dáil,' Mr Blythe told me, 'I had no profession to fall back on. I was in a bad way financially. One morning I came down the stairs and found a package in the hall. It contained three hundred pounds, a lot of money then. There was no note, nothing written on the package; but it must have been from someone who knew about my problem. Now, that really happened, and things like that do happen; but if that same thing was in a play nobody would believe it.'

When he finally – after nearly two hours – got round to discussing what I had come to talk about, Mr Blythe blithely (I can't resist the pun) dismissed the readers' opinions he had sent me. With a laugh and a wave of his hand, he said, '*Ná bac leo!*' (Don't take any notice of them). When I pointed out that he had asked me to rewrite my play with reference to these anonymous readers' opinions, he was even more emphatic.

'They don't know how to write plays,' he said, 'and we here in the Abbey don't know how to write plays. If we could write them, we would. But *you* know how to write a play, and this is a very good play, and we want to put it on, but we feel that it can be improved.'

'So, what am I to do?' asked the perplexed playwright.

'Read over these opinions again,' said Mr Blythe, 'and pick out anything you think might be useful. And send us in the play as soon as you can.'

He made only one practical suggestion of his own.

'Get rid of that little girl you have in the play, you don't really need her.'

I explained that I did really need her. She was a twelve-year-old daughter of one of the families in the tenement, and she represented the future generation who, unless things improved, would be doomed to live in the same conditions as her parents.

To this argument, Mr Blythe came back with, 'We don't like child actors here; they usually come from some acting academy and the first thing you have to do is get them to forget all they have been taught.'

I suggested that a petite actress of eighteen or twenty could easily play a girl of twelve. This caused him to observe that the cast was very big anyway, and it might be no harm to consider getting rid of one or two other minor characters, such as the two political canvassers I had in two short scenes. I was beginning to feel that if I stayed much longer, Mr Blythe would have eliminated all my characters except one, reducing my play to a monologue for the Abbey's resident comic actor, the genial Harry Brogan.

I rewrote my play, sent it to the Abbey, waited three months, and received another bulky package from the postman. The second version of my play, Mr Blythe informed me, was better in some ways than the first, but in other aspects it seemed to have been weakened. Enclosed I would find – readers' opinions! Again, A,B,C,D,E,F, were in disagreement. What A praised as an improvement, another lamented as a mistaken change. And so it went on, exactly as with the first version. I decided that the Abbey was run by lunatics and that no writer could maintain his integrity if he had to deal with such a system. I threw the second version of my play into a drawer with the first version, and directed whatever time and energy I had to spare for creative writing to other projects.

An item in the newspapers about a public course of lectures in drama, to be given by a visiting American professor, caused me to drift in and listen to a big pleasant man from New York whose name was Arnold Sundgaard. Hearing him reading extracts from Synge and others to illustrate his talks, I noticed that he did not understand the difference between the long monosyllable, sure, meaning certain, and the short Hiberno-English one, sure (pronounced shur) which is a meaningless interjection, so that he misread phrases like 'Ah, sure (shur) maybe they'll come,' and 'Sure (shur) how would I know?' I decided that he should not be allowed to go back to his university in New York handicapped by this misapprehension which he would obviously inflict on his students. When I took occasion, after one of his lectures, to apprise him privately of the difference, he was grateful with the humility of the scholar; he also made a note of my explanation that our common colloquialism *shur*, not given in English dictionaries, is probably derived from *'sha*, itself an abbreviation of *wisha*, from the Irish interjection, *muise* or *mhuise*. In subsequent chats over a cup of coffee, he told me of his amazement at finding that most Irish people seem to believe that they could write poems, plays or novels if only they set their minds to it. He encountered the most amazing, and amusing, instance of this literary proclivity when, soon after arriving in Dublin, he checked in at the local garda station. When he informed the desk sergeant that he was a professor of drama from New York and that he would be spending a year in Trinity, the sergeant beamed at him as at a soulmate.

'Do you know now,' he said, 'I have a great interest in the theatre myself, and listen to this – I wrote a play, would you believe! And maybe while you're here in Trinity College you might read it some time and tell me what you think of it.'

'Can you imagine walking into a police station in New York and meeting up with a cop like that?' the professor asked me, still shaking his crew-cut head in delight and astonishment. I can imagine that he regaled many of his classes and colleagues with that incident for years afterwards. When I told him of my own play and its second semi-rejection by the Abbey, he asked to read it. I gave him the first version and his verdict was that the Abbey should have accepted it as it was. Any such verdict from a friend must obviously be treated with caution but it is at least as good as a cup of Bovril for an author suffering from that sinking feeling of rejection.

About three months after I had thrown my play aside in despair, a letter from Mr Blythe arrived. He wanted to know when I would send in the new version of my play, which, he said, they were very anxious to read. By now, the very thought of trying to chop and change the play yet once more made me want to devote the rest of my life to writing novels; but having taken counsel with some people more prudent and experienced than myself, I decided that it would be worth having another go at the script if it meant that for the future I could call myself an Abbey Theatre playwright. My experience of the Abbey to date had disillusioned me brusquely of my naïve attitude towards that institution and its board of directors, but my new friend, Professor Sundgaard from New York, assured me that the cachet still carried a lot of prestige in the US and would be valuable if I wanted to look for a job as writer-in-residence or even in submitting literary work to magazines.

Feeling humbly like Beethoven writing his *Leonora* (No.3) overture to the opera, *Fidelio*, I put the plot, characters and dialogues back into my brainbox, mixed them up well, and worked out a third version of my play, noticing that it was actually working its own way back to be very much the first version with some slight changes, including the elimination of the little girl and another minor character. This version was accepted within a month – after I had agreed to make a few more changes in the Third Act! I was then invited to meet the producer (called *director* nowadays), Ria Mooney, who had been a noted Abbey actress in her younger days. I met her in Mr Blythe's office, with himself introducing us. In one hand she held the script of my play, in the other the last two pages of that script which she had removed.

'We'll have to change this ending,' she said emphatically, 'it's too like the ending of one of O'Casey's plays.'

I protested that I knew nothing of O'Casey's plays, never having seen or read them, and that even if some people in the audience thought my play had an ending like one of them, it was likely that such similarities could be found in many dramas and novels. Mr Blythe sided with his lady producer, pointing out to me that because my play was set in a Dublin tenement, the critics were likely to begin, as they usually did, by comparing it with O'Casey's plays; so, if the ending reminded them, etc., etc. It was arranged that I would meet Ria Mooney a few nights later in the bar of the Queen's Theatre, the Abbey's temporary home, during the interval of the play which she was currently directing. This was another comedy by John McCann, whose Dublin comedies were the mainstay of the Abbey and the butt of the literati during those lean years. When I met her, we sat in the little galley of a bar, hearing the 'noises off' of the play on the other side of the wall. And just as Mr Blythe had treated me to the history of the Abbey, as well as his views on theatre and on life in general, before briefly referring to my play, I now had to listen to this gentle lady telling me about her career and about her frustrations, the latest of which she had suffered at a recent Wexford Festival which featured a visit by the Abbey company. Some of the actors had apparently entered into the festive mood by drinking too much and when the lady producer remonstrated with them, she was called a stupid old bitch, among other things. As Mr Blythe said, things happen in life that would not be believed on the stage. If I had a scene in my play, in any play, in which a young writer had to sit and listen to an ageing actress actually sobbing as she complained about drunken actors, Mr Blythe himself would have told me that the critics and the audience would regard it as far-fetched and incredible.

17

CURTAIN UP

When I was informed that my play would have its first night at the end of November – the year being 1959 – I still had enough optimism in my soul to hope that this would be a turning point in my career as a writer. When I attended the dress rehearsal – as a writer with a full-time job, I was unable to see the preliminaries – my optimism was somewhat dampened when one of the actors gloomily admonished me thus, 'You shouldn't have let them put on your play just a few weeks before Christmas; it's suicide,' and an actress loftily informed me in a throwaway line, 'It's not much of a part really but I'll do my best with it.' But I felt sympathy for the young actress who took me aside during the tea-break and said timidly, 'Could you not have done something better with my part?' It transpired that Mr Blythe had decided after all that having a young girl in the plot, representing the coming generation, was a good idea; but there was no need to *see* her; so, without discussing the matter with the author, he and Ria Mooney had decided that it would be sufficient if the child's voice was heard calling out to her mother in a few scenes. For the duration of the play, therefore – and at least one member of the cast was surely praying that it would only last a week – this young actress was to sit on a box in the wings and watch as intently as the cymbalclasher in an orchestra for the great moments when she would cry out immortal lines like, 'Mam-mee, they're comin'!'

Mr Blythe's protective personal secretary asked me how many tickets I wanted for the opening night and would I be making a speech. From my general reading of novels and newspapers, I thought all authors were supposed to respond to the cry of 'Author! Author!' (provided, of course, some voice thus led the pack, I having no supportive clique or hired claque to do the job). 'Some of them go on too long,' she complained. 'If you want to say anything, just thank Mr Blythe.' Which, of course, I did, but I also thanked the producer and the cast, and even the small orchestra, which entertained the audience before the curtain went up and during the intervals. The leader of the orchestra was the pianist, a young composer named in the programme as John Reidy BMus, who would later become Seán Ó Riada and go back to his ancestral sources of culture to achieve fame with the music for Gael Linn's historic documentary, *Mise Éire* (1956). His death at an early age was as tragic as that of the writer, Donncha Ó Céileachair, who was born in the same west Cork Gaeltacht in which Ó Riada went to live.

During an interval in the play my wife and I were interviewed by Terry O'Sullivan, who was in those years a popular social columnist with the *Evening Press*, a paper now sadly extinct like the other two papers in the Burgh Quay trio that began when de Valera founded the *Irish Press* in 1932. Terry-O, as he was known, had the reputation of being cynical behind his suave manner but on this first encounter we found him to be pleasant and in no way disconcerting. He asked about our children and whether we expected to make money from the play, and seemed amused when I said we'd be sure of a turkey for Christmas anyway. His piece in *Dubliner's Diary* the next evening, however, gave me a shock and a lesson. Under a picture of the author and his lovely young wife, the man gave a nice write-up of the event and of our conversation, and then spoilt it all and mystified myself and my wife, by concluding with the statement, 'In another capacity, the author is secretary of the League of Decency.' I was not aware of the existence of any such league, nor had we discussed decency or its opposite during our chat in a corridor of the Queen's Theatre. I wrote to Terry-O asking him to inform the readers of the *Evening Press* to this effect. The correction appeared as a brief sentence mixed in with his annual paragraph acknowledging Christmas cards from various sources.

I have been wary of journalists ever since, especially of the failed writers who have to earn their bread in a profession which is both potentially noble and potentially sordid. Strangely enough, in many subsequent meetings, I came to know Terry O'Sullivan (or Tomás Ó Faoláin to give the man his real name) fairly well, and we developed a reciprocal respect based on my side on the belief that he was a very talented writer who had probably been frustrated by one or more of those 'enemies of promise' analysed by Cyril Connolly. My sympathy became empathy when I learned that this brilliant gossip columnist had been, like myself, a teacher in his young days. I began to envisage parallels between my own early struggles as a writer and what might have been his, and to wonder if he had written plays and fiction but had suffered rejection to the point of giving up. In a recent book, his journalist daughter, Nuala O'Faolain, has given some indications of the enemies of promise that may have blighted his creative literary talent. I asked him on several occasions why he did not write a book about his experiences as a journalist – his *Sunday Press* articles on visits to the US and to Jerusalem and Lourdes (a place that shook his cynicism, he told me) would have been the basis for an enthralling book. I was glad and he was sincerely appreciative when I was able to pay his work the tribute it deserved by dedicating the book of my play on the poet Raftery, produced by the Abbey in 1973, to a writer who seemed to me to be a modern version of that rambling nineteenth-century journalistic poet.

The morning after the night before has a special significance for the dramatist. The magazine stories and the gossip columns paint a glamorous picture of the party going on all night and the excitement of reading the reviews in the early editions of the papers. After my curtain speech on the opening night of *In Dublin's Fair City*, my wife and I were allowed to go on our way without even being offered a drink or a cup of tea. We stood on the pavement under the awning of the theatre waiting for the rain to ease off before walking home, a taxi being a luxury beyond our means. The morning after the first night of my play found me far from the so-called glamour of the theatre. I was standing, as I did on every working day, but understandably somewhat more schizophrenic of soul than usual, before my class in the primary school in Drumcondra, not even having had an opportunity to buy the morning papers to read what the critics had to say about my play. Some time during the morning my bleary eyes observed in the corridor outside my classroom (all the walls in that school were of glass panels) the president of the training college, Dr Cregan, CM. He had succeeded Fr Kilian Kehoe, the man who gave me the job in that school.

He was beckoning me to come out. When I did so, he said he had read the papers and he had come down from the college to congratulate me on the excellent reviews. Unfortunately, he added, he would be unable to see the play himself as the clergy were not allowed to go to the professional theatre. This Jansenistic regulation was made all the more ludicrous by the fact that an amateur drama group, with the local curate or teacher as producer, was one of the principal fund-raising activities in almost every parish in Ireland, and that every successful Abbey play was sure to be put on in the village hall as well as being adapted for broadcasting on Radio Éireann. The memory of that courteous gesture on the part of my clerical manager, and of similar incidents involving other priests, would help me to keep my spiritual equilibrium in years to come when I encountered more boorish and ruthless clergymen. When I did get to see the papers at lunch-time, I found that Desmond Rushe in the *Irish Independent*, Michael Mills (later to become Ireland's first Ombudsman) in the *Irish Press*, and Seamus Kelly ('Quidnunc') in *The Irish Times*, were unanimous in their high opinion of my play, two of them judging it to be the best new play seen in the Abbey that year. Only Seamus Kelly brought up the O'Casey comparison that Blythe and Ria Mooney had foreseen as inevitable but he did so in order to add further praise to my effort at depicting life in a Dublin tenement a generation after O'Casey's trilogy.

In spite of the critics' praise, Mr Blythe informed me that my play would have to be taken off after two weeks so that rehearsals for the Christmas pantomime in Irish could begin but he promised me that when the pantomime ended its run in February, my play would go on again. As a patriotic lover of the Irish language, I had to feel glad that the annual pantomime at the Abbey would give audiences the chance to realize that the language was not merely a school subject or a politician's tool, but as a tyro dramatist hoping for fame and fortune I was inclined to agree with those who maintained that the Abbey should not neglect its *raison d'être* for seven or eight weeks in the year by devoting its entire resources to a pantomime. When the pantomime eventually folded in mid-February, my play resumed – for one week only. I learned then that even while the pantomime was running, yet another Dublin comedy by John McCann was in rehearsal, and my play was put on for a week in February only because the pantomime petered out before the new McCann comedy was ready. Another lesson in the hard school of experience.

Among the distinguished visitors to my play during its two-and-one weeks run were my mother, Harry S. Truman, ex-President of the USA and Joseph Tomelty, the Belfast playwright. Each of them gave me a line to remember. My mother refused to come from Limerick for the opening night, saying she would be too excited. Sadly, my father did not live to see the play; he had enjoyed my early radio plays and stories – and joked that he should have got half the fee for some of those stories as they were a mere reshaping of yarns he had told us from the family history. When she finally came for a weekend, we brought my mother to the play and established her in the centre of the front row of the dress circle in the old Queen's Theatre, the equivalent of the royal box in an opera house. As the lights came up after the first act of the play, I turned to her and asked, 'Well, Ma, what did you think of that?'

'Well, glory be to God,' says she, 'haven't they words at will!' That left her playwright son temporarily dumbfounded, but when I told it later to some of the actors they said it was the best compliment they had ever received.

A night at the current Abbey play was *de rigueur* in those days for all distinguished visitors to Dublin and when Truman came to town he and his entourage were brought to see my play. He told me that he enjoyed it very much – but added with a smile that he thought I was too hard on politicians.

I was introduced to the white-haired Joseph Tomelty in the bar one night. I told him that I had seen his play, *All Souls' Night*, performed by the College Players in Limerick before I ever tried to write a play. He told me that I had the most important talent of a dramatist, invention, and then he asked me a question that brought my mind back to that night in the foyer of the old Abbey when Ray McAnally stunned my naïve mind by asking me if I had a contract for the writing of lyrics for the Irish pantomime. The question put to me by a dramatist much more experienced than myself was, 'Did you count the house?' It took me some time even to grasp the meaning and the import of the blunt query. When I admitted that I had not, in fact, 'counted the house', he shook his white head and said in his Belfast twang, 'Ah, now, you should always count the house.' I remembered his pragmatic Northern counsel when I received my royalties from the Abbey. The contract set out payment on a sliding scale, from ten per cent of the box office for a full house, down through seven-and-a-half, to five per cent for half the house or less. I had visited the theatre at least three times after the opening night, and each time the house seemed full to capacity; but my nightly royalty varied between the two lower rates, never reaching the full ten per cent. When I queried this with Mr Blythe, he shook his bald Northern head and leered most amiably as he told me that many free tickets would be included in any seemingly full house. Why the author should be at a loss if the management gave away free tickets he was unwilling to discuss.

And so my dream of fame and fortune by means of an Abbey play proved to be a mirage. I accepted that I must continue to labour in the chalk mines, like many a good man and woman before me. But at least I could now impress anyone who thought it a sign of artistic achievement with the new line in my CV, 'Abbey Theatre playwright'. And I would never again believe any of the mushy drivel dished up in magazines and newspapers about the theatre and those connected with it in any capacity, nor would I believe that everything I saw on any stage or read between the covers of any book, was actually the work of the named author.

18

IN MOZART'S FAIR CITY

I was long enough on the snakes-and-ladders road of life to know that the disappointment resulting from the Abbey Theatre's production of my play would pass away in time, even if the disillusionment remained as a hard-earned protection for my spirit in future literary ventures. Even before the final curtain came down on my play I was reaping some benefit from what was, in spite of everything, a literary achievement of some measure. Some friends had suggested that I should apply for a Fellowship at the Salzburg Seminar in American Studies (the title nowadays says *European* instead of *American*). This institution was based in Mozart's native city in Austria, and it had been initiated after the Second World War by some American graduates in order to promote peace by bringing professional people from all the countries of Europe together at month-long courses in their respective fields. The building they acquired for this purpose was an eighteenth-century mansion, the Schloss Leopoldskron, originally the home of the aristocratic archbishop of Salzburg. Before the war it was owned by a famous theatre director whose name I forget, and during the war it became the headquarters of the local Nazi Gauleiter. In recent years, while still functioning as those American postwar idealists intended, it has become a special item on the itinerary of the tourist coaches because it was used as the stately home of the Von Trapp family in the film, *The Sound of Music*.

I applied for a fellowship at a course in *Literature, Drama and the Mass Media*, and the American who conducted the interviews in a Dublin hotel was so impressed by the fact that I was the author of an Abbey Theatre play, as well as having written all kinds of everything in Irish and English, that when I told him I could not afford the residence fee, in whole or in part as stipulated, he told me that in the case of people with achievements like mine who were considered to be likely to contribute something of value to the discussions but who were in straitened financial circumstances, the fees for maintenance and lectures would be waived; all I would need would be my return fare to Salzburg and whatever pocket-money I could bring along. My heroic wife, who would be left caring for our three young children, came along with me to the local bank in Drumcondra, where a benign manager demanded only the deeds of our new house as surety for a loan of one hundred pounds. The bankman made our day by turning to my wife and saying, still with a benign smile, 'Of course, you know that if he doesn't come back, *you'll* be in a bad position.'

As had happened when I was offered a six-month period in the Gaeltacht eight years earlier, I encountered no opposition from my school manager – the same Dr Cregan, who had done me the courtesy of coming down to the school to congratulate me about my play a few months earlier – or from the officials of the department of education. It was required, of course, that I employ a substitute teacher and pay him from my own salary. Dr Cregan told me that he had visited Salzburg himself, that it was a beautiful city and that he was sure I would benefit as a writer from the European experience.

Air travel in 1960 was still confined largely to the rich, or to emigrants who had saved up or been sent the fare to America. I went to Salzburg by trains and ships. Of the mailboats plying between Dún Laoghaire and Holyhead in those years, the *Princess Maud* was the smallest and the most likely to make the traveller leave his last meal with the seagulls. On the Friday night when I boarded her, she was packed to the rails, the usual complement of passengers being augmented by the rugby alickadoos decked in green-and-white scarves on their way to Saturday's international between Ireland and England at Twickenham. When we were half-way across the Irish Sea, Mother Nature tried to frighten them with a display of thunder and lightning but it only caused them to sing louder and drink more. I went from London to Harwich by train, boarded another ship to the Hook of Holland, and from there made the final train journey through Holland and Germany, arriving at the station in Salzburg, just inside the border of Austria, on Sunday morning. By that time, the train was so packed with groups of weekend skiers and their equipment that it was almost impossible to move along the corridors.

My first impression of Salzburg was blue and white, the ground being covered with snow, the sky a cloudless blue. Since the Church authorities in Rome had not yet adverted to the fact that the first Mass was an evening one, celebrated as the conclusion to a meal, Catholics were still obliged to fulfil the Sunday obligation of worship before midday and fasting from midnight if they wished to receive Holy Communion. I decided to attend Mass before making my way to the Schloss Leopoldskron. When I got off the train I spotted a young nun who seemed to be waiting for someone. I approached her and told her in Hiberno-Deutsch that I was *aus Irland gekommen* and that I would like to find *die Kirche* so that I could hear *die Messe*. Having got over the shock of being thus accosted by a big unshaven foreigner carrying a heavy travel bag and a big black box (my trusty Underwood ever-portable) the girl went into a giggle of excitement and proceeded to lead me out of the station, meanwhile spouting eloquently in her native tongue about

Irland and *Frank Duff.* Most of what she said about them was beyond me, but I threw in the *ja, ja*, here and there as if I were a personal friend of the good man who founded the Legion of Mary in Dublin.

Whoever that little nun was waiting for at the station must have made their own way, because she brought me through several streets to a church where people were going into Mass. A tall, thin old priest in a grey Franciscan habit was standing chatting to some people. My guardian angel for the day introduced me, and when she got to the bit about *aus Irland gekommen* the old priest's gaunt face lit up and he raised his hands as he beamed at me.

'Ich bin Virgilius,' he announced. I could see that he meant me to be impressed, but I was too tired to appreciate why he was telling me that his name was Virgilius. It wasn't until I made my first tour of Salzburg that evening and saw four statues on pedestals outside the cathedral that my refreshed brain made the connection. The statues are of St Peter, St Paul, St Ruprecht, principal patron of Salzburg, and St Virgilius. The last-named was known in his native Ireland as Fearghal. He was one of the Irish missionaries who brought religion and learning to Europe after the Dark Ages. Arriving in Salzburg around 746, he first became abbot of a monastery and later the second bishop of Salzburg. His relics are preserved in the cathedral. In 1974 the city of Salzburg commemorated with great ceremony the founding by Fearghal of the first cathedral in 774, and throughout the whole year in 1984 events and ceremonies commemorated his death in 784. Among the Irish clergy and scholars at the celebrations was the late Cardinal Tomás Ó Fiaich, a professional historian whose lifelong study of the Irish missionaries in Europe resulted in his fascinating book, *Gaelscrínte san Eoraip* (1986) an enlarged edition of the original *Gaelscrínte i gCéin* (Foilseacháin Ábhair Spioradálta, 1960). I paused before the statue of Fearghal/Virgilius on many other days during my stay, and what I had felt to be

the hardships of my own trip to Salzburg seemed a luxury compared with the journeys those missionary Irish monks had made.

While Salzburg is for the Irish pilgrim the city of Fearghal, for the music lover it is the city of Mozart. Happy the visitor who can combine the two aspects into a memorable experience. Having to count out carefully the cost of a cup of coffee or a glass of beer in the local *Gasthaus*, I was unable to do more in the Mozart line during my month in Salzburg than admire his pigeon-soiled statue in the square and visit the *Geburtshaus* where the childish fingers of the little Wolfgang were first placed on the strings of a violin.

Having thanked God through the Mass – with a special word to my personal patron, Kristopheros, patron saint of all travellers – for having brought me safely all the way from the Island of Saints and Scholars to Fearghal's place of holy exile, I made my way to the Schloss Leopoldskron, where I was welcomed by a pleasant American woman who, when I identified myself, said, 'Ah, you're the Irishman!' To which the weary Gael replied, 'No, I'm only *an* Irishman, there's a few million more of us back at home.' She explained to me in plain terms, as such efficient people do, that I was the only person from Ireland taking part in that particular session.

As my school manager had foretold, I found the European experience of benefit. It would have been of even more benefit but for the fact that Europe had been partitioned by the so-called Iron Curtain that cut off the communist countries of Eastern Europe, so that the only communist country represented was Tito's independent Yugoslavia. The people at the course were all experienced in their respective fields, the mass media, theatre and literature, and the faculty were Americans who were distinguished in their own disciplines. The theatre specialist was Edwin Burr Pettet, professor of drama at Brandeis University in Boston. He had first-hand knowledge of Ireland – at our initial interview he showed me the label, *Clery's*, on the inside pocket of his jacket – and he had no time for stage Irishism or for 'Oirish' antics in literature, in films, or in life. We had been advised to bring scripts and any other material of interest, and when, at a later session, I showed him an item of practical professional interest, viz. the detailed royalty statements from the Abbey, he sat back in his chair and shook his head in disbelief. 'No wonder Irish writers leave that damn country!' he commented, a sentiment with which I could only partially agree.

Towards the end of the month, he offered me the opportunity to leave 'that damn country' myself. Having read the script of my Abbey play and the first version of a new one, he asked me to come to Brandeis University the following year as playwright-in-residence. I promised to discuss the offer with my wife when I went home. Although, as narrated in a previous chapter, I had on three successive occasions applied in vain for a drama scholarship that would enable me to spend a year at a university in the US, in the event, having considered the pros and cons with my wife at our own fireside, I eventually turned down Dr Ed Pettet's offer, as I did later with two similar offers from the universities of Notre Dame and Arizona. We could have gone as a family, with the assurance of suitable accommodation, but foreign travel was not the commonplace experience then that it is now, and we were reluctant to disrupt the children's lives at that stage. While my wife, with her usual selflessness and grace, would have agreed to my going alone, on the one hand I knew the added burden my absence for even a month at Salzburg must have imposed on her; on the other, I had seen enough evidence, both in the lives of some other Irish writers and during my own stay at the Salzburg seminar, to know that such separation poses a threat to marital fidelity and personal integrity. No bags of dollars could ever compensate for the loss of those things that money cannot buy.

In addition to the formal lectures and more informal discussions, we had regular literary evenings at which writers read samples of their work. At one such, a large and earnest Yugoslav woman gave the males of the species a catchphrase when she read a chapter of her war novel in which a gallant major was 'grawnted wawn night uv luff' by a beautiful peasant girl. After hearing one of my short stories, a faculty wife asked to read some others and then advised me to send some to magazines in the US, especially the Catholic magazines whose editors and readers would appreciate my attitude to life – she commented that she would like to live in Ireland where people seemed to be sane and decent; in America, she said, there were too many books and stories about violent and horrible things.

The Americans judiciously lightened the academic aspect of the seminar with the social dimension which gave more opportunity for the promotion of the ideals of the founders of the Salzburg Seminar. Even when dining at round tables which seated twelve – the dining-room was the original ballroom of the mansion, with the musicians' balcony still intact and probably haunted by the ghost of W. A. Mozart who had once been employed as the Archbishop's resident composer – we had international and transatlantic points of view to share. I confess that I had to swallow hard and think of Ireland's honour when, towards the end of dinner one evening, one of the American faculty (he was a retired editor of the *St Louis Post Dispatch*) asked me if I would favour the company, there and then, with that lovely old song, *Mother Machree*, which was their Irish favourite. I stood up and gave it my 'level besht' like the tinker in John B. Keane's *Sive*. I don't know what the ghost of Mozart thought of it but the company there present gave it a generous round of applause and an Italian woman asked me later to write out the words for her. The genial American ex-editor said to me, 'If I were the head of the tourist business in Ireland, I'd give you *carte blanche* and let you wander around in the United States.' Unfortunately, he was not the head of the Irish tourist business when the day came, not so long after, that my talents were placed at the service of Mother Machree Kathleen Nee Houlihawn.

Weekend parties, as well as occasional dances to which some prominent Salzburghers were invited, helped to establish friendships and show that some nations are better than others at letting their hair down. I hope the Angelic Doctor, St Thomas Aquinas, theologian and occasional hymn-writer, forgave the exhibition put on at one of the parties by the only Irishman and the only coloured man, a New Yorker named Mel who qualified as a European because he was living in Paris. (He was also one of those 'working on a novel'.) Like myself, he had been an altar boy in his boyhood, although he had since given up religion. After we had consumed too much wine, he began to reminisce about his altar boy days and trying to recall the standard hymns sung at Benediction of the Blessed Sacrament. We ended up sitting on the floor with a bottle and glasses, giving a spirited if unspiritual rendering of the 'Tantum Ergo' and the 'O Salutaris Hostia' for the edification of Swedish Lutherans, English agnostics, communist Yugoslavs and all others of any or no religious affiliation or belief. Even that discordant echo of his boyhood devotions seemed to have awakened something in his soul; on the following Sunday he decided to come to Mass with the Irishman and a few Italian women. His conversion was shortlived, however – he left half-way through the Mass, telling me that the cathedral was too so-and-so cold.

After another weekend party, I was awakened at about three in the morning by two drunken Swedes – a glass of wine seemed to make them tipsy. They were always sombre in dress and manner, so that when they shook me awake my first impression was that I had died and the undertakers had arrived to put me in the box. 'Christopher, we wish to speak with you,' says one chap. 'I'll talk to you tomorrow,' I groaned. 'No, no, we would like to talk now because it is quiet.' They planted themselves one on each side of the bed. I decided to give them what we call 'a blasht' so that I could get back to sleep. 'Will ye go away to hell outa that, for God's sake, and let me sleep!' It had the opposite effect. 'Ah, yes, that's it, about God, that's what we wish to talk about.' The only way to get rid of the eejits was to sit up in bed and talk, and listen. They thanked me next day for what they called a 'very interesting discussion', although I had only a vague memory of what the chat was like. One of the lasting impressions I got from the month in Salzburg was that, just as in pubs in Dublin, the people who wanted to talk to me about God and religion were those who seemed to have little or no religion themselves, including my drama tutor, Dr Pettet, who had been reared as a Jew, and the German radio journalist who asked me one day to explain why I went off to pray in a church every Sunday when I could just as well kneel down and pray to God in the dormitory or the grounds of the Schloss. That same German had a degree in English literature from Oxford, spoke English better than the English, and kept a notebook in which he wrote down some of the words and expressions I used, as well as my 'Irish' pronunciation of words like 'imperturbable', 'film', 'girl', etc.

It was only fifteen years since the end of the war, from the horrors of which Ireland had been saved by de Valera's policy of neutrality; but even in casual conversation I learned something of what the war meant for ordinary people all over Europe. One of my new friends, a mild-mannered Viennese schoolteacher, told me how, late in the war, when he was a youth of seventeen, he had one day received a letter ordering him to report for military service. When I asked him what fighting he had seen, he shrugged and laughed. 'I was lucky,' he said, 'I never fired a shot. They looked at me and decided to make me assistant to the company cook. We were in the north of Italy when the Allies came along. One day, I was peeling potatoes when we were ordered to get our rifles but before we could move, the Americans came up the road and we just put up our hands. They put us in a camp and gave us chocolate – they said we were only kids. I remember that chocolate – we were starving. Later they shipped us off to Texas and we were working on farms for two years. That's how I learned English, and when I got back home I was able to take a degree in English at the university and become a teacher.'

Like the Americans who founded the Salzburg Seminar, my Austrian friend hoped that there would never be another war but I came back to Ireland with a more pessimistic attitude, having observed how, from the general camaraderie and goodwill of the early days, as the weeks went by there were indications of exclusive little groups and friendships developing and even mild squabbles which on a few occasions warmed into heated arguments. A French Jew who had lost most of his family in a concentration camp could not for long conceal his hatred of all Germans, and even the usually ebullient black New Yorker from Paris, having been afforded too generous treatment by Americans and Europeans alike, turned on some of us one night and declared that we were all white pigs who would be eliminated when the black race took over the world. When I asked him if that applied also to the Finnish blonde who had taken a fancy to him and who was even then cuddling him, he threatened to smash his wineglass in my ugly Irish face, but refused my Irish invitation to try it. So, although I made a few lasting friendships, and enjoyed the literary discussions, I came home with the realization that, as the Scripture says, there will be 'wars and rumours of wars' as long as the human race lasts. The First World War of 1914–18 was confidently described as 'the war to end wars' until the Second World War broke out only twenty-one years later. My despondency was not lightened by the fact that my journey home took me through the port of Dunkirk.

Yet in spite of all human experience there is something in the human spirit that dreams of establishing a heaven on earth. My European experience brought back to me the words of that great European humanist, Sir Thomas More, Lord Chancellor of England, a man who gave up wealth and power, and in the end life itself, rather than risk losing the real heaven. In his book, *Utopia* (written in Latin, first printed at Louvain in 1516, and not translated into English until 1551, sixteen years after his execution) in which he philosophised about the ideal state, he wrote: 'To have everything turn out well assumes that all men are good, and this is a situation that I do not expect to come about for many years.'

19

'OUT OF THE FRYING-PAN . . .'

I had lugged my Underwood ever-portable all the way across Europe to Salzburg because I was confident that I would be able to recover the deeds of our house from that benign bank manager by writing a series of radio talks or articles about the journey and about my experiences at the Schloss Leopoldskron. In spite of the cautious whisperings of my angel guardian, whose celestial memory recalled that since I first began to submit material to Radio Éireann as an apprentice writer, none of my stories or talks in English had been accepted by Francis MacManus, I felt sure that these talks would be of such interest that he would consider them worth broadcasting. Not for the first time, or the last, I was wrong.

I posted the first talk from Salzburg. In it I gave an account of my journey from Dún Laoghaire to the city of Mozart and Fearghal. When I arrived home from Salzburg, among the items in the accumulated post was the rejected script, with a note from MacManus telling me that, although it was very well written, my talk would not be suitable for broadcasting because it was almost a mile-by-mile description of my journey. Now it so happened that before I went to Salzburg I had listened to a series of six radio talks by Mervyn Wall, a novelist who was also Secretary of the Arts Council.

These talks, each of which lasted fifteen minutes, described a journey in West Cork, and one of them covered the distance from Bantry to Bandon. In a talk lasting the same time, fifteen minutes, I had described a journey from Dún Laoghaire to Salzburg. With apologies to my forewarning angel guardian, I wrote to MacManus pointing out the anomaly, reminding him of his rejection of my previous efforts over a period of nine years, and telling him that he would never again have to go to the bother of rejecting my work. He did not reply but again I was wrong. Before going to Salzburg, I had submitted my Abbey play, *In Dublin's Fair City*, to Radio Éireann. It was almost a matter of course that any new Abbey play would be broadcast as the Sunday Night Play, thus not only earning a fee but being brought to the attention of the amateur groups all over the country. My play, a realistic drama set in contemporary Dublin, was found to be unsuitable for broadcasting, no reason given.

I have already stressed that for the writer, as for everyone else, life is a matter of ups and downs and I have recommended that children be introduced at an early age to the age-old game of Snakes and Ladders as a philosophical preparation for life. So my angel guardian did not need to remind me that hope is one of the three major virtues and that it springs eternal in the human spirit. Nevertheless, I was shocked into feeling that someone in heaven was putting in a good word on behalf of myself and my dependants when, shortly after MacManus rejected my first-of-a-series talk and my Abbey play, a letter arrived from my Salzburg drama mentor, Professor Edwin Burr Pettet, now back at his post in Brandeis University in Boston. He renewed his offer of a year as dramatist-in-residence but also asked me if I would like to write a series of articles about my experiences at the Salzburg Seminar, to be published in a magazine of which his wife was editor and at a fee which was three or four times the amount I would have got from Radio Éireann, payment prepaid if I agreed to supply the articles. Some people don't believe in miracles. I do, and I believe that they occur at various levels of experience and often in manifest-ations more commonplace than the inexplicable physical cures that have been stringently scrutinised and meticulously documented at the Lourdes medical bureau.

Having observed that Mr Blythe of the Abbey Theatre pulled my play off the stage as soon as a new comedy by John McCann was ready, on my return from Salzburg I decided that I would try the Abbey with a comedy. When it came back to me after a few months it was in the theatrical limbo in which my first effort had suffered before eventually coming alive on the stage. It was neither accepted nor rejected. 'We like this play very much,' Mr Blythe wrote, 'and it shows again that you have great dramatic talent. But we feel that you could improve it here and there, and you could also shorten it so that we could put on a one-act play in Irish with it.' Enclosed, of course, were the readers' opinions, just as contradictory as the set he had sent me with my first play. And his suggestion that I shorten the play was accompanied with the practical advice of a pragmatic northerner: all I need do, said Mr Blythe, was get a blue pencil and delete a sentence or two here and there, a counsel that proved to the dramatist that the managing director of the Abbey Theatre had no notion of the nature of dramatic dialogue. His mention of a one-act play in Irish gave me cause for ironic amusement, the Abbey having already rejected two such plays of my own.

I wrote to Mr Blythe and thanked him for his advice but pointed out that I had spent nearly two years working on the script of my previous play trying to satisfy contradictory opinions of anonymous readers. I was not willing to go through the same frustrations again but if the Abbey would accept the play and sign a production contract (*Thanks again, Ray McAnally*! I commented in my learning soul) I would discuss any changes suggested by the person who was to direct the play. Mr Blythe replied to this with a severe reprimand. He told me that the board of directors had spent a lot of time over my other play but that obviously I had not learned anything from their efforts because I was too headstrong. In spite of this, being the man he was, he again invited me to rewrite the comedy, which I did not, and to continue to submit plays to the Abbey in the future, which I did.

Year after year, in the belief that a job that was in any way connected with writing would be more congenial than the daily grind in the chalk mines, I had applied for any such position advertised in the papers. A few months after my return from Salzburg, an ad appeared for a job that seemed to my optimistic soul to be just made for me. Bord Fáilte Éireann (the Irish Tourist Board) wanted a writer for the publicity department whose duties would comprise writing about cultural affairs in Ireland, acting as courier for visiting writers and journalists, and writing scripts for promotional films and radio and television programmes. (A national television service was in the pipeline; it began about eighteen months later, on 31 December 1962.) The main qualification was writing experience and a knowledge of cultural affairs but a university degree and a knowledge of a continental language would be considered advantageous. I had some ten years' experience in writing of all kinds, in Irish and English, and I had what I felt was a competent knowledge of Irish cultural matters. I had an honours degree in English added to my teacher's qualification and besides a good knowledge of Spanish and French, I had a smattering of Italian and German. I also had a qualification not mentioned in the advertisement but one that I considered essential in such a position: I loved Ireland and considered the work of Bord Fáilte to be something more than a business or an industry. As a writer, I would be proud to spend my working day writing about Ireland in such a way as to attract tourists and I would be eager to impress visiting writers with the qualities that might cause them to write about Ireland in laudatory fashion on their return home. In short, I was patriotic, idealistic, naïve, and looking through green spectacles at that ad in the newspaper.

I had given up hope of a reply to my application when a letter arrived some time during the school summer holidays inviting me to come for an interview on the date appointed. I put a lot of effort into preparing for that interview, swotting up on Irish history and cultural affairs, getting up early to put in a few hours on my continental languages, staying up late to listen to foreign radio stations. At the interview, I was confronted by three men behind a table, *moi* placed, as is the style, on a chair. Later I learned the identity of the three – personnel manager, publicity department manager and his assistant manager. While they put questions to me in English things went along fine but I was waiting for the moment when one or other of them would switch to Spanish or French, the languages I had claimed to be fluent in, or even to Italian or German. Maybe, God knows, even to Irish, this being, after all, an interview for a job with Bord Fáilte Éireann. Divil a bit, as we say, of any language but the good old Anglo-Saxon was heard out of any of them. No need to explain why.

A few weeks later, I was called to a final interview where I again met the manager of the publicity department, accompanied this time by the director-general of Bord Fáilte, Dr T. J. O'Driscoll. This interview was more informal, the three of us sitting on armchairs and having what purported to be a nice chat. The DG told me pleasantly how impressed he was with my qualifications and experience, that I was top of the short list of candidates, etc. And then he asked me whether there were any factors that might militate against my obtaining the position. To which I replied that I had been thinking on positive rather than negative lines, on why I was suitable rather than unsuitable for the job. To which the suave DG countered with, 'But haven't you been working as a teacher, and aren't teachers inclined to be dogmatic?'

There is much that could be said about such a question, and its being asked by such a person. But an answer was awaited. 'If they are,' said the writer/teacher, 'they're dogmatic about the only thing one can be dogmatic about.'

Pause then, let him wait, watched by his underling, the manager of the publicity department. Let him wait, and ask. Which he did. 'And what is that?'

'The truth.' He gives a little cough and a flicker of the DG eyebrows, turns to the manager and says, 'I – eh – I don't think we have any more questions – ' then turns to me, ' – unless you want to ask anything yourself?' The only question I had was about salary and contract. The manager enlightened me. The initial contract would be for a six-month probationary period, after which, provided my performance was considered satisfactory, I would be given a permanent contract and placed on an incremental salary scale. With formal handshakes all round, I was told that the job was mine.

So I bade a fond farewell to the chalk-and-duster trade, to the daily grind of teaching children the elements of everything, little realising as I did so that I was jumping out of the frying-pan into the fire.

In the classroom, the teacher is independent and undisturbed except by occasional pests like school inspectors, parish priests or a busybody principal. In my solitary writing at home, I was used to sitting at a desk banging on a typewriter, but in the cramped office to which I was assigned in Bord Fáilte there were two other desks on which colleagues were doing likewise. I also found it strange to be 'working to' the assistant manager of the publicity department, which meant that each morning his secretary brought me my tasks for the day, magazines or newspapers for which an article was required, letters of enquiry from abroad to be answered. To these, a slip of paper was attached (note the word) which contained some direction which always included 'see *attatched*' (italics mine).

I was not long in the job when I happened one day to have to visit an office where four girls worked in a typing pool (the computer age had not yet arrived; the standard equipment in offices comprised the phone, the typewriter, the female typist and the female secretary). One of them asked another, 'Did we give him the test yet?' When another checked at the door that no management interference was likely, I felt the understandable nervousness of a mere male trapped by four females who were obviously up to something. What they were up to was to give me a spelling test. One of them provided me with paper and a pencil, another called out a short paragraph containing phrases like 'the accumulation of essential accommodation'. When they checked my effort, they united in congratulating me as the first person to have got it all right. I modestly pointed out that as a writer and a teacher I had for many years been vigilant of my own spellings and those of others.

I was made into a secretary myself when the manager of the publicity department asked me to function in that role for an inter-company committee comprising the publicity managers of Bord Fáilte, Aer Lingus, Córas Iompair Éireann and Córas Tráchtála, which met once a month to discuss cooperation in their publicity activities, each company taking it in turn to act as host. In this way I enjoyed a monthly dinner which I earned by listening to a lot of waffle and making notes, these to be expanded later and typed up by the girls in the typing pool. I was also charged with compiling a monthly bulletin on cultural affairs in Ireland for worldwide distribution. This bulletin was the cause of the only reprimand I suffered during my probationary period – in the November issue I used a forbidden four-letter word. Not much of tourist interest was happening in Ireland in November and so, having stared at a blank page in my typewriter for some time, I began poetically thus: 'Although in Ireland the days may be shortening in November, the birds still sing after every shower of gentle rain and the sky brightens etc. etc.' My typed script, passed by the assistant manager, came back down from the manager himself with a red circle drawn around the four-letter word; a note in the margin said, 'We do *not* use this word in Bord Fáilte.' The offending word was *rain*. Later, the lads in the photographic section of the publicity department told me that the sky is *always* blue over Ireland.

I was only a few days in my new job when I began to feel uneasy. On the very first day, the man to whom I was to work, the assistant manager of the publicity department, brought me to the office I was to share with two others, introduced me and then showed me a steel cabinet of files and a jumble of papers and documents in the drawers of my desk and on the floor. He commented that my predecessor had been unsatisfactory and had left things in such a mess that it would take me a few weeks merely to sort out the files and records and get organized for work. In spite of which, the flow of 'see *attatched*' new work began next morning and continued daily. I noticed also, with some apprehension, that most of my new colleagues had a very negative attitude towards the senior management and the work of Bord Fáilte. A woman who was in charge of a minor section, to whom I had to go for information on one of my assignments, gave me as her forthright opinion that I must be mad to have left a secure profession like teaching in order to come to work 'for this crowd of phoneys'. A man ten years my senior told me that he had spent the last ten years in frustration and disillusionment, applying in vain for any and every position that might give him more job satisfaction and more money. Having been a paid-up member of the teachers union (Irish National Teachers' Organization) since I got my first permanent appointment, I was disconcerted when my new colleagues informed me that the employees of Bord Fáilte were not members of a trade union but that there was a staff association with an elected committee. When I learned that the main function of this body was to organize functions like the Christmas party, I decided to join the NUJ (National Union of Journalists).

I was only a month in the employ of Bord Fáilte when all the staff were invited to attend an afternoon meeting at a hotel for the purpose of discussing the annual report which semistate bodies like BFÉ were obliged to provide for government consideration each year. After a synopsis of the report had been read to the gathering by the public relations manager, the director-general, Dr O'Driscoll, invited comments and questions. When one man queried the annual grant given by Bord Fáilte to the Dublin Theatre Festival, pointing out that the Festival did not attract tourists, I was doubly interested, firstly as a playwright, who might wish the grant to continue, secondly as an employee of the national tourist board, who should wish to see all of our state funds put to the best possible use. My dilemma was not solved when the director-general replied to the query in words that gave me a story to tell my wife that evening and left us both feeling the initial stirrings of unease about the move I had made. 'You're welcome to your opinion, Mr –,' said Dr O'Driscoll, and then, to the assembly in general, 'any more questions?' And this, I thought, was the man who had asked me whether I might be unsuitable to work as a writer with Bord Fáilte because teachers, he said, were inclined to be dogmatic.

As the weeks went by, I began to feel further unease and more than a little frustrated, when my daily tasks seemed to have very little to do with 'cultural affairs in Ireland', as when I was instructed to *'see attatched'* and supply a magazine in Sweden with four thousand words on 'motoring in the West of Ireland' or when I was ordered as a matter of urgency to write a series of articles on holidays in Killarney and west Cork for provincial newspapers in Britain. (These were returned with the instruction that they needed to be rewritten as they were 'too good'.) When I enquired on a few occasions about when I was to use my foreign languages by supplying material to France and Spain and about work for radio, television and films, the assistant manager replied with vague but persistently negative remarks. I never got to see the films already made by Bord Fáilte itself or in association with the other semistate companies; all of these were kept locked away in his office. And on a day when my prescribed tasks included the instruction to check and update the Irish hotels and guesthouses in an American tourist guide, I began to wonder if I had only imagined the wording of that advertisement for 'a writer on cultural affairs in Ireland'.

Although a day spent sitting at a typewriter churning out articles about any aspect of Irish affairs was much less stressful than a day in the classroom trying to educate, or at the very least teach, forty or fifty pupils of varying ability, temperament and personality, I soon found that the first of those four elements for which Herman Melville had sighed, *time*, was now in much shorter supply. The school day ended two hours earlier than the office day and the clear-cut five-day week of the primary school had not yet become the norm in business and industry, although it existed in the chopped-up form of the half-day's work on Wednesdays and Saturdays. I used to walk to and from school in five minutes; now I had to face a double bus journey across Dublin morning and evening. After a late dinner – works cafeterias and pubs serving midday lunches were still unheard of – I scarcely had time and energy to maintain the role of paterfamilias let alone settle down to do any creative writing. And my standard quip about there being twenty-five hours in a day was of little consolation to my spirit when even that twenty-fifth hour seemed to be at the disposal of the Bord Fáilte management – a telephone call from the asst. man. late in the afternoon could mean that I had to make a similar call home with the news that I had been instructed to attend a press conference or some other function. I soon realised that I was deputed only to the least important of such functions.

I must record here, with some ironic satisfaction, the events at one such conference. The asst. man. of the publicity department told me, late in the afternoon as usual, that he would be unable to attend a conference at the Gresham Hotel and that I was to go there as the representative of Bord Fáilte. He gave me directions as follows. 'It's some people from Kerry who want us to give them a grant for a local festival based on the song about the Rose of Tralee. Just listen to them and say we think it's a good idea but tell them we can't make any promises; we have lots of groups looking for grants for local festivals.' Having more cultural affinity with the Kingdom of Kerry than with Bord Fáilte management, I took care to let the hospitable stalwarts at the press conference know that I was only the most humble servant of Mother Ireland, a mere messenger boy (or *penny boy* as my mother used to say) for my masters in BFÉ. Also that I was a native of Limerick and that I had lived in Dún Chaoin for six months and that I loved everything about Kerry, the football, the people, the scenery, and the music – especially that beautiful song, the *Rose of Tralee*. After a few convivial jars had mellowed their justifiable anger and frustration, one of them turned into a prophet – no bother to a Kerryman – and gave me a message for my bosses. 'You can tell them fuckers in Bord Fáilte,' he said, 'they don't want to know us now but the day will come when they'll be breakin' their arse tryin' to get in on our Rose of Tralee festival.' Being a mere *penny boy*, and not a Daniel with miraculous immunity in the lions den, I did not convey that forthright message verbatim; but it often echoed gloriously in my memory in later years when I watched the RTÉ host of the *Late Late Show*, Gay Byrne, chatting up the competing Roses from all over the world in what had become as prominent an item in the Bord Fáilte publicity literature as the Dublin Horse Show.

The other aspect of my new job, acting as courier to visiting writers, which in the newspaper advertisement seemed so attractive and potentially interesting, turned out to be an enlargement of my knowledge of the human race but at the cost of many hours of tedium and occasional disruption of domestic life. Some guests wanted only to spend a few days in Dublin, others had to be taken farther afield, in which case I sometimes had to drive a visiting journalist or writer around the country for up to a week, staying at the best hotels, of course, and eating many a fine dinner in honour of Mother Ireland. This could involve enduring uncongenial company but for the representative of Bord Fáilte it meant being always on guard lest the guest should have cause for complaint to headquarters or in an article on return to the typewriter from which he or she had come.

A pleasant young woman journalist from Manchester who was to write some articles about Dublin confessed, after I had brought her to the Zoo and the Museum and dined with her in the Gresham, that Mummy had been very worried about her coming for this, her first visit to Ireland, and had warned her not to talk about politics or religion because the Irish were liable to become very violent about these topics. On the second day of her three-day exploration of Dublin, she asked if it would be possible to take a trip to some place in the countryside where we might see a leprechaun. I told her it was not the right season just then but if she could return in May she might be lucky. Another and more glamorous female journalist came to spend a few days visiting Dublin's fashion houses. I escorted her each morning and afternoon to meet Sybil Connolly, Irene Gilbert, Nellie Mulcahy and others, leaving after the introductions to read the paper and enjoy a pint in the nearest pub, collecting her for lunch and later for dinner. The ritual visit to the Abbey Theatre was a bore for me as I had already seen the play; it also proved enlightening for me as a writer with regard to the legal question of circumstantial evidence when two people, a man in McDaid's pub and one of the typists in the Bord Fáilte pool, told me separately, and in the same insinuating tone, that I had been seen with a lovely blonde at the Abbey Theatre and in other places. When I protested that it was all in the line of duty for Mother Ireland and that I would much rather have been at home with my wife and family, the comments were along the lines of 'Ah yes, that's what they all say.'

I renewed acquaintance with the man who had presided as official Church witness at my marriage in Limerick eight years earlier, the cultured Monsignor Molony, when I had to escort an elderly and somewhat eccentric American professor to various places in Dublin and then drive him to Limerick and deliver him at the parochial residence in the Ennis Road where he was to be a guest. But the visitor who made the most lasting impression on me was a German journalist. He was to write articles about Ireland for his paper and I was to drive him around for a week, showing him the beauties of Ireland in general, and especially anything of German interest, such as the Liebherr factory in Killarney. The week in question happened to be Holy Week, the week before Easter Sunday, when as a teacher I would have been starting my ten-day Easter vacation, enjoying life on the family hearth and finding some time to work at my true vocation in life as a writer of literature.

When I went to hire a car in the name of Bord Fáilte, I was asked to sign an insurance form. Under *occupation* I entered *writer*. When she checked the form, the girl looked at me with regret and said, 'I'm sorry, but we don't insure writers or actors.' *(Proper order, all bloody lunatics, liable to be composing a poem or reciting "To be, or not to be" instead of watching the road . . .)* I explained that I worked for Bord Fáilte as a writer but that I also had to drive people around, etc. 'Oh, that's all right!' she assured me. On a fresh form she told me to write *company executive* and all was in order.

The German journalist turned out to be a plump, dark, bespectacled chap of about my own age – I was then thirty-three – and he proved to be a man of two moods, taciturn and phlegmatic all day while I drove and talked, but undergoing a post-prandial metamorphosis after a few glasses of wine had loosened his Teutonic tongue. His most recent assignment had been in the Congo, where some Irish soldiers were killed in a clash with Baluba tribesmen, but all I could get from him on this was a grunt and the word *bad*. The Cliffs of Moher and the Lakes of Killarney rated a few grunts apiece. Bord Fáilte having been recently involved in the restoration of Bunratty Castle in County Clare, about twelve miles out on the Shannon Airport road from my native Limerick, I was keen to see for myself what in my boyhood days had been a ruin where cows poked around in the nettles and jackdaws nested and where a young man who had been my schoolmate sadly decided to solve the problems of life by hanging himself. The German refused to get out of the car, shaking his head and grunting a negative in response to my invitation. With a genuine Bord Fáilte smile, I cursed him profusely in Irish and left him brooding in the car while I toured the castle. In fairness I must record that he told me in one of his late night bursts of eloquence, that as a boy of fifteen he had been a member of an anti-aircraft battery outside Munich. 'That must have been terrible,' I commented. 'It was not so bad,' he observed, 'because, you see, we were given free tickets for the symphony concert every Sunday afternoon.' So, the kind Führer only asked that you sit at your AA gun every night under the Allied bombs and on Sunday afternoon, if you were still alive, you could hear half-starved retired musicians playing Wagner and Beethoven, for free.

It was in Killarney, on the night of Good Friday, that Fritz (we'll call him that) gave me cause to mark him down as unique among the various international visitors I had been paid to charm on behalf of Mother Ireland. After dinner in the Great Southern Hotel – checking in at such places, I always felt faintly guilty as I heard an inner voice tootling, *We're a couple of swells, we stop in the best hotels* – my glum

Deutscher brightened into his usual post-prandial vivacity. 'What will we do now?' he asked. I was wondering what my wife and children were doing in our semi-detached in Drumcondra just then, around nine o'clock in the evening. I suggested a walk – I would have welcomed the exercise after a day in the car. 'No, I don't like to walk,' said the guest of Mother Ireland, 'I think I would like to go to the brothel.' My own mother used to tell me fondly that I was born with the gift of the gab but this was one occasion on which I was totally at a loss for words, looking out of my mouth, as we used to say in Limerick.

As I write these lines we are approaching the millennium and in the hedonistic Ireland of today there may well be, for all I know, brothels in Killarney and other such tourist centres as there are in Dublin's fair city; but on the night of Good Friday in the year of Our Lord 1961 even to mention such a word in Killarney or anywhere else in what was then Catholic Ireland could result in grievous bodily harm being inflicted by the outraged citizens. To my cautiously-worded explanation of the non-existence of such an institution, Fritz uttered uncomplimentary remarks about Ireland in general and then entertained me and consoled himself with lascivious reminiscences of his recent assignment in the Congo. We went for a walk in the silent town and discovered a cubby-hole of a shebeen where a grumpy man who was probably Killarney's only atheist was serving bottles of stout to two disciples. It was obvious that they regretted not having bolted the door but when I explained that we were just passing through and that my friend was from Germany (no mention of Bord Fáilte, of course!) two bottles were produced and payment accepted, with little more than a few grunts in place of the usual Kerry eloquence. Even that begrudged refreshment was spoilt on me for two reasons; my Catholic conscience accused me of carousing on this fateful night when the nation was mourning the death of Jesus on Calvary and as I watched Fritz gulping the black stuff, I wondered what was he going to write about Killarney when he got back to base in Germany.

A guest whom I never met added to my uneasy feeling that the day-to-day reality in a job with an organization like Bord Fáilte could be very different from the image conjured up in my mind by that alluring advertisement for 'a writer on cultural affairs in Ireland' to which I had eagerly replied. One day when I had occasion to discuss something with the assistant manager, he digressed to tell me that for some days past he had been showing a French countess around. 'You'd have been very interested in her,' he told me blandly, 'because she's very keen on the theatre. I took her to meet Brendan Behan last night and we had a marvellous evening.' I made no comment and I make none now.

I was about half-way through my six-month probationary period when my wife, who had recently given birth to our fourth child, gave me further proof of what we mere males call female intuition. One night as we sat over a late cup of tea, in the middle of some unrelated conversation she suddenly remarked, 'You're not happy in Bord Fáilte, are you?' I could not deny it. 'Maybe you should think of going back to teaching,' she suggested. I thought I should wait and see if the situation would improve when I got a permanent contract and started on the incremental salary scale. Like many a man before me, I should have been guided by female intuition.

20

WHAT POLONIUS SAID

On the penultimate day of my six-month probationary contract – during that six months I had written many thousands of words for Bord Fáilte, but hardly a page of creative writing of my own – a telephone call from the manager of the publicity department summoned me to his office. There he went officiously through the motions, telling me that I had worked for six months on a temporary contract, at the end of which period, if my performance proved to be satisfactory, I was to receive a permanent contract and be placed on the incremental salary scale. I sat across the desk from him and listened, waiting to go through the formality of signing the new contract. And then he gave a few little coughs, as such people do, and said, 'I have to tell you that the Bord considers that your performance has not reached the standard required by the Bord and so you will be offered a second temporary contract for six months. If your performance reaches a satisfactory standard then, you will be given a permanent contract and you will be placed on the incremental salary scale.'

When I got over the shock, I protested that no one had found fault with my work throughout the six-month period. I reminded him that the only fault he himself had found with it was on the day when he instructed me not to use the word *rain* – that all my written work had been used by Bord Fáilte, and that all the guests for whom I had acted as courier had expressed satisfaction in formal letters and in their subsequent articles, his only reply was that he was not at liberty to discuss the matter with me. 'I have the new contract here,' he said, and pushed the form across the desk, 'all you have to do is sign it.'

'I can't sign this,' I told him. 'If I sign it, I'm admitting that my work was unsatisfactory and that is not true. No fault has been found with any aspect of my work, no complaints have been received, nobody has shown me any examples of this standard which you say my work has not achieved. Therefore I am entitled to the fulfilment of the terms of the contract I signed with Bord Fáilte six months ago, a permanent contract and an incremental salary.'

'This is the contract I am instructed to offer you,' he said. 'This is your new contract.'

'If I don't sign it, what happens?'

'I must give you a month's notice.'

'Do that,' I said, and walked out. The formal letter of notice arrived on my desk about an hour later.

With the creation of the office of Ombudsman and the setting up of the Fair Employment Tribunal in the 1980s, the pendulum of moral justice in industrial relations has swung so much in favour of the worker that nowadays it is difficult to get rid even of a truly unsatisfactory employee but on that day in 1961 when I walked out of the office of the publicity manager of Bord Fáilte I had no such government appointed arbiters to whom I could take my case. I had the option of finding another job within a month or of getting the management of Bord Fáilte to rescind the decision some person or persons unknown had taken in my regard, a decision which I regarded as totally immoral and contrary to the most basic principles of industrial relations. I also, of course, had to go home that evening and tell my wife of this development. When I did so, she seemed to have been expecting it – more of that female intuition – and she advised me again to look for a job in teaching; but she insisted that whatever happened I was right not to accept a second probationary contract, no matter what the consequences.

In my own soul I decided that if anyone in Bord Fáilte thought that, like Longfellow's Arabs in the poem, I was about to fold my tent and silently steal away, that person was very much mistaken. I have earlier in this chronicle adverted to the basic principles of survival into which I was inducted in my boyhood in Limerick, one of which was that if you are hit or kicked, even by a bully much bigger and stronger than yourself, there is no point in lying down or running away. You must let the bully know that he has been in a fight. It is the story of the Irish race in its resistance to the English conqueror. So, I resolved that if I was going out of the employ of Mother Ireland, as represented by the bureaucrats in Bord Fáilte Éireann (literally, the Welcome Board of Ireland) I would go out with all guns blazing and leave them with a distinct impression of wrongdoing on their conscience.

Being now a paid-up member of the National Union of Journalists, I decided to bring my complaint to the notice of the union officials and see what they could do for me. The official who interviewed me was blustery in manner and trenchant in speech. Even before I outlined my problem, as soon as I told him I worked for Bord Fáilte, he launched into a virulent tirade against that state-sponsored body. 'We're a long time trying to get a foot in there to do something about those bastards,' he informed me. When I got a chance to tell him the details of my situation, he put on a fierce scowl and commented, 'You see now, the problem is, we have no fuckin' clout there, none at all; but if you could get more people to join a union, talk to some of the people that work with you – '

I suggested that the NUJ had members in all the

newspapers and in Radio Éireann, and that perhaps – he waved the suggestion into the wastepaper basket. No way, we couldn't do anything there, not for a case like this.' He got rid of me by telling me that he had an important meeting to go to and urged me, as he ushered me out, to keep in touch and let him know how I got on – and get other people to join our union or any other union. I came away pondering the fact that his suit was as expensive, his office as spacious, his desk as big as those of the publicity manager in Bord Fáilte. Except for his blustery style and his more vehement vocabulary, they could be switched. I realised that trade unionism had come a long way since James Larkin and James Connolly began their struggle for workers' rights, so that industrial relations was now a business, just as much as Bord Fáilte.

What the union could not do for me, the law might. The only solicitor I knew was the man to whom we had been directed by the builder when we bought our house. His name was Liam Cafferky, and he had offices in the buildings where the Stephen's Green shopping centre now stands. He was a courteous, serene gentleman and he listened to my story while he leaned back in his chair and puffed his pipe. He told me that, given the facts as I had outlined them, there was no doubt at all that a grave injustice was being perpetrated, and then he advised me to forget about Bord Fáilte and go back into teaching as quickly as I could find a job. He reminded me gently that law and justice are not synonymous. If I brought a case against Bord Fáilte, they would be able to hire the best available legal experts and they would conjure up all sorts of reasons for their decision – including intangible aspects like personality and reliability and so on.

'How did you get on with your colleagues?' he put it to me as if in cross-examination.

I told him that my work, especially when writing that monthly bulletin for world-wide distribution, entailed consultation with people in all departments of Bord Fáilte. I had never had any problems or unpleasantness with anyone. I told him also that some of my colleagues, considering me under that over-estimated title, 'Abbey Theatre playwright', had asked me to form an amateur drama group in Bord Fáilte, in emulation of those in other state and semi-state departments. By courtesy of Carolyn Swift, as a trial of talent we put on three one-act plays in the small Pike Theatre near our offices, inviting the staff of Bord Fáilte as audience. The only person with whom I had any problems during my six-month stint was the man to whom I was working, the assistant manager of the publicity department, not in direct confrontation, but in his seeming reluctance to let me broaden the scope of my work from repetitive journalism to the areas indicated in the advertisement which had caused me to apply for the job. My counsel took the pipe from his mouth again to warn me not to make any accusation, even by implication, of malice on the part of anyone in management; if I did, they could bring a case against me for defamation.

'And as for your colleagues,' he added, 'what they say to you in private about Bord Fáilte is probably their true opinion; but the question is, how many of them would be willing to appear in court and give evidence in your favour against the management of Bord Fáilte?' A question to which I had no answer. My counsel answered it for me: 'Not one.' And then he repeated his advice to forget about Bord Fáilte, put the whole thing down to experience, find another job. I could, of course, decide to go on with an action, and he could engage a barrister; but if I lost my case, I would lose my house and my shirt, and if I applied for a job with any other company or organization, my name would be known as that of a troublesome and unsatisfactory employee. In the unlikely event of my winning the case – Mr Cafferky thought the odds were about a hundred to one against – how did I think I would be treated by Bord Fáilte management?

I bought the papers every day and applied for every teaching job in the Dublin area. In the meantime, within a few days of my interview with the publicity manager, most people in Bord Fáilte seemed to have heard of my predicament. The woman who had greeted me in her office six months earlier with the opinion that I was a fool to have left teaching to come to work for Bord Fáilte now reminded me with the inevitable 'I told you so'. An assistant manager from another department, a grey-haired edgy man whom I knew only slightly, met me one day in a quiet corridor and actually shook hands with me. 'I admire you,' he said, 'you're the first person to tell them to fuck off for themselves.'

'But they're telling me the same!' I reminded him. He told me that a colleague of mine had served three temporary contracts before being given a permanent one. Having looked around furtively as if afraid we might be seen together, he advised me to consult the Staff Regulations. I told him I had never heard of them. 'Your manager has a copy,' he said, 'but he'll probably refuse to show them to you.' He was right. 'If you can't get them, ring me and I'll get a copy to you.' He did. In the booklet I learned that any employee of Bord Fáilte whose work was not satisfactory would have this pointed out to him at once by management; also that in the event of a dispute between an employee and management, the employee had the right to make a direct appeal to the director-general. Fair enough, it seemed. I wrote a formal letter to Dr T. J. O'Driscoll, Director-general of Bord Fáilte, setting out my grievance and requesting an interview.

Before he replied, I was summoned by phone to an interview with the personnel officer. He had learned of my request to the Big Boss and he wanted to advise me. His advice was to sign the second temporary contract: 'These things happen in organizations like this,' he said; and he was sure that I would get the permanent contract eventually and he had been told that Bord Fáilte really considered me very promising material for a management position in the future. When I pointed out to him that I could not sign a contract which stated that my previous work had been unsatisfactory, while I and everyone else knew that this was not true, he changed his tune and reminded me that I had a wife and children to support. If I did not sign the contract, I would find it very difficult to get another job anywhere – because I would have to tell any prospective employers about Bord Fáilte and they would contact BF and so on and so on.

And so the month wore on, no teaching job was in prospect and the day for my interview with the director-general arrived, with less than a week remaining of my month's notice to take my talents elsewhere. But I remained fully confident that when I sat face to face with Dr T. J. O'Driscoll, and put the facts of the case to him, man to man, he would have no alternative but to agree that my performance during the six-month probationary period had been satisfactory. How often does fate have to kick a confident man in the teeth or in the posterior before he begins to learn that nothing in this world can be taken for granted except that we all die and the world itself will end one day?

Like the small but important sums of money I have mentioned in previous pages, we remember very clearly also certain hours that were crucial in our lives – nobody forgets the hour and date of their wedding. My appointment was for 11 am at Bord Fáilte's head office in Merrion Square (the building is now occupied by Bord na Gaeilge). The new Bord Fáilte offices at Baggot Street Bridge were then abuilding and staff were scattered at several locations, the main premises being two adjacent houses in the crescent at St Stephen's Church near the canal bridge in Upper Mount Street. I arrived at five minutes to eleven and was told by a female secretary to seat myself on a chair on the landing. I sat there until twenty past eleven, observing to myself as the minutes passed that if I had been five, or ten, or fifteen minutes late for this or any other appointment, it could be used in evidence to show that my performance was not up to the standard required by Bord Fáilte. My writer's mind noted also that this delay, allowing the individual to stew in his own anxiety for twenty minutes before the interview, was a useful ploy on the part of management; it was like a scene from Kafka's psychological novel, *The Trial*.

When the secretary appeared again and invited me to enter, my confidence in the result of the man-to-man interview evaporated like a summer's fog on the River Shannon. The interview was not to be man to man, but *three* men to a man. Facing me from behind a large boardroom table was the director-general, with my own manager on one side and the personnel manager on the other. As usual, the victim's chair was set in the middle of the floor space. We went through the motions, I stating my case and the DG replying – but before he answered any point I made, he turned left and right and engaged in a whispered consultation with his management acolytes. When I pointed out that the Staff Regulations stated that an employee would be told at once if any of his work was not satisfactory, and that this had not happened in my case, the reply, after consultation, was that Staff Regulations applied only to *permanent* staff. When I replied to this that it was in accord with the same Staff Regulations that I was having this interview, another consultation produced the explanation that this interview was granted to me as a favour on the part of the director-general. The main thrust of the management case, as expressed by the DG, was that I was trying to impose my own assessment of my performance on the management, and that no company or organization could function if this were to be allowed to happen. I countered this by asserting that all the written work I had done for Bord Fáilte during six months had been passed by my manager and sent all over the world, that all the guests to whom I had been assigned as courier had expressed total satisfaction, and that the publicity manager himself had appointed me as secretary to the inter-company committee of publicity departments, an added task which I had performed each month without any complaint from my own manager or any of the others. I concluded by declaring that I was morally entitled to the fulfilment of the contract I had signed when I came to work for Bord Fáilte. The reply to this was a general waffle about my performance of individual tasks being satisfactory but on the overall picture, it was judged that there was room for improvement in certain aspects, and this was why I had not been dismissed outright but had been offered – generously, it was stressed – a second probationary contract.

When I walked into that room and saw a triumvirate behind the table, I felt that I had little hope of achieving justice from the management of Bord Fáilte. Before the interview ended, I had no hope at all. A few days later, I received a letter from Dr T. J. O'Driscoll informing me that, having considered my application, he could see no reason why the decision of management in my case should be altered. On the same day, the personnel officer phoned me again and urged me to accept the second probationary contract which, he stressed, was still available. A few days later, my employment with Bord Fáilte ended. I did not realise until a few years later that I had a readymade play in my head as a result of my experience. All I realised as I headed for home that evening was that I had no job, that I had a wife and four children to support and that it was little consolation to know that I had followed the moral advice of the garrulous old counsellor, Polonius, in *Hamlet*: 'This above all, to thine own self be true, and it must follow as the night the day, thou canst not then be false to any man.' I knew I had to follow my conscience and preserve my integrity but had I the right to cause suffering and deprivation to my wife and children by doing so?

When I eventually wrote the play, I made the commercial mistake of writing it in Irish instead of English (other circumstances influenced that decision, as will be seen in a later chapter). I called it *Is É Dúirt Polonius* (What Polonius Said). The Abbey accepted it for production in the small Peacock Theatre downstairs – the new Abbey had opened in 1966 – and Mr Blythe reminded me yet once more of the difference between real life and the art of drama. I thought the basic point of interest in my play was that there was no *apparent* reason for the dilemma in which I had been placed, to choose between losing my job or losing my integrity. The audience in the theatre, said Mr Blythe, would not accept this because most people would believe that there must have been *some* reason for the management in Bord Fáilte to act as they did. I quoted Robert Emmet in his speech from the dock when he mockingly told the judge, Lord Norbury, 'Ah yes, there must be guilt somewhere!' When I suggested that envy or malice could be the reason, or a policy on the part of someone in Bord Fáilte to make the new employee feel insecure and therefore more subservient, Mr Blythe was dubious about working such themes into the play; but when I mentioned that I had joined a trade union in my first week with Bord Fáilte, he jumped on this as a plausible dramatic reason that the audience could accept as possible or probable – whether true or not in the events that gave rise to my play.

I had hoped that the play would be directed by Tomás Mac Anna but he informed me that he was giving it to a trainee director, a young man from Galway named Frank J. Bailey, who eventually put on the noisiest, craziest, most distorted production I have ever seen of any of my plays or indeed of any play. (He was tragically killed in a road accident in Galway some years later.) When I met Bailey, the first question he asked me was, 'Tell me the truth, is this play about what happened to me in Radio Éireann?' When I sat in at a rehearsal, an Abbey actor sitting beside me said, 'Do you know, this play could be about the Abbey.' A year later I was invited to Galway to see a production of the play in An Taibhdhearc where Seán Stafford directed it with artistic fidelity and creative style, as he did several other plays of mine (the lead role was impressively played by a young actor named Mícheál Ó Maolalaí, later to become better known as Mick Lally and a television personality in his role of 'Mylie' in the popular soap-opera, *Glenroe*). On the train to Galway I was walking along between seats when a man caught me by the arm and spoke to me in Irish. 'You don't know me,' he said, 'but I'm from Galway. I saw your play *Is É Dúirt Polonius* in the Peacock last year and actually I'm going home now to see it again in the Taibhdhearc. But tell me this, I work in the Civil Service, and when I saw your play I felt sure you must have worked there some time, did you?'

These reactions, and others like them, caused me to feel that my play was more universal in its theme and implications, and making a broader comment on the human condition, than the personal tragic tale I thought I was presenting in the form of dramatic art; but that, of course, is what distinguishes literature from mere storytelling. They also prompted me to hope that an English version of the play would be of even wider appeal and perhaps achieve more commercial success than the Irish one, which lasted only a week in the Peacock and earned me the sum of twenty-five pounds. I wrote the English version and it was turned down by Tomás Mac Anna, who had become artistic director of the Abbey when Ernest Blythe retired.

When I walked out of Bord Fáilte I did not know that I was beginning what the captain of a plane might describe to his passengers as a period of severe turbulence. For the next three years, my family could be classed as itinerants, moving through three counties and seven houses until the storm passed and we came to settle in 1964 where I am writing this book, in a new semi-detached house on the slope of Killiney Hill above the seaport town of Dún Laoghaire. By one of those little tricks of fate, our wanderings came to an end on the other side of Killiney Hill from the residence of the Director-General of Bord Fáilte – a topographical fact which was to become of some literary note some years later. Shortly after we settled into our new house, I took our dog – or he took me – for an early morning walk on Killiney beach, so early that I could see only one other person on the long strand. This man also was accompanied by a dog. As he and his dog came towards me and my dog, the dogs ran to say 'hello' in doggy lingo. I did not run to say 'hello' to the dog's owner. The previous time I had seen that man, nearly four years earlier, he was sitting behind a big boardroom table, flanked by two bureaucratic henchmen. As we pretended to be two strangers passing by on a deserted strand, and exchanged a civilized wish of 'good morning', I looked T. J. O'Driscoll long and hard in the face and I wondered what were the thoughts in his mind. And as I walked on I looked at the sea and thought of those lines of Dante in the *Divina Commedia* which I have prefixed to this book:

> *E como quei che con lena affanata*
> *uscito fuor del pelago alla riva*
> *si volge all'acqua perigliosa e guata . . .*

And from the sea I saw the hero, Odysseus, struggling breathless and battered to safety on the beach of the island of Scheria, where he would find refuge and hospitality with the princess, 'white-armed Nausicaa' and I remembered the words of Homer: 'There comes a time when a man who has had bitter experiences and travelled far can take comfort from the memory of his sufferings.' I walked on, thinking of my wife and children safe at last in our new house on the other side of Killiney Hill. I looked up at where all mortals look when they think of God, and I said, *'Buíochas le Dia.'*

21

WHAT'S IN A NAME?

That haven and sanctuary in the shape of a new semi-detached house in Glenageary, on the inland slopes of Killiney Hill, was still three years in the future on the day I parted company with the Welcome Board of Ireland in 1961. I spent a few months again considering the lilies of the field, an occupation in which I now had enough experience to qualify as a professor. The Cassandra predictions of the hostile personnel officer and of my benevolent solicitor came to pass, not that I was myself over-eager to become the hireling of any other organization or company like Bord Fáilte. Finding a job as a teacher in Dublin proved equally difficult and before long I was applying for a post anywhere. When the summer vacation ended I found myself installed as principal of a two-teacher school in the village of Newcastle, near Greystones in County Wicklow. Having again availed of the professional services of Mr Liam Cafferky, this time to sell our house in Drumcondra, we bought a small car and told our children that we were going to live in a much nicer place, beside the sea and the mountains, where we would some day own a pony and sheep and 'live happy ever after'. The building boom of later decades which saw houses sprouting like mushrooms all over the south Dublin and north Wicklow area had not yet begun;

in fact, hardly a single new house was being built in the Greystones area, so that over the year we spent there we moved from rented house to rented house. Our briefest stay was in a dilapidated and rat-infested summer chalet, our longest in a secluded estate of continental-style houses one of which was the residence of Cearbhall Ó Dálaigh, the Chief Justice, later to resign as President of Ireland because of the refusal of the Taoiseach, Liam Cosgrave, to dismiss a minister who had referred to the President in public as 'a thundering disgrace'. In the process of moving from one temporary abode to the next, my harassed wife and I came to envy the parish priest and his two curates – each of those three celibate ministers of the gospel lived in his own spacious bungalow and each had a paid housekeeper to cook and clean for him.

The parish priest was a decent man from County Limerick who sometimes changed his Roman collar for a white silk scarf, donned a bowler hat, mounted his horse and rode to hounds with the Wicklow Hunt. Unfortunately, although he was officially the manager of the three schools in his extensive parish, he left school affairs and other matters like parochial fundraising, to his curates. The cleric in charge of my little school seemed to have the notion that my wife and I would fit nicely into his various fundraising schemes, while we were desperately trying to raise funds to recoup my loss of salary and feed our children. Since the new principal had the reputation of being an Abbey Theatre and Radio Éireann dramatist, it was only to be expected that he would be a godsend to the amateur drama group – my wife also was invited to join. From the day when we both declined gracefully to engage in that or any other fundraising activities, our curate looked on us with disfavour. In my own case, this turned to absolute enmity when we had a difference of opinion on the matter of monthly confession for the children in my school.

Once a month this priest came to tell all the pupils who had made their First Communion that today was the day for confession, then drove off to the church in Newtownmountkennedy, over two miles away, where he would hear their confessions – after they had *walked* to the church. They would then walk back to the school, most of them having already walked a mile or two to school that morning, with the same walk to do back home when school finished. When I learned from some of the senior pupils that a previous curate used to hear their confessions in the school, I suggested to the present incumbent, on his next monthly visit, that this would be a more reasonable arrangement, sparing the children, some of them just seven years old, the trek to the church which involved going out on to the main Dublin-Wexford road. The man of God told me, in effect, to mind my own business of teaching and that he would look after his priestly duties as he saw fit. He never spoke to me again during the rest of the year we spent in that territory, refusing even to hear the First Confession of the children we were preparing to receive their first Holy Communion because it would involve meeting me at the church. The gregarious fox-hunter parish priest, filling in for his own curate, explained to me that Father X was not easy to get on with. 'He's a good man in his own way,' he said, 'but he's the sort that says, "He that is not with me is against me".'

The people in the Newcastle area were so friendly and their children so pleasant and civilized that as a teacher I would have been happy to settle there; however, it soon became apparent that the combination of the lack of permanent suitable housing and the hostility of a domineering curate would compel another move. The difficulty of finding a rented house was compounded by an element of which we had little or no experience up to then. The house agent, himself a Protestant, told us candidly ('But don't quote me') that some of the houses he might have offered us were owned by Protestants who would not let to a Catholic tenant. I was assured later by an ancient local historian that at the turn of the century Greystones was one of the most Protestant towns in Ireland and that it used to have an

Orange parade on the Twelfth of July that was the biggest outside of Belfast. (Samuel Beckett said that in his youth the morning train from Greystones to Dublin contained only one Catholic, the guard at the rear of the train). He also asserted that as the area south of Greystones had for many centuries been the border of the Pale, the natives there were, as he put it, 'the seed, breed and generation of Irish whores and English horse-soldiers'. We found that bigotry is reciprocal when we were advised by an elderly Catholic woman to stop buying petrol from our usual local source but to get it from a man in Newtownmountkennedy who was 'one of our own'.

My reputation as a playwright caused the local postman occasionally to detain me in discussion on matters theatrical when he called to the school. 'We used to have a great drama group here one time,' he told me. 'One of the plays we did was *Willie Reilly and His Own Colleen Bawn*. Did you ever see that play?' I had to confess that I had never seen it. 'Ah, that's one great play, Master,' he assured me (the title *Master* was, of course, commonly given to the local teacher in rural areas – see next paragraph!). 'But we had great trouble getting it,' my dramatic postman recalled. 'How we got it was like this: there was a travelling company doing it and we followed them around from one village to another; we'd write down a few lines, each of us in turn, and then take it up again; the next night, we'd try and get a few more; and so on until we had the whole thing for ourselves. And we put it on ourselves the year after.' I thought Shakespeare would have loved that man and that story.

A decent woman who came to tell me one day that her daughter was unwell gave me another perspective on the complications of life. Having given me a graphic account of the little girl's symptoms, she informed me that the important thing was 'to keep her bowels open' and this she was doing with a prescription from an old relative who 'had the cures from the old times.' She promised to give me the cure in case my own children might need it. And then she gave me food for thought when she said, in a confidential tone, 'I hear your mistress is pregnant.' My wife and I had a wry laugh that night as we imagined that news travelling on the bush telegraph until it reached the ears of some of the lads in McDaid's pub or my former colleagues in the Drumcondra training school or in Bord Fáilte.

Now that I was again earning the crust in the chalk mines, I was able to allocate some time at night and at weekends to my vocation as a writer – and what a relief it was to my spirit to sit at the typewriter and not have to cook up yet another rehash of articles about Killarney or Connemara or the delights of Dublin's fair city, and to be free to use the word *rain* if and when it was artistically necessary. The peace and quiet of Wicklow were conducive to production and during that winter I wrote a play the idea for which I had first jotted down during my six-month sojourn in Dún Chaoin eight years earlier. I used the same setting, with an offshore island on which ruined houses told of the demise of a community. My central character was a mute young man whose widower father was a noted teller of folktales and legends. He was also a rough and unsympathetic parent who regarded his only child as a moody idiot, useful for doing some fishing and other jobs. A woman artist from England, recently divorced and seeking spiritual recuperation, establishes a rapport with the boy, while an American academic folklorist concentrates on the father as an unsophisticated source of material. Apart from the basic theatrical entertainment of plot and character, I thought I was writing a play about the interpretation of the metaphysical element in human nature. The mistake I made was in the title. When Shakespeare said:

What's in a name? that which we call a rose
By any other name would smell as sweet

he meant that Romeo would be just as handsome if he were called Tom, Dick or Harry. His dictum can also be applied to a book or a play, meaning that no matter what the title,

223

the contents remain the same. But I was to learn to my cost that a title can sometimes be misleading in a way that militates against the work and its author.

Thinking as I was of the autistic young man as my central character and imagining in my mind what was going on in his, especially the effect of hearing his father's heroic and romantic old tales over and over again – in each act I introduced a surreal scene in which the young man and the English artist became a prince and princess in one of the old tales and spoke in blank verse – thinking also of how his father regarded him as a simpleton, I called my play *Romance of an Idiot*. I thought it the perfect title when I sent the play to the Abbey Theatre. When it came back, rejected outright, I was so stunned by what Mr Blythe wrote about the play that it took me a long time to realise that the title was the worst I could have chosen. Hindsight is a great clarifier and some years later, after this play had caused even more trouble for me than a rejection by the Abbey, I realised how the very title had pointed the minds of the Abbey directors and others towards a totally wrong interpretation of the play. If only I had called it *Land of the Living*, as I renamed it many years too late, their minds might have recollected the words of the Psalmist:

I am sure I shall see the Lord's goodness in the land
of the living: hope in him, hold firm and take heart:
hope in the Lord.

The phrase, *Tír na mBeo*, also occurs in some of the old Irish stories which gave me the idea for the play.

The only words in the title, *Romance of an Idiot*, that had been acceptable to Blythe and company were 'of' and 'an'. They had fastened on the common meanings of the words 'romance' and 'idiot', with the result that Mr Blythe, having praised the construction, characterisation and dialogue of the play, went on to tell me (in Irish, as usual) that they were rejecting the play, and he explained why. 'Our readers feel,' he wrote, 'that this play would disgust the audience'. (Some readers may find this statement incredible, and so I quote the exact words in Irish: *Is dóigh lenár léitheoirí go gcuirfeadh an dráma seo déistin ar an lucht féachana)*. He continued: 'It would remind people of those blackguards who, from time to time, receive prison sentences in the courts for having put poor stupid half-witted girls in the family way.' The forthright Mr Blythe concluded, as usual, with words of encouragement, the kind that butter no bread and pay no rent. 'It is obvious from this play, even if you had written nothing else, that you have great dramatic talent but we feel you should keep away from fantasy and stick to themes and characters which would be somewhat realistic.'

I could not understand the workings of the minds that had interpreted my play in so absurd and moralistic a manner. There was not the slightest suggestion of any sexual relationship between the man and woman, not even in the dialogue of the play. And as for their advice that I should 'keep away from fantasy', apart from the brief vision scene in each act the play was as realistic as could be. On a personal level, I took offence at the implication that my play was somehow immoral. I wrote to Mr Blythe and told him so. I pointed out that as a Catholic I would consider it an immoral abuse of my talent to write anything that was immoral. I also directed his attention and that of his colleagues on the Abbey board to the fact that they were misinterpreting my play and rejecting it on non-artistic grounds; in other words, engaging in literary censorship.

I sent copies of the play to Hilton Edwards at the Gate Theatre, to Mary O'Malley at the Lyric Theatre in Belfast and to some of the leading amateur groups. Edwards and MacLiammóir were enthusiastic about the play and assured me that they would produce it if a certain London impresario showed an interest. (The Gate did not have a subsidy at that time, and I understood that they hoped their production would be funded as a preliminary to the West End one.)

Nothing came of this because the man in London had other shows in the pipeline. Mary O'Malley accepted the play and so did the Guinness Players, an amateur company composed of employees of the St James's Gate brewery, who had recently won the All-Ireland amateur drama competition.

The Guinness Players planned to give the play its premiere in their own hall, the Rupert Guinness Hall at the brewery. When they told me that they were going to give the play a trial run in a drama festival organised by Dublin amateur groups and that this would take place in the Father Mathew Hall in Church Street, I had some misgivings – not, of course, about my play or the ability of the amateur champions of theatre to do it justice but because the hall in question was owned by the Capuchin Fathers, whose church gave the street its name. On the night of the performance, I found myself seated in a row of bearded Capuchins in their Franciscan habits and I was unable to enjoy the play. If Blythe and company at the Abbey thought the play would disgust the audience, what would these bearded Capuchins have to say to it? The man on my right-hand side was Fr Henry, the editor of the *Capuchin Annual,* a literary cum religious compendium to which many leading writers contributed.

At the first interval he turned and congratulated me, saying that he was very impressed. When the play ended, he shook my hand and spoke in terms so laudatory that I was nonplussed. I pointed out to him that Mr Blythe had rejected the play on moral grounds. 'Ah, yes,' he said, with a dismissive laugh, 'I saw that on the papers; but you see, there are morals and morals!' That left me mystified but reassured. When we joined the cast for a cup of tea, the other Capuchin priests praised the play so much that I began to feel that they, like the Abbey directors, were seeing things in it that I had not intended but this time in a positive and even spiritual sense. A few months later, Fr Henry wrote to me about the play. I quote from his letter: 'The more I think back over the play, the more I like it. There is a great challenge in it for professionals, who would, I feel, establish its message and beauty as it deserves.' I don't think he meant to imply any slight on the Guinness Players production, which was one of the finest I ever saw of any of my plays. The director, Paddy Ryan, was later to be engaged by the Dublin Grand Opera Company to direct several of their productions. One of the cast, Val McGann, was an artist and the company presented me with his oil painting of the imaginary locale of the play in the west of Ireland.

When the play was put on for a week at the Rupert Guinness Hall, I was able to relax and enjoy it, secure in the *imprimatur* bestowed on it by the Capuchin sons of St Francis. I had been interviewed by the *Sunday Independent* and I made no bones about what I thought of the Abbey's rejection of the play on moral grounds. I thought the newspaper critics, and all the opponents of literary censorship who were just then vociferously championing the cause of Edna O'Brien because of the banning of her first novel, *The Country Girls*, (1960) would be eager to see my play and make their opinions known. The silence was deafening. Like a voice crying in that wilderness, *The Irish Times* critic, Alec Reid, alone wrote about the play as I had hoped all the critics would. In view not only of the Abbey's rejection but of the further recriminations caused by this play and the injustice subsequently perpetrated by self-righteous moralists on me as author, and indirectly on my dependants, it is of interest to record the verdict of Mr Reid:

> Here is an original and beautiful play, provocative in the best sense, a most encouraging protest against the mediocre and the trivial. *Romance of an Idiot* has on its first night established itself as a play controversial in the grand manner of *The Silver Tassie* or *Waiting for Godot*. It has been rejected by the Abbey and, while this is not of itself proof positive of quality, it strongly suggests distinction and vitality. This is a play about

which indifference is impossible – either one is enthralled with its cunning mixture of symbolism and realism, of low comedy and high romance or one rejects it as a pastiche or dog's dinner. One admires the skill with which the author works on his audience, leading them from a quiet first act to a passionately exciting third, or one succumbs to the novelty and battens on to the comedy to the exclusion of much else. Those who seek stimulating theatre will be greatly heartened by this play. *Romance of an Idiot* is essentially an experience of illumination; the very language has a fine sweep about it. "Evil is the leaven in the bread of good," says one of the poetic lines, and another likens Expediency and Hypocrisy to fattened twin monsters who will eventually devour the king foolish enough to pamper them at his court. Some people may dismiss such lines as arrant nonsense; to others, however, they will have the welcome ring of true dramatic poetry. Inevitably, then, I think this play will inspire argument; but in the desert of tedious banalities this should be as welcome as a generous shower. At the moment, O'Flynn seems to have all the passion that distinguished the earlier O'Casey.'

Soon after the Guinness Players production of the play, it was put on at the Lyric Theatre in Belfast by Mary O'Malley, who directed it in a setting by the artist Rowel Friers, and I had the opportunity of seeing how the same play can be interpreted in different ways by various directors. A few years later, I sent the play to my Salzburg friend, Edwin Burr Pettet in Brandeis University in Boston. He put on a production with his senior drama students and also caused them to write a long critical essay about the play. When he sent me a copy of these essays I learned amazing things about my play: one student included diagrams relating the characters to one another in the various stages of the play.

22

A Belt of a Crozier

Meanwhile, before *Romance of an Idiot* went on the stage in Dublin, after ten years in exile in the Pale, the author and his patient wife, with their children and their goods and chattels, such as they were, had moved from County Wicklow back to their native city by the Shannon. We had never lost hope of finding a job in Limerick that would enable us to return to the native heath, and an advertisement for a position in a two-teacher school in Pallasgrean, fourteen miles from Limerick city, was doubly attractive in our present circumstances because it offered an official rent-free residence. The Victorian bureaucrats who planned railway stations, military and police barracks, schools and work–houses, all over Britain and Ireland, were practical officials who added living quarters or an official residence to all of these developments. Hence, when a school was built in a rural area it was usually matched by a commodious house for the teacher. The house was rent free, but it did not belong to the teacher. Like the school itself, the house was vested in the local manager, who in the system set up under the National Schools Act of 1831 was almost everywhere the parish priest or rector. Like the schools also, these official residences were often allowed to fall into disrepair, the clerical manager being unwilling to allocate parish funds to their upkeep, while the teacher was naturally reluctant to spend any of his income on the maintenance or improvement of a house that would never be his own property and which he would have to leave when he retired.

In this context, it is of historical interest to quote some articles from the contract form I was given to sign when I became principal of that two-teacher school in County Limerick in 1962 (the school, one of several in the parish of Pallasgrean, was known as Nicker National School, a name which gave rise to lewd comments from some of my monoglot acquaintances but which is, in fact, a sad comment itself on our linguistic deprivation, the original Irish word being *coinicéar*, which means a rabbit warren). The contract was as Victorian as anything in Dickens, full of terms like *whereas* and *notwithstanding* and each item began with impressive capital letters. It was apparently a standard item in the employment of teachers in the archdiocese of Cashel, in which that part of County Limerick is included, and probably in other dioceses also.

'No Act Or Thing which shall or may be or might become a nuisance, damage, annoyance or inconvenience to the said schools or occupants of adjoining or adjacent premises or the neighbourhood shall be done upon the said premises or any part thereof.' (Since the school in a rural area was usually in an isolated position and the residence some distance from it, it remains a matter of conjecture what antics country teachers in Victorian times were likely to get up to that might 'become a nuisance, danger, annoyance or inconvenience etc.')

'The Teacher will from time to time and at all times during the subsistence of the Licence hereby granted, clean and repair all Glass, clean all Sanitary Arrangements and Ashpits, gravel and keep in good order the Grounds and Walks, keep and maintain the fences and the surface Channels in good order and condition, thoroughly sweep and keep swept all Chimneys, and well and substantially repair, cleanse, paint, maintain and keep the interior of the said Premises in good order, repair and condition.

'The Teacher shall insure the said Premises in some responsible insurance office to be approved of by the Manager.

'The Teacher will punctually pay and discharge all rates, taxes, charges and assessments of every kind payable in respect of the premises.

'The Teacher shall in each year pay to the Manager a sum not by way of Rent but to enable the Manager to provide monies out of which such external or structural repairs of the said Premises as may from time to time be carried out by the Manager in his discretion may be paid for.'

I doubt if St Thomas Aquinas himself could deny that these terms contradict, *de facto* if not *de iure*, the meaning of that phrase, *rent free*, which had seemed so attractive when read in a newspaper advertisement. In plain English, they state that the teacher is to pay the cost of maintaining the interior and grounds, pay all rates and taxes, etc., insure the house, and then pay an annual sum to the reverend manager 'out of which' external repairs 'may from time to time' by carried out – but only 'at the discretion of the Manager.' In correspondence, we had been told by the reverend manager that the residence was 'a fine house', and that the teacher who was now retiring had added a bathroom. When we drove with our children to see it, the house proved to be a fine one in terms of space, having been designed as a pair of semi-detached houses at a time when the local population was such that the school had an enrolment requiring a larger staff than the two which was now the usual complement in such rural academies. For many years now, however, only one half was occupied, and it was very obvious that the practical terms of the contract had not been adhered to on either side, so that inside and outside the residence was not only in need of what the euphemism calls 'a lick of paint' but was in serious need of a complete renovation.

That is exactly what the nearby school was about to undergo, as the reverend manager had also informed me. And as anyone knows who ever attended one of those Victorian rural schools or taught in one, the government's Board of Works was never in a hurry to carry out such a renovation until the very rats were in danger of being drowned by the rain. The added bathroom turned out to be a lean-to shed which certainly contained a bath; but in order to make use of this modern amenity pots of water would have to be heated on the kitchen stove. And since the retiring teacher and his wife had removed the Aga cooker, leaving a gaping black hole in the kitchen, even bathing by this carrying of pots would prove impossible as things stood. The final disillusioning touch was added to our viewing of this damp and crumbling Victorian residence when we saw iron hooks in the ceiling of the musty pantry, on which we assumed the housewife in former times used to hang meat. But that was not the last straw. We had already decided that we could not bring our young children, one a baby of a few months, to live in this spacious but insanitary dwelling when the reverend manager casually informed me that, because the school had to be stripped down to the stone walls and the rebuilding would take a year, he had decided to put the seventy or more pupils, ranging from infants of five years to teenagers of fifteen, into the other half of the semi-detached residence, with as many of the old school desks as could be squeezed in, and with a temporary toilet in the back garden.

The reverend manager and I had our first tentative altercation when I told him that even if we considered the house habitable, which we did not in its present much neglected condition, we would not agree to live in our half while the other half was used as a temporary school, and that in justice to the teacher and his family, the residence, built at the same time as the school, should now get the same total renovation. The black clouds loomed on the horizon. I record, as a matter of fact, that the reverend manager's own house, like most parochial residences, was an impressive and well-maintained building that would have done credit to a landlord in Victorian times. Another item of interest, on the day when we drove with our children from County Wicklow to see the school and residence, and called to the parish priest's house to meet the man himself, he never asked us if we had a mouth on us, as the saying goes.

On that first visit also we were courteously greeted at the residence by the retiring principal teacher and his wife. While our spouses chatted in the house – my wife listened to some cautionary tales, and to expressions of regret that the old teacher had resisted his wife's suggestions over the years that they move to a house, and possibly a job, in Limerick city – the man himself showed me the school and the garden. The latter area included a small orchard, much neglected. 'Only for those apple trees,' the old teacher told me, 'I might have been born in Dublin. My father planted them when he came here as a young married man and later when he was offered a good job in Dublin he couldn't bear to leave them.' That reminded me conversely of Chekhov's story, 'Gooseberries' about the civil servant whose fulfilment of his lifelong dream of retirement in the country is symbolised by his childish relish of the fruit that his visitor finds hard and sour.

Having boldly laid our parental cards on the parochial table, so to speak, we decided to rent a house in Mayorstone in Limerick City until such time as the official residence was made suitable for habitation – in our opinion rather than that of the reverend manager. We found a good house in Mayorstone, near the famous rugby grounds at Thomond Park, and when the summer vacation ended I began to drive the fourteen miles to my latter-day hedge-school in Pallasgrean every morning from Monday to Friday. My new mistress was ensconced, with the infants and junior pupils, in what some Victorian architect had designed as a kitchen, while I earned a niche in the history of education in Ireland by becoming the only teacher ever, as far as I know, to have taught mixed classes in a bedroom. With the desks pushed together so tightly that the lads and lassies had to clamber over them, and the blackboard on its easel leaning against the wall beside the tiny fireplace, we were such a sight that RTÉ should have made a documentary on the situation. Even the local school inspector was aghast when he paid us a visit. He consoled me by telling me that it would be all worthwhile when the renovated school reopened in a year's time, with all mod cons, toilets and washbasins and electricity. When I met up with the local contractor who was tearing the old school apart, he told me ('Don't tell him I told you this') that the parish priest had asked him to 'fix up' the residence by putting a fireplace in the kitchen to fill the black hole left by the Aga cooker, and to do a few other things, like boarding over the hole in the floor of one of the bedrooms, 'but he told me not to go beyond about forty pounds' – after all, he had given him the big contract for the school.

It was my new mistress, a courteous lady who was married to a local farmer, who enlightened me when I asked about the row of hills we could see in the distance. 'They're the hills of Doon,' she said. When we had our first music session, I asked my new pupils to sing me a song about their own locality but they told me they had never heard any such song. I promised to make one for them. Driving home to Limerick that day, I remembered that phrase, 'the hills of Doon.' I made the song, to the air of Kickham's 'She Lived Beside the Anner at the foot of Slievenamon' and although the hills of Doon had claimed the refrain, I managed to squeeze in enough references to Pallasgrean to make it valid for the natives. Some years later, I realized with salutary humility that that ballad may very well be the only item in all my corpus of writing that will be known in times to come. I was told by Donncha Ó Dúlaing of RTÉ that when he was doing a programme about Sarsfield's Rock in Ballyneety, near enough to Pallasgrean in East Limerick, a young girl who was lined up to contribute a song told him she would sing *The Lovely Hills of Doon*. 'I never heard that one,' says Donncha. 'Will you sing a verse for me till I hear how it goes?' She did, and when Donncha asked her who wrote it, she replied, 'It was made by a master that was in Pallasgrean a few years ago,' and gave my name, already well-known to her interlocutor with whom I had done several radio interviews in the intervening years.

The black cloud that had loomed on the horizon as soon as I told the parish priest that we would not move into the 'rent-free' residence began very soon to blow across what had been the clear blue sky of our expectations when, after ten years in exile in Dublin and Wicklow, we moved back to our native Limerick. And the straw that showed which way the cloud-bearing wind was blowing was a little item called a rosary card. During our ill-fated sojourn in Wicklow we had become acquainted with the Columban Sisters, a missionary order of nuns whose headquarters in Magher-amore were not far away. One of the ways in which funds were raised for the missions was by the distribution to schools of the so-called rosary cards. These were small cards on which a picture of Our Blessed Lady was surrounded by rosary beads. The children would ask their relations and neighbours to prick one or more of the beads with a pin, collecting a penny for each bead. I had raised a few pounds for the Columban Sisters by this humble system while I was principal in Newcastle in County Wicklow and when a new batch of cards was forwarded to my Limerick address I decided to enlist the children of Nicker school in this worthy cause. The day after I distributed the cards, one girl brought her card back to me and said the priest had met her when she began collecting, (the priest being my reverend manager, the parish priest of Pallasgrean), and had ordered her to desist at once. 'He said it would be interfering with his collections, and I was to give you back the card.' I recalled the rest of the cards and returned them to the Columban Sisters, informing them of the serious harm their simple fund-raising gimmick could have done to the church finances in the archdiocese of Cashel.

In our crowded and insanitary hedge-school bedroom I was also given one of the most moving moments of my literary life. One day, a girl came up to me shyly and proferred some pages from an ordinary exercise copy. 'My mother said you might like to read that,' she said. 'What is it?' I asked, seeing lines in longhand that looked to be verse. 'It's a poem my sister wrote when our brother was killed on the buildings in England.' Her words took me from that musty and smelly bedroom to the foot of a gallows. One of the most moving folk poems in the Irish language is an anonymous composition by a girl for her brother, *Donncha Bán* (Fair-haired Donncha), who was hanged by the English on the word of an informer. Here's the first stanza:

> *Is ar an mbaile seo a chonaic sibh an t-ionadh*
> *Ar Dhonncha Bán is é dá dhaoradh,*
> *Bhí caipín bán air in áit a hata*
> *Agus rópa cnáibe in áit a charabhata.*
> (It's in this town ye saw surprise
> On fair Donncha being sentenced to die,
> Instead of his hat a white cap he wore,
> And his cravat was made of hempen rope.)

The poetic sister of Donncha Bán gives us the name of the traitor, but not her own name, the family name, or any details of place or time. But her poem links her with Eibhlín Dubh Ní Chonaill, whose poetic outpouring of grief for her murdered husband, Art Ó Laoghaire, gave me the material for one of my first dramatic efforts, and they were both linked now with a girl here in this area of County Limerick who had expressed in verse, albeit in English, the grief of her whole family for the boy who died on a building site in England. I confess that I read those handwritten lines on a few pages of a school copybook with more emotion, and with more awareness of the true nature and function of poetry, than I have ever experienced from the architectonic sonorities of Milton's *Paradise Lost* or the calculated euphony of Yeats. My regret is that I did not make a copy of that humble poem on that day and that subsequent happenings gave me such pressing concerns that I forgot to do so later.

The black cloud that had loomed on the horizon as soon as the parish priest realized that we would not move into the official residence in its present dilapidated condition and under present circumstances now spread quickly across the sky. Now that he was bidding a final farewell to the two-teacher academy of Nicker, to the parish of Pallasgrean and to the house where he had been born sixty-eight years before when his father had been the teacher, my predecessor unburdened himself – in confidence, of course! – of his true feelings about the clerical managers under whom he had laboured and especially about the present incumbent. All teachers were politely saddled by the bishops of the time with doing the clergy's task of teaching Christian Doctrine and preparing the children for the sacraments of Penance, First Communion and Confirmation; but in rural parishes or in small towns, in addition to his job in the school, the teacher was an unpaid general factotum in the parish, expected to be at the beck and call of the priest, to collect the offerings at the church – and to be secretary of any and every society or club. He or his wife, who was often also a teacher, would be expected to train the church choir, if any, and to play the harmonium at Sunday devotions, at retreats and missions, and at the evening devotions in May. But even with my recent experience of a dictatorial curate in County Wicklow, I was surprised to learn from this mild and courteous pedagogue that he had also been given charge of the parish registers and told to issue baptismal or marriage certificates to applicants at home or abroad – 'he nearly expected me to dig the graves!' he concluded bitterly. It will be seen that in desiring us to move into the official residence without delay, the parish priest was not motivated by reasons educational.

Another factor in this situation came to light at Christmas when the reverend manager called in one day at lunch break. The children were playing around the area of the residence while the master and the mistress were having a cup of tea in the kitchen-classroom. After a few preliminary remarks about the weather, he produced a notebook and said, in a tone that might fairly be described as brusque or blunt, 'Mr O'Flynn, I see here that you owe me twelve pounds ten.' Having swallowed hard as they do in the best and worst of novels I told him that I was not aware that I owed him anything. He explained. 'Seven pounds for Christmas dues, and five pounds ten shillings for stations.' In the less religious Ireland of today, it may be necessary to explain what 'dues' and 'stations' meant and still mean for some people. One of the laws of the Catholic Church is 'to pay dues to our pastors', in other words, that the faithful contribute something, usually at Christmas and Easter, to support their clergy. In rural areas, and in many small towns, the clergy also receive a contribution when they hold a Mass-station in a house in the parish. This custom arose in former times when there were few churches, and the priest travelled from one place to another saying Mass in a selected house and then administering the sacraments to the local people. Apparently, the parish priest of Pallasgrean, like many others of his kind, did not leave the amount of the contribution to the individual parishioner but decided for himself what they should 'offer' by way of support for their pastor. And the teacher in Nicker school was listed at seven pounds for Christmas dues, five pounds and ten shillings for stations. (These must have been held in a house in the locality some time recently).

I informed my clerical employer that I didn't owe him

anything. I was not yet, I said, a parishioner of his, and I would be obliged to pay my Christmas dues to the parish priest of the parish of St Munchin's in Limerick, Monsignor Molony, with whom he could check. Nor had I been present at any station in the area; so, I did not see that I should be expected to make a contribution in that regard until I came to reside in the parish and took part in stations. While the unfortunate mistress tried to sip her tea and nibble at her sandwich, the reverend manager reiterated that the teacher in Nicker school had to pay the sums in question and the Limerick-domiciled teacher told him again that I owed him nothing.

'Are you refusing to pay your dues?' he shouted.

'No, Father,' I replied, with the calm of a noble of the *ancien régime* mounting the steps to the guillotine, 'I told you, I'll pay dues to the priest in the parish where I live and where I receive spiritual ministration, and you can check with him. If and when I come to live in this parish, I'll pay dues here.'

'But you work here as a teacher,' he countered, 'and so you must pay your dues here.'

'If that were the case,' I said, 'the parish priest in Shannon Airport would be the richest priest in Ireland; but surely all the workers in Shannon who live in Limerick or Ennis or other places pay their dues to the priest in the parish where they live?'

He left without bidding us adieu. And under my teeth I wished him *à diable*.

Some time before this visit, when I noticed that the supply of coal for our two small fireplaces was running low, I gave a note to one of the pupils who lived near the parish priest, requesting a fresh supply of fuel. (The Department of Education gave an annual grant to the school manager for the heating, lighting and maintenance of the school.) A few days later, on a frosty morning in December, no coal having arrived, we shivered in our overcoats, in kitchen and bedroom respectively, until I noticed that there were lots of old bushes and trees growing around the double residence. I ordered the pupils to go out and play (it should be remembered that this was when there were not even indoor toilets in schools, let alone a telephone). I sent some of the bigger boys who lived nearby to ask for a saw or a hatchet in their homes and we warmed ourselves for a few hours by cutting and chopping anything that looked dry enough to burn. I probably earned myself a mention in the local folklore by this desperate remedy for a desperate disease; but I was also unwittingly giving the reverend manager material that could be used in evidence against me as an eccentric writer who was not a suitable person to be in charge of the education of the children of the parish.

A fresh supply of coal arrived two days later, and on the following day the reverend manager called to ensure that we were safe and warm. We had stacked our logs and chopped branches in one of the empty bedrooms. 'I see ye have a fine pile of logs too,' the reverend manager observed, as he stood on the landing before departing down the stairs. 'We have,' replied the Principal of Nicker Academy. That ad-hoc pile would come in for mention in another context later.

When the Guinness Players informed me that, as national amateur drama champions, they had been invited by the committee of Féile Luimnigh (an annual cultural festival) to come to Limerick for a weekend with a play of their choice, and that they had decided to put on my play, *Romance of an Idiot*, which they had recently produced in Dublin, I was elated as a dramatist. I was also ironically amused at this further evidence that the curse of St Mainchín (Munchin), patron of Limerick, which I had blamed for my failure to find a job in my native city, was now being lifted in my case. (When the natives of Limerick refused to build a stone church for Mainchín, whom St Patrick had placed in charge after converting the locals, high and low, the fiery little monk reacted in a most unChristian manner by threatening them with his pastoral staff and cursing Limerick thus: 'May the stranger flourish in you, and the native perish in you.'). Here was I with a job at least within driving distance of the city, and hoping that some day I might move to one in the city itself. We were also negotiating the purchase of a house near the one we were now renting. And now I was about to be presented to my fellow-citizens as a playwright. In fairness to the holy Mainchín, however, and as evidence of the power of an episcopal curse, I should admit that no play of mine has ever been produced by a local company in Limerick, before or after the production of *Romance of an Idiot* by the Guinness Players. And little did I know that Mainchín was about to have the last laugh, because this play would be the means of bringing that black cloud across the entire sky, and another pastoral staff was about to give me a belt that would send me even farther into exile from my beloved Limerick than the Pale of Dublin or Wicklow.

There is nothing so intensely satisfying for the creative writer as the experience of writing a play and seeing it produced with artistic fidelity in a packed theatre to an appreciative audience. I enjoyed that experience on two nights in succession when the Guinness Players came to the Belltable Theatre in Limerick and packed houses responded to *Romance of an Idiot* just as the audiences in Dublin had done. But it was a week later that I was paid a compliment that still lingers in my soul and has often been a source of solace when rejection or nonsensical criticism caused me to wonder if the whole business of writing was the romance of an idiot. On the Saturday after that dramatically glorious weekend, I happened to be browsing in O'Mahony's bookshop in O'Connell Street, the mecca of all booklovers in the city and surrounding territory, where the O'Mahony family and the shop manager, Arthur O'Leary, consistently defied the curse of St Mainchín by promoting Limerick writers as they had done with myself since my first efforts were published. I was approached by Arthur O'Leary, himself a talented amateur actor, who said that a woman on the other side of the shop would like to meet me. As we moved across, he told me that this woman had very poor sight but that she had been to my play and had asked to meet me when he told her I was in the shop. She told me that in her young days she had been an amateur actress but failing sight forced her to give up that pastime. However, she still loved to go to the theatre and by sitting near the stage she was able to follow the action of the play from the dialogue. 'And I have never enjoyed a play so much as your beautiful play,' she said. 'In fact, I could imagine myself *in* the play. I enjoyed it so much that I went again the second night.'

I got an opposite reaction when I drove out to Pallasgrean on the following Monday morning. During the course of the morning, the reverend manager paid a visit. He clomped up the creaking stairs to my hedge-school in the bedroom and told me to send the pupils out to play, as he wanted to talk to me privately. When we were alone he said he had come to tell me that he had gone into Limerick to see my play. 'I'm very interested in the theatre,' he told me, 'and I often helped the nuns in Doon with their productions.' He went on to tell me that while the play was in general very good, he understood why the directors of the Abbey Theatre had rejected it on moral grounds (the controversy had been revived in Dublin and local papers in connection with the production in Limerick). 'You'll have to rewrite the play,' he said, and proceeded to make practical suggestions. 'I'm only trying to help you, you understand,' he commented, while I again 'swallowed hard' and tried to think of my wife and children so that I would not kick him down the stairs from this hell-hole of a hedge-school bedroom. 'You shouldn't end the play with that boy committing suicide,' he said. My mute hero was reported as having been seen walking into the sea but in his mind, and in that of the dramatist, he believed he was going into 'the Land of the Living.' To explain this to my parish priest employer at that point in time was beyond my power and my patience. He gave me a new ending for my play. 'Let him fall off the cliff and hit his head on a rock. This will cure him, and then he can marry that English artist woman.' *And they can live happy ever after, and pay dues to their pastors*, etc.

In spite of his theatrical achievement in helping the nuns in Doon with their productions, I pointed out to my clerical employer that I had no intention of accepting his suggestions or of changing my play in any way. When he began to tell me again that the play was immoral, but could be 'fixed up' to make it satisfactory, I had no option but to tell him that as a teacher, I was willing to listen to anything he had to say about matters educational but with regard to my play and to all my work as a writer, I was independent and would do my writing to the best of my ability and according to my conscience. 'But that's not the way I see it,' he said, 'and that's not how the people will see it. And I as the parish priest have to take all things into account.' I knew what that implied. I told him that as parish priest he should look after the spiritual welfare of his parishioners and not presume to tell me how to write my plays. He told me that I was a gifted writer, he could see that from my play, but that I was not writing as a Catholic writer should. On that theological note, he departed to look after the spiritual welfare of his flock, while I rounded up my innocent flock to resume earning my daily bread by broadening their minds.

Anyone who has read my chronicle of my boyhood in Limerick, *There Is an Isle*, might remember the optimistic dictum of my Granny Connolly: 'We never died o' winter yet', which that hardy woman verified in her own case by falling down the stairs and so departing this vale of tears. Her maxim would have been more than apt with regard to our survival while I taught my mixed classes in a musty bedroom and my wife cared for our five children, one of them a baby (the three eldest were settling into local schools) in a rented house in Limerick during what was one of the severest winters for many years. With the coming of spring there came the chance to buy a house in the same area in which we were pouring money down the black hole of rent. There came also catastrophe.

I drove home from Pallasgrean one Friday feeling only the usual weekend fatigue, and a few hours later I was lying as low as the Croppy Boy in the poem who was *sínte ar thaobh an tsléibhe agus piléar trína ucht* (stretched on the side of the mountain with a bullet through his chest). The bullet that laid me low was identified by our family doctor, Ambie McCann, as viral pneumonia. His initial examination having caused him to consider my case as serious, he returned later that night with a specialist colleague, Dr John Leahy, who prescribed some magic pills and advised that I be shifted to St John's Hospital the following morning. I was not very much aware of what was going on in 'the Land of the Living' when my solicitous brother-in-law, Kevin Beegan, transported me in his car to the benevolent care of the Blue Nuns in St John's. Dr McCann provided my wife with a medical certificate which she posted forthwith to my clerical employer in Pallasgrean. On receipt of the sad news that I was thus stricken down by pneumonia and shifted to hospital, he being a priest immediately phoned my wife to offer his sympathy and drove into Limerick to visit me. Anyone who believes that last sentence would believe that little green creatures with periscopic eyes live on the moon and are preparing to invade the planet Earth.

By return *registered* post, my wife received from the parish priest of Pallasgrean the following, which I reproduce here in facsimile because it might not be believed if I just quoted it:

Parochial House.
Pallasgreen,
Co. Limerick.

29 March 1963

To
Christopher O'Flynn
N. T Nicker N.S.

Dear Mr. O'Flynn,

In accordance with the terms of the agreement between us dated 16 October 1962 I hereby give you notice that I shall terminate your employment as teacher in Nicker school, three calander months from tomorrow March 28th. 1963.

Signed Patrick J. Lee,
Manager.

Countersigned:
+ Thomas Morris
Archbishop of Cashel.

When I saw this document on my coming home from hospital, I was so appalled that my mind sought equilibrium by fixing tritely on one word while the import of the whole letter was causing a rush of blood to my head. Apparently, you could become a parish priest without being able to spell a word like 'calendar', just as you could become part of the management of Bord Fáilte without being able to spell *attached*. My wife told me that on the day she received the registered letter, Dr Ambie McCann, calling to the house to see the baby, who had also contracted pneumonia, found her in a state of distress. She showed him the letter which had come as a riposte to his medical certificate; whereupon the doctor, who was also an army doctor, rang up the parish priest of Pallasgrean and gave him hell (I speak, alas, metaphorically). I knew my reverend manager well enough by now not to be surprised by his action; what surprised me, even scandalised me as a Catholic, was that the Archbishop of Cashel, my boss's ecclesiastical boss, a man I had never met, had countersigned this letter of dismissal which was as brutal and unChristian as any notice of eviction given by a landlord in the days of Ireland's Great Famine. Without interviewing me or giving me any chance to discuss the matter, the archbishop was in effect putting me and my wife and family out on the side of the road, and eventually, like many of those victims of the landlord class, on the emigrant ship.

23

FAREWELL TO INIS FÁIL

All trouble is comparative, just as life imprisonment is considered a less severe penalty than capital punishment and a rich man can shrug off philosophically the loss of a thousand pound bet on a horse while the loss of a shilling might mean no supper for a pauper punter. So, in the week when I was recovering from pneumonia and I had been told that in three months' time I would once more be without a job, my wife and I had an even greater worry keeping us awake at night. Our baby, who had contracted pneumonia shortly after me, was still in hospital and not showing signs of recovery. As he had been placed in the Regional Hospital, while I was in St John's, my wife had been compelled to do the grand tour of the city on her bicycle every day to visit us both. The doctor and the nurses told us that the child was getting weaker because he was refusing nourishment. The mother took command of the situation by taking the baby home, where the addition of total *love* and care to the stuff on the spoon or in the bottle caused an immediate improvement in his condition. I often wondered afterwards how many babies die in hospitals because they 'will not take their nourishment' and whenever my wife and I saw the saintly Mother Teresa of Calcutta on television saying that the little orphan babies she and her sisters picked up off the streets needed love more than food or shelter, we knew from experience the truth of her assertion. Our baby began to grow stronger by the day; eventually he made a full recovery, thank God, and grew to be as fine a man as his father, who only a few days ago enjoyed a few pints with him and one of his brothers in a pub in Greystones.

Since neither the parish priest nor his ecclesiastical director-general had given a reason for sacking me – at least the gaffers in Bord Fáilte had the neck to state that my work had not reached the required standard – I wrote to the reverend manager and demanded one, *inter alia* letting him know what I thought of his action and of the fact that the Archbishop of Cashel had put the weight of his crozier behind the punitive pen of the parish priest. In reply, he stated that he required a teacher who would live in the parish. When the local schools inspector called to my bedroom academy some days later, he told me that he had to make a report to the department with regard to the condition of the desks, whether they could be used in the renovated school or whether new furniture would be needed. I told him that it was no concern of mine, as I would not be teaching in the renovated school. When I explained why, he told me that the manager could not dismiss me because I did not live in the parish, a fact I knew already. I told him about my argument with the manager about my play and he told me he had seen the play himself in Limerick and enjoyed it.

He asked me if I intended to fight the case through the courts or through the Irish National Teachers Organization (I was back in that union after my brief and enlightening spell with the National Union of Journalists). Without going into the history of the hard lessons I had learned by my experience in Bord Fáilte, I told him that I felt the best course would be to find another job. He agreed and his advice was redolent of the sage counsel uttered by the solicitor who had urged me to forget about Bord Fáilte and return to the chalk mines. 'The union wouldn't be keen to take on an archbishop,' he said, 'and even if they did, you never know what sort of stuff the church's lawyers might bring out in court, especially about your play. And even if you won the case, you'd be regarded here as the immoral writer fellow who dragged the parish priest and the archbishop into court when they were only trying to protect the children.' A brief discussion with local union officials, all of them teachers, convinced me that the inspector was right; they agreed that a gross injustice was being perpetrated but they considered that the matter of the play and of my being a writer as well as a teacher, would complicate the case. They gave me the impression that they would prefer if I found myself a job in the Aran Islands or some other salubrious but distant region rather than compel them to match their union pens against the crozier of Cashel.

I thought I detected a twinkle in the inspector's eye when he produced a document and said, 'I'm afraid I have to check with you on this.' It was an official form which the reverend manager had filled in with regard to the fuel supplied to the school in the previous quarter. The inspector pointed out the information he needed to check with me: 'a half ton of coal and a quarter ton of blocks.'

'Is that correct?' he asked. I knew by his smile that he must have heard about a day in December when the mad teacher from Limerick had organized the cutting down and chopping up of the bushes around the school and residence.

'Well, if the Reverend manager says it,' I replied, 'who could doubt his word?'

The inspector wished me good luck and promised to let me know if he heard of any impending vacancy in his bailiwick.

I set about trying to find a job before the expiration of my three months' notice. I answered every advertisement for a teacher in the primary schools, everywhere and anywhere, in Dublin, Achill Island, Miltown Malbay, the Curragh Camp (where they seemed regularly to need a seventh assistant in the school) and places I had never heard of until I read that they needed a male principal or an assistant teacher. Because the teaching profession in Ireland was structured in three separate systems for primary, secondary and vocational schools, with different training and qualification procedures for each, teachers were restricted to the kind of school for which they had initially qualified. The two-year live-in course in the teachers' training colleges, leading to what was then known as the qualification of national teacher, allowed graduates to teach only in the primary school. To qualify to teach in a secondary school, a university degree was the basic requirement but to this there had to be added a one-year university course in education resulting in the grandly styled Higher Diploma in Education. Having eventually been compelled, some years later, to add it to my primary teacher's qualification as a meal ticket, I could never make out why it was deemed to be *higher* than the two-year, live-in, more intensive and professional course required for teachers in primary schools.

This compartmental system was, and still is, detrimental to the whole educational process, resulting in the obvious anomaly that a university graduate with a poor pass degree in any subject, to which was added a similar scrape-through in the H.Dip. in Ed., was allowed to teach up to the level of honours Leaving Certificate in the secondary schools, while the most talented and dedicated of primary teachers, even if they added a first-class honours university degree to their credits, could not teach at any level beyond sixth standard in the primary school simply because they had not also added the professionally superfluous Higher Diploma in Education to their other qualifications. And even if they added this, there was a financial obstacle to moving from one kind of teaching to another because the teacher would have had to start at the lowest point in the other salary scale. There was also a marked difference in the salary scales, the national teachers being on a lower salary scale than those in the post-primary schools. This injustice was defended by secondary teachers by claiming that their work was more difficult because it was on a higher level and involved preparing pupils for the public examinations. In my own experience of all kinds of teaching, I found a year spent trying to teach junior infants the most stressful, while university lecturing was the easiest of all.

I was made painfully more aware of the anomalous aspects of the Irish educational system when a priest friend of mine in Limerick contacted the heads of the Jesuit Crescent College and the diocesan St Munchin's College and asked them if they could offer me a position. An interview with each of them resulted in the same crux. Since neither of them was a parish priest, they seemed unperturbed by my narration of events in Pallasgrean – the Jesuit, especially, treated the matter with a supercilious shrug and a remark that was highly uncomplimentary to the cultural status of the secular clergy. They were both impressed with my academic qualifications and my literary achievements and each of them expressed what seemed to be a sincere desire to employ me but although I had an honours degree added to my national teacher qualification, they could offer me only the token annual salary of three hundred pounds. This was the basic sum paid to teachers by the managers of secondary schools in order to ensure their control of the hiring of staff, the bulk of the salary being then paid by the Department of Education. Since I did not have the higher diploma, the department would not agree to supplement this token salary and since we were not a family of mice we could not live on three hundred pounds a year. That put the kibosh on any prospect of my earning a living by teaching pupils in the secondary schools. The president of St Munchin's, who was what the journalistic cliché used to call 'an Irish language enthusiast', urged me to try to survive for a year while acquiring the Higher Diploma, as some national teachers did, by means of the weekend lectures at the university in Galway. (Limerick did not have a university until 1989, a development of the National Institute of Higher Education which was established in 1980.) It was not the first time I noticed that the celibate clergyman has little idea of how the daily bread arrives on the table or how the building-society wolf is kept from the door of the mortgaged semi-detached.

When the summer vacation arrived and I shook the dust of Pallasgrean off my feet if not off my soul, I had already applied for so many jobs in teaching and other areas that I was beginning to grow sick at the thought of typing out yet more copies of my glowing references and academic and literary achievements. Most of the school managers to whom I wrote did not reply. A few had the courtesy to inform me that the position was filled. A few interviewed me, all with the same interest until the inevitable question came up: 'And where did you teach last, Mr O'Flynn?' The most sardonically amusing example of that halting point in the interview came about when an old priest in a parish near Pallasgrean was telling me how impressed he was with my credentials. 'You're the sort of a man I'm looking for,' he told me warmly, 'because we'll be getting a new school and I'd love to have a man like you in charge. We had an old couple here and – ah well now, I'll say no more, but you know the way it is; sure I'm getting old myself and I know how it feels. But tell me now, where were you teaching last?' I had no option. The old man looked puzzled. 'In Pallasgrean? D'you mean, with Father Lee?' *The very man.* 'And why did you leave there?' If the eyes are the windows of the soul, that old priest's soul got a right shaking as I explained how Father Lee and this excellent and highly-qualified teacher had parted company as a parochial educational team. Like others before and after him, the poor old man mumbled that he would let me know as soon as he made a decision. I could see him already crossing my name off the top of the short list and shaking holy water on the chair where I had sat so deceptively trying to lead him into trouble.

By the time the schools reopened after the summer holidays, I had come to the conclusion that there must be a black list in operation in Maynooth by which parish priests were able to check up on applicants for teaching posts. The Jesuit editor of an Irish language religious magazine, *An Timire*, to which I had contributed articles and stories as a donation towards the shortening of my purgatory hereafter, rang me one night from Dublin to tell me that, in his own words, he had put on his hat and gone from his base in Milltown to the parish priest in Phibsboro, whom he knew, to ask him to consider me for a job he had advertised in his school. He came away fit to eat his hat when the parish priest asked him only one question about the man he had been recommending in laudatory terms as a teacher and a writer. 'I know his name,' said the reverend manager, 'isn't he the fellow who wrote that immoral play I read about on the paper?'

It was during this limbo period, with hell threatening, that a new and hopeful prospect opened up in my career as a writer. Since leaving Bord Fáilte and finding myself with time to write, I had taken the advice of that American faculty wife in Salzburg who had been so impressed with the few short stories I read at the literary sessions there. Results in the form of an occasional cheque began to appear from my submissions to the US market. I had been advised to concentrate at first on the Catholic magazines, of which there were many, and some of which had editors of Irish-American connection. I found a welcome for my poems as well as my short stories and one magazine commissioned an article on the position of the Catholic writer in the modern world.

I felt I was on the threshold of a more potentially lucrative market when one of my stories was retained for further consideration by the *Saturday Evening Post* but that magazine folded before I got on their list. Subsequent events prevented me from exploring the US market for some years to come, and when I tried again I collected only rejection slips from magazines like the *New Yorker* which seemed to have certain Irish writers on its retainer list. Even before I gave up sending material across the Atlantic, I had begun to feel distinctly uneasy about the dollar market when some editors to whom I submitted a few stories selected the one I thought of least merit, and I realised that I got more fulfilment, in literary and cultural values, from my unpaid contributions to *An Timire* than from the cheque for a few hundred dollars from one such editor in the US who said he would welcome more stories from me – 'especially stories of Irish *whimsey*,' he added. I had to read it twice to see that he had not said 'whiskey', and I consulted an American dictionary just to be sure what the decent man had in mind. As a matter of literary interest, I quote from it now what I read then:

1 A tendency to have or show a fanciful, often humorous approach to life
2 An odd or capricious idea; an idle fancy
3 Anything quaint, fanciful or odd

I got the feeling that editors like this man could do to me what Hollywood did to Barry Fitzgerald and other Irish actors. I understood also the reason why the stage Irishman, in literature or in theatre, is a continuing phenomenon in the Anglo-American culture, and why a clown or a facile scribbler is more likely to achieve recognition and material success in that world than a genuine actor or a true writer.

The autumn leaves were falling when my wife and I came to the decision that we would have to emigrate to England. I had written to publishers, to newspaper editors, to Irish language bodies, even to the Department of Education, in my search for a job, with no result other than a few sympathetic letters and lots of sincere good wishes. I had a married sister living in Worcester and a brother in London but I did not wish to tag on my own troubles to whatever personal troubles they might have in life. Also, of course, the family pride as exemplified in the motto which gave me the title for this book urged me to 'paddle my own canoe.' I decided to go to Liverpool, find a job there, and then bring the family over. The week before I left, RTÉ broadcast a new radio play of mine called *One Night Stand*. This was one play above all others that made me wish my late father had lived to hear it (for all I know, maybe they can hear things like that in heaven). The play was based on an event in my father's life.

In *There Is an Isle* I have recorded with filial gratitude how he and my mother reared their family of eight in the hard times of the Thirties. My father kept food on the table and clothes on our backs by working at two contrasting jobs, selling coal by day and playing the saxophone in casual gigs at night. In his later years, after the war had put an end to the slavery of the horse and cart, and with the family reared, he was able to enjoy playing with a small dance band called *The Sylvians* in a weekly stint in Limerick city and additional gigs up and down the country. It was when they were returning from a distant job on a stormy winter's night that their car ran into a flood on a country road. Stranded in total darkness, and with the water rising slowly in the car, they had to get out and clamber on to the roof. The band leader, Earl Connolly, who was a strong swimmer, swam back in the direction from which the car had come downhill into the flood and located the road a short distance away. My father was no swimmer but he was over six feet tall and with the band leader he was able to help some of the smaller members back to safety. They walked back along the road until they saw a light in the distance and eventually came to a farmer's house where they were given blankets and a cup of tea. Readers who share my religious view of life will be interested to learn that my father told us that the first thing he saw in that farmhouse kitchen was a picture of Our Lady of Perpetual Help to whom he had a great personal devotion.

Like most families in the Limerick of my childhood, we had that picture hanging in our house, devotion to Our Lady under that particular title having been promoted by the Redemptorists when they came to the city in the previous century.

The personnel of the dance-band in my radio play differed very much, of course, from that of the Limerick *Sylvians*, and the play ended in tragedy. But it was an ironic twist of fate that just as everything was falling down around us and I was preparing to say goodbye to my wife and family and set off for Liverpool, one of my most satisfying and successful pieces of writing should be going out on the national radio network. The play was produced by the late Seamus Breathnach, who also directed a new production in 1978. The late P. J. O'Connor, who produced several of my radio plays (he eventually became head of the radio drama department in RTÉ and a radio drama competition for amateur groups has been instituted in his memory) told me that he and his colleagues regarded *One Night Stand* as one of the best radio plays ever broadcast by RTÉ and recommended it as the RTÉ entry for the international Prix Italia. As a matter of record, apart from the Board of Directors of Taibhdhearc na Gaillimhe, Paddy O'Connor was the only person in Ireland who ever commissioned work from me.

A few days after listening to the first broadcast of that play, I drove from Limerick to Dublin, made a quick sale of our small car to a backstreet dealer, sent the bulk of the money to my wife and on a rainy night sailed down the Liffey on the old green-hulled *Munster*. Strange the things that stick in the memory. I can still see the floating carpet of litter on the water between the ship and the wall of the quay. And I can remember thinking, as any writer would, of James Joyce's bombastic effusion as he goes into exile at the end of *A Portrait of the Artist as a Young Man*: 'I go to encounter for the millionth time the reality of experience and to forge in the smithy of my soul the uncreated conscience of my race.' My own emotions were less conceited and my plans more pragmatic. The fire was out in the smithy of my soul, and the conscience of my race was a matter between them and God. I was wondering how long my wife and children could survive and how long it might be before I could bring them to join me in England. As I leaned on the ship's rail, I spat into the Liffey's litter and cursed the people, known and unknown, who had 'hand, act or part', as my mother would say, in depriving me of the opportunity to make a living in my native land.

24

LIVERPOOL BLUES

When I walked down the gangplank in Liverpool, dragging a heavy suitcase and my portable Underwood, ghosts walked with me. At the turn of the century, when he was six years old, my father walked down a similar gangplank here in Liverpool docks along with his mother and four siblings. His seafaring father, finding that his voyages began and ended in Liverpool, decided to bring his family to live there in order to save the extra travel and expense of coming from and going home to Limerick. My grandmother, Bríd Bhán (née O'Donohue), was pregnant when she arrived, and after a year, having given birth to another son, she decided that living among strangers in a dockland tenement in Liverpool was not in any way an improvement on living in a tenement among her own people in Limerick; so, back to the old city by the Shannon she went with her children. She died some years before I was born but I could hear her now telling me that I should not bring my wife and family to this foreign land.

I asked a taxi driver to bring me to a cheap, clean, respectable bed-and-breakfast establishment. The house he brought me to was a tall old house in a Victorian terrace. It was clean and it was respectable – there were a few permanent guests, including a retired lady violinist, and some of the occasional customers included orchestral musicians and minor business executives – but it was not as cheap as I would have wished. The proprietors proved to be courteous and civilized, the wife more of an intellectual than the ex-RAF husband who had some business interests that took him away to other cities and towns. They seemed to be impressed by my story that I was an Irish writer who had come to Liverpool to write a play – I thought that was a lie, but I didn't know what the Holy Spirit was up to – and that I would be staying for some time and so would prefer to pay weekly rather than nightly. I added that I hoped to find some work in journalism or teaching as a change from my daily writing and in order to get to know the city and the people. I was ensconced in a small room on the top floor, a room as sparsely furnished as the cell of a medieval monk and only mildly heated by a midget electric fire that looked as if it had been recovered from a scrap-heap. And it was in that room that I wrote, in ten days, a three-act play that was to bring me more notice in the literary world than anything else I had written and that was also to prove to me that lightning, even of the ecclesiastical variety, can strike twice.

The next morning I made my way to the offices of the local education authority and was greeted by an affable official who, having swallowed my line about being an Irish teacher who wished to make a career in Britain, began to blather about his holiday in Ireland in a way that made me think he must have swallowed some of the stuff I had written for British newspapers and magazines during my brief career as a publicist with Bord Fáilte. He told me that my diploma from the teachers' training college and my university degree would qualify me to teach at any level in Britain, even in a university, and that the shortage of teachers in England would make it easy for me to pick and choose where I would settle down in a permanent position. I would have to submit official evidence of my professional and academic qualifications to the Ministry of Education in London in order to obtain recognition and, as this was likely to take some time, he offered to place me in a temporary job in Liverpool.

I began the next night in a college of technology, paid by the hour to teach English to two classes of adults, some of whom were English tradesmen wishing to take a certificate in their own language, others a variety of immigrants trying to improve their knowledge of the language in general. I found them to be more attentive and eager to learn than any students I ever taught or lectured. At our initial meeting, I explained that I was Irish and that my accent might present some difficulty but after the session even the native English assured me that they understood me better than some of the English-born teachers.

My offer to discuss any problems with any student, perhaps over a cup of coffee in the cafeteria, produced one result that would not have enhanced my pedagogic prospects in England if it had come to the ears of the authorities. After the second class one night, I was approached by two men who told me in stilted English that they were from the Yemen and would like to have a talk with me. When we settled down at a table in the cafeteria, I asked what was the problem. 'You are Irish,' the older one said. I had told them so on the first night. 'We would like to talk with you about de Valera and freedom,' said the spokesman. They knew more about Dev and the Irish struggle for freedom from British rule than many Irish people. Three years later in 1966 when the Irish people were commemorating the golden jubilee of the Easter Week Rising of 1916, it so happened that one day I was in a room in Áras an Uachtaráin, presenting a book of mine, a long poem in Irish about the Rising, to the Man himself, Éamon de Valera. I told him my Liverpool story about the lads from the Yemen. He nodded and laughed. 'Ah yes,' he said, 'we caused a lot of trouble for the British far beyond our own country; it would have been wiser of them to give us Home Rule in Gladstone's day.'

From my first earnings I rushed off five pounds folded

into a letter to my wife in Limerick. A few days later, a woman rang at the door and gave her the torn envelope which she had found somewhere in the neighbourhood; the letter was intact but there was nothing folded in it.

While waiting for recognition of my qualifications from London, I decided that I could usefully fill in some of the day by earning some extra money. I offered my talents as a journalist to newspaper offices and my skills in dishwashing to hotels; the former had no openings but showed interest and took my phone number, the latter wanted me to work at night which I was already doing. A newspaper advertisement offering part-time work as a salesman on commission asked anyone interested to phone. I did and learned that the commodity to be sold consisted of brushes, not for the floor but for the person. I went for an interview the same day and found myself in a very bleak room in an old building – the room looked as if it had been rented for the short term – listening to a chirpy chap with brilliantined hair and a slimline moustache. He seemed satisfied when I told him that I had worked in the drapery and tourist trades in Ireland. I did not tell him that my drapery experience consisted of summer holiday work as a delivery boy at the age of twelve nor that I had been selling Ireland itself for six months until found to be unsatisfactory by management.

He showed me the goods, fancy brushes for the discerning female, all neatly arranged in a presentation case. 'Just the thing for the blokes to give 'em for Christmas,' my mentor told me, and his model sales talk was mostly on that line. Women, he said, would spend a long time examining and admiring the brushes, and then tell you that they actually had very nice brushes already, thank you; but get the chap who wants to splash out on something nice to give her for Christmas, convince him he'll pay twice the price in the shops, that this was a special consignment from a firm in Paris that went bankrupt, that we have only a few dozen left in stock and if he looks the type tell him that the Queen has a set exactly like this in her bedroom at Balmoral. He made me go over that palaver a few times – my mother never told me I looked *that* stupid – and he showed me a map of Liverpool on which he marked out a few streets not far from where I was now domiciled. I was to be on trial for three days, and if I brought in enough orders I would be given the job on commission up to Christmas. He took five pounds as surety on the sample set I was to hawk around which he claimed to be worth twelve pounds but which could be knocked down to eleven or even ten.

My career in fancy brushes lasted only two days. By that time I was feeling like Willy Loman in Arthur Miller's *Death of a Salesman* felt after a lifetime. The few men who opened a door were truculent and hostile, unwilling to open their ears to my rehearsed sales talk about Paris and the Queen. One big black man in an apartment block told me that the brushes were stolen goods and threatened to report me to the police. In the next street a native Liverpudlian with a twisted face told me, with a liberal use of impolite language, that he had not gone through six years of the war against Hitler to come back and find his home town being invaded by blacks and Irish. As the snazzy chap in the office had foretold, the women in general showed a lot of interest but gave me no orders. I thought I already had enough problems in life but my test period as a salesman added another when I began to realise that some of the women who opened a door seemed to be more interested in me than in the gift case of fancy brushes; my mother never told me I was *that* handsome. After the initial chat about brushes evolved into more personal conversation, it didn't surprise me to be told sympathetically that I looked very tired, but to be asked if I would like to come in and rest for a while and have a cup of tea caused a little warning light to flash somewhere in the brainbox.

I finished my first afternoon without a single order but with some new perspectives on the human condition. After a second day slogging from door to door and up and down stairways in an apartment block, with the same negative results and the same variety of personal encounters, I was glad to be told by the spiv in the office that I was not suited to the job and need not come back for the third day. I collected my fiver and went away footsore and dejected, having now been found to be unsatisfactory by a Liverpudlian spiv as well as by the parish priest of Pallasgrean and the Archbishop of Cashel, and the Director-General of the Irish Tourist Board. Perhaps it was as a psychological effort at self-defence that when I got back to my small room in the boarding-house I put my typewriter on the bed and started to write the play that had been developing in my mind for about ten years.

Apart from a few sessions at a garage washing cars during those first weeks on Merseyside – the automatic car-wash was not yet part of the equipment – I made no more forays into the casual labour market. I got some further hours teaching in the technological college, and, when my clearance arrived from the Ministry of Education in London, renewing my frustration with the constraints of the Irish system by confirming that I was fully qualified to teach in any kind of school, college or university in Britain, I was offered a full-time post. By this time, however, I had seen enough of Liverpool and of the industrial midlands of England to agree with the spirit of my paternal grandmother, Bríd Bhán O'Flynn that this was not the place where I wanted to live or to rear our children. Unlike that strong-willed woman, however, I could not just go back up the gangplank to a ship that would take me back to Shannonside.

I was still hopefully applying for every teaching job (primary schools only, of course) advertised in the papers in Ireland, or I should say that my wife was doing so on my behalf. Along with our debts and a pile of bills, I had left my beloved a pile of signed letters of application, with copies of references, and she kept me informed as further refusals added to the pile I had already accumulated before leaving Limerick. From my address in exile, I began to apply for jobs in London and the South of England. Before leaving Ireland, I had seen advertisements in the papers for teachers in various African countries – that decade of the Sixties saw a new development in the recruitment of lay volunteers and teachers for schools run by the missionary religious orders – and my wife and I had discussed this as an alternative to joining the Irish nation in exile in Britain.

I had sent off a few letters of enquiry, and I continued to do so while in Liverpool, the Catholic papers in England having the same kind of job offers. As the weeks went by, I was surprised and somewhat confused by the number of positive replies I received, both for positions in England and in Africa. Among the former, there was even an invitation to an interview at the Benedictine boarding school in Ampleforth, where the future Cardinal Basil Hume was then a monk and a teacher; but as the courteous letter contained the caveat that the position would probably suit a single man rather than a married man with a family, I declined the invitation with thanks. After further discussion with home base, I selected a job in a modern secondary school in Southend as a temporary measure, principally because the board of management (who believed that I wanted to settle permanently in Britain) provided a modern semi-detached house at a nominal rent, and a job in Dar Es Salaam in Tanganyika, now Tanzania, on a long-term contract, teaching English and drama in a girls' college run by a German order of nuns ('we have thirty-three different nationalities in our school,' the head nun wrote) to which we would proceed in the following September, all expenses paid and living accommodation provided.

We never got to Africa, of course, but Africa came to us one night when I was at home in Limerick during the Christmas vacation. It was not shaping up to be a happy Christmas. We were in the process of selling the house beside the rugby field at Thomond Park which we had bought early that year and we had arranged for the transport of our goods and chattels to England in the new year. A stranger rang at the door one night and asked to speak to us. He turned out to be the bishop of a diocese in Sierra Leone, home on holidays in his native Limerick. Among the jobs I had applied for there was one in his diocese. He told us how impressed he was with my credentials, how pleased he would be to put me in charge even of the teachers training college in his diocese but that he wanted to tell us honestly that he did not think West Africa was a salubrious place for young children like ours. He advised us, if we were still keen on going to Africa, to look for a job on the East coast. When I told him that I had found one in Dar Es Salaam he wished us good luck and said that as a writer I would find that city, and the whole experience, interesting and profitable. When that decent man left us, my wife and I laughed ironically at the thought that an archbishop had sacked me and in effect put us out on the side of the road by causing me to be apparently blacklisted by every clerical school manager in Ireland, while missionary schools all over Africa were so eager to make use of my talents that a bishop had actually come calling at our soon-to-be-sold house, and those German nuns in Dar Es Salaam were willing to wait until September to get me on their staff.

I was in London for two interviews one weekend, staying in the house where my brother was the sole lodger with a childless and very cultured English couple, when my wife rang with the exciting news that the principal of a religious order school in Galway city had written to my home address asking me to come for an interview. I rang him and explained that I had been offered several jobs in London and had planned to bring my family over in the New Year but that we would much prefer to live in Galway. However, I thought there was little point in coming for an interview unless he could promise me the job. He told me that I was the man he wanted, that I was at the head of a very short list but that he needed to interview me before making a decision. We arranged an interview for the following day. I went by train to Holyhead, crossed the Irish Sea once more and went on to Galway by train, arriving there literally penniless.

The religious headmaster told me that the short list now contained only my name and that of a local man, but that he was impressed with my credentials. I had no option but to answer truthfully his queries as to why I had not taught in Ireland since the previous June and why I was at present teaching in Liverpool and seeking a permanent post in the South of England. He made no comment but said that he would let me know as soon as he got approval for my appointment. He did not say from whom but I was told later that Bishop Browne of Galway would have had to give his episcopal nod. Bishop Browne was one of the more dictatorial of the tribal popes who ruled in Ireland from the so-called Catholic Emancipation in 1829 until the latter half of this century when the Second Vatican Council brought the winds of change to blow Maynooth Jansenism out of St Patrick's Island of Saints and Scholars – unfortunately blowing much of Patrick's orthodox religion and Catholic faith along with it.

Like the parish priest of Pallasgrean, the religious headmaster in Galway never asked me if I had a mouth on me, which I had, and a big one, not having eaten since I left London. I walked out the road and hitched a lift to Ennis, another to Limerick where I was reunited with my family for one night before heading back to Liverpool. Two days later my wife phoned me with the message from Galway, that the local man had been appointed to the job.

Another interview lingers in my mind for a reason that links language with national culture. In a London school, I was courteously invited by the headmaster to meet the staff at the teabreak. As I chatted with some of them, the glamorous female art teacher turned to another teacher and said, 'Hasn't he a lovely brogue!'

'Actually,' I growled, 'I have two of them,' and left the lady gaping while I moved on to be introduced to the next group. (Most readers will get the point; for those who don't, the Irish word *bróg* means a boot or shoe).

My landlord in Liverpool, like many of his generation, had been conscripted during the war and his conversation consisted largely of reminiscence about his experiences in the RAF. Unfortunately for my digestion, he liked to stand with his back to the fire in the dining-room, tilting his big bulk on his toes and talking while I tried to eat as much as possible of the breakfast which was usually the main meal of my day and sometimes the only one. 'I'm a man of few words myself,' he would begin, 'but I like to think . . . ' He usually went on to prove himself a man of far too many words for my liking. But he was typical of the civilized English middle-class and he manifested a polite interest in my writing although his own literary bent was solely towards books about cricket and the war. Like my Garda Inspector landlord in those early years in Dublin, he sometimes benevolently interrupted my writing by inviting me to accompany him when he drove to Manchester and some other areas on business. It was on those trips that I saw those black mountains called slag heaps about which I had often read. Along with the huge factories and warehouses, and the tower blocks and warrens of red-brick houses, they convinced me that my family would be better off living in a mobile home in Kilkee, if only I could support them, than joining the many Irish immigrants in the industrial cities of Britain. Some of the families of both Irish and other immigrants whom I encountered during my brief career as a fancy-brush salesman or during my freelance slumming as a writer – I used to knock on doors and say I had come from Ireland and was looking for a cousin of mine named XYZ – caused me once more to realise that there are many degrees in the scale of misery and deprivation. This reminded me once again of that poor woman in the pawnshop in Gardiner Street in Dublin whose desperation made me ashamed of the self-pity I had felt at having to pawn my typewriter.

When he felt that I was not the Brendan Behan model of Irish writer, my amicable landlord brought me to his club one night, where I was reminded of Chesterton's dictum that such clubs are socially successful because all the members are of the same class and have the same opinions. My landlord introduced me to some fellow-members as an Irish writer who had come to Liverpool to write a play, and this obviously made more of an impression than if I were a rank-and-file member of McAlpine's Fusiliers who had just finished another day digging tunnels or making roads. Although the IRA campaign of the Fifties had petered out and the more recent Northern Troubles had not yet begun, the convivial ex-RAF types who were showering hospitality on me wanted to discuss the IRA and Ireland's reluctance to be part of Great Britain just as eagerly as my friends from the Yemen but of course from a different perspective. They seemed to believe that de Valera was the real head of the IRA and had used their power to prevent the Irish people from agreeing to support Britain during the war. I could not even begin to unravel the complications of Irish politics for them but at least I could let them know about the internment camp on the Curragh of Kildare, where most of the IRA had spent the war years acquiring a university education from some of their academic members, and where German and British airmen were better fed, the latter being discreetly released and allowed to slip across the Border into Northern Ireland and so to return to their units in Britain. For my part, I took away material for my writer's notebook when the discussion turned to the increasing number of black immigrants in Liverpool and in Britain generally. Chesterton's analysis received some support in their unanimous opinion that these people were an inferior species: 'You need only look at them,' one moustache said, 'and you can see that they're only just down from the trees.' They believed that they should all be shipped back to wherever they came from.

A club of a very different kind to which I was invited would have been closed down and its members shipped back to Hong Kong if that xenophobic gent in my landlord's club became a British Hitler. In my rambles around the city, I had come across a small Chinese restaurant in one of the poorer areas where a three-course meal, consisting of a liquid grandiosely called soup, rice with the usual Chinese add-itions, and a cup of tea, could be had for half-a-crown (two shillings and sixpence). As I was sending home whatever money I could spare – I had taken on a few private lessons in English with some of my more affluent foreign students in the night classes – I was really counting my pennies. I was also learning exactly what my fellow-writer, Luke the physician, meant when he said of the starving Prodigal Son that he would have liked to fill his belly with the pigs' food. I was sure of a breakfast every day, but the breakfast provided by the proprietors of a bed-and-breakfast establishment is worked out on a commercial basis of profit-and-loss. Sitting at the typewriter in my half-heated room on a November day, I tried not to think of food while I pulled my overcoat tighter around me and banged out more lines of dialogue in my play. Wandering around the city streets, I sometimes stood at the window of a confectioner's shop, of which there were many in Liverpool, and considered the items I would gorge myself on if I had the money; my preference was unwaveringly for some of those chocolate éclairs, of which concoctions I am a connoisseur.

On a day that stands out in my memory, I had subsisted from breakfast onwards on a bag of apples bought for a shilling in a street market. I was walking to my job at the college, absolutely penniless and hoping that my friends from the Yemen or some other eager students of 'de Valera and freedom' might invite me to coffee and a chat (and possibly a bun!) when I saw a limousine draw up outside an expensive restaurant. Out of it there came two couples, the women in furs, the men in evening dress, all of them grossly overweight. I could see the people at the tables inside. It struck me that these four fatties were going to pay exorbitant prices and consume piles of food that they did not need, while I would have been glad of the crumbs that fell from their table.

I became a fairly regular consumer of the half-crown three-course Chinese dinner; so much so that a middle-aged waiter began to chat to me one night when I was the only customer. We discovered that we were companions in distress, he having a wife and children in Hong Kong to whom he hoped to return some day when he would have saved enough to start a little business of his own. Once again I found my misery lessened by comparison when he envied me the fact that I was hoping to bring my wife and children to live in England. He pointed out to me then that the two younger waiters, also from Hong Kong, were having their own meal in a curtained-off alcove at the back, and he told me that if I came in at about that hour any night I could eat with him or them, free of charge, provided the boss was not around. That was an offer I could not refuse, although it ultimately had undesirable consequences for my digestive system. I got to know the three of them so well that the senior man asked me one night if I would like to go to their club. In doing so, he warned me not to get involved in gambling or card games there and lamented the folly of his two young colleagues who were already in debt to older gamblers and were also repaying the fare from Hong Kong to their employer.

The visit to the club proved on that account to be a quiet but pleasant evening for me, enjoying a mild beer with my friend and some older people, while the two younger waiters did some preliminary dancing with their friends in a small room before disappearing into what I assumed must by the den of iniquity where they would lose more money. That night is memorable in my writer's mind mostly because of a sentence uttered by one of those younger men. I had arrived at the closed restaurant at the time appointed. I was admitted by the older man, spruced up for his night out. One of the younger men joined us. As we waited for the other one, the older man looked at his watch and complained. 'Where is he?' he asked. 'He coming, he come quick now,' the young waiter explained with a meaningful grin. 'He bombing Tokyo.' I remember thinking later that the ex-RAF chaps in my landlord's club might have relished that image professionally, but for an Irishman it had even more significance, reminding me that the invincible secret weapon of any conquered race is satire.

My landlady was more interested in artistic matters than her placid and pleasant husband. She knew something of O'Casey's plays and was curious about my own writings. One night she asked me if I would like to see a French play, in translation, on the television. The ex-RAF man went off to bed, saying he had to travel to some other city early next morning. I enjoyed a very nice tea along with the play. And here is where I hear a voice that is not angelic suggesting that I could now give the reader three or four pages describing how the attractive landlady and the writer in exile enjoyed a bout of sex on the rug before the fire, the kind of stuff that helps to sell many books and films. I refer the Tempter to the passage from Hermann Hesse which I quoted among my forewords: 'Conscience provides us with an unerring standard. Consequently literary conscience is the only law that a writer must under all circumstances obey and cannot evade without injury to himself and his work.' After we had chatted about the play and other matters, I thanked my gracious landlady for a very pleasant evening, we said goodnight and I went up to my little room where I put on my overcoat, huddled near the small electric fire and wrote a few pages of notes.

I was called from my room one afternoon by the landlady, who told me that there was a phone call for me from America. I came down to the phone in the hall, to be astonished by the voice of my Salzburg friend, Professor Edwin Burr Pettet, calling from Boston. He had rung my home number in Limerick to tell me that he wanted to put on a production of *Romance of an Idiot* and when he learned about our situation from my wife he asked for my phone number in Liverpool. After giving me a brief telling off because I had gone on working in Ireland, where I was subject to the kind of treatment recently dished out to me by the clergy, instead of accepting his offer of a year in his drama department in Brandeis University, he said bluntly, 'I suppose you could do with some money right now?' I could not deny it. 'I'll send you a hundred pounds,' he said. I asked him to send it to my wife, and promised to repay it as soon as we got settled in a job in England. 'This is not a loan,' he said. Later, he sent a fee for the play and wrote to tell us that he had arranged a small monthly gift that would be of some assistance to us. It amounted to about ten pounds, which in the mid-Sixties represented a very significant addition to our resources, and it continued for some years until his own income was reduced on his retirement and he and his wife went to live in Mexico. He was the only person who ever gave me practical help during those troubled years. I later sent him the original script of *The Order of Melchizedek*, the play I was writing in that room in Liverpool on the day he phoned, and when the Irish version of the play, *Cóta Bán Chríost*, was published by Sáirséal agus Dill, I dedicated it to Edwin Burr Pettet of Brandeis University in Boston.

Meeting with or hearing about Irish emigrants less fortunate than myself in Liverpool and London gave me the material from which I made my first play for television. A Welsh policeman in Liverpool with whom I got into conversation one night asked me why we were allowing young people from Ireland to go to Britain without money or any prospect of a job. He pointed out to me the porch of a shop where a few nights previously he had found a young girl huddled and shivering. She was penniless and hungry, and was able to tell him only that she had come from Ireland the day before with another girl, who had gone off with a woman they met in a café. The policeman took her to an Irish agency from where she was sent back to Ireland. On my way back from the college one frosty night I was accosted by a prostitute in a faded fur coat who asked me if I would like a nice time. At that moment I would have liked very much a good feed of bacon and cabbage and spuds. I told the girl that she should look for some customer who had money. She asked me if I came from Wexford because I talked like a man from Wexford she had known once. She was Irish herself, she told me, from the Midlands, but she had come over a few years ago to her sister, who turned out to be in this business and led her into it.

In London in an Irish club I met a young man who told me that he had come from Ireland the year before with a friend. On the train from Holyhead to London, they were befriended by an Irishman who had lived for many years in London and who said he would get them work. He brought them to a pub where they were to meet the man who would give them jobs. They met him, with their guide and some others, in the yard of the pub where they were beaten and robbed. I wove these true stories into a television play called *The Lambs*. When it was shown on RTÉ in 1967, after a delay of three years, a priest who was doing the religious spot at night used it in one of his talks and suggested that a copy of the play should be sent to every school in Ireland, while a critic on the *Evening Press* named Maurice Kennedy dismissed the incidents of the plot as incredible – 'a string of middle-aged clichés', says he – and made sophisticated mockery of its theme of the innocents abroad.

In addition to material that I later worked into a television play, my dark days and nights in Liverpool provided me with some incidents that developed into short stories. I never got round to making the collection I planned, with the title I have used for this chapter, *Liverpool Blues*, but I wrote a few in Irish and English later on. One such was based on an altercation I witnessed one night as I walked along by the Mersey. I came across a hot gospeller bellowing anti-Catholic clichés to a small crowd while he waved the Bible as if he were Moses coming down from Mount Sinai with the Ten Commandments. He didn't wave it for long. Two Irishmen beside me began to shout at him and when he said something against Our Lady they rushed him. The fiery preacher would have followed his Bible into the river if the police had not come on the scene so quickly that I assumed they must have been watching from somewhere nearby. The Paddies were hauled away to cool off in a cell for the night.

Mention of that television critic named Kennedy reminds me of another member of that ancient clan which bears the name of the father of Brian Boru. Most people who were adult at the time remember exactly where they were on 22 November 1963, when the world was stunned by the news of the assassination of John F. Kennedy. I was in my room in Liverpool, typing words in my new play, when the landlord knocked on the door and told me. (To whom it may concern: the Belfast-born academic and writer, C. S. Lewis, died in Oxford on the same day. A topic for discussion: which of the two did the more good for humanity?)

Liverpool being the 'nearest parish to Dublin' on the east, as Boston is to Galway on the west, I was not surprised to find a strong Irish presence there but I was appalled to read in the museum the statistics of mortality among the Famine Irish who poured into the dockland cellars from the ships that many of them thought would be the first stage on their escape to a new life in America. An Irish priest helped to put me off looking for a permanent job in Liverpool when he asked me during an interview the professionally irrelevant question, 'Tell me now, are you a member of the Legion of Mary?' In my rambles one evening I came across a theatre where an amateur company of Irish people were putting on a play. After the show, I made myself known to them and was flattered to find that some of them had heard of me and one of them had seen my play in the Abbey a few years before. They brought me to the pub and showed me true Irish hospitality. I was a guest some time later in the home of two Dubliners among them, Una (née O'Keefe) and Denis Minto, to whom I was to be further indebted when, having resettled in Dublin years later, they maintained their interest in my work and put on professional productions of two of my plays.

25

COME BACK TO ERIN

I have often been asked, by believers and non-believers alike, why I did not give up the Catholic religion, if not belief in God altogether, when I was in exile in Liverpool as a result of the injustice inflicted on me and my family by the clergy – and there is more of the same to be chronicled. The blunt answer, eschewing false modesty, is that I consider myself to be an intelligent man. In the story of my growing up in Limerick, *There Is an Isle*, I have recorded how as an altar boy in St Mary's Convent of Mercy I was one day given a slap in the face by a priest and on another given a shilling by another priest to go to the 'pictures'. Thus I was given an early lesson in the fact that the truth of the Catholic religion does not depend on the behaviour of its ministers, from the Pope down to the ordinary priest. And as an adult, I had recently been given the further lesson through my experience in Bord Fáilte that it is not only a priest or a bishop who can inflict an injustice. Even if the unChristian actions of some clergymen were to be considered as a reason for giving up the Catholic faith, the truly Christian lives of so many priests should conversely be an argument for keeping the faith – all the more so since the good ones are so much more numerous than the others. Who but God alone knows the benefit to the human race of the life of even one good priest or nun?

Emotion, of course, can prejudice reason, as it did in the case of a friend of mine, now gone to God's mercy, who told me many years ago that he gave up the Catholic religion because a priest shouted at him at Confession. The shouting might have been a touch of hyperbole in the story, but from what he told me of the stuff he was pouring into the cocked ear of the confessor, who might have been sitting cramped in that cell of the confession box for several hours, I would have felt like giving him a telling off just as much as the priest. In more recent times, with the confessional in danger of being relegated to an item for a Dickensian old curiosity shop, the tendency for some Catholics is to adapt the doctrines of the faith to suit themselves or even to swap the dogmas of the faith for a vague but morally lenient spirituality of one kind or another, best described as spiritual cannabis.

While honestly acknowledging that I am intelligent, however, I humbly admit also that I am very far from being in the same class as St Thomas Aquinas, Dante, Descartes, St Teresa of Avila, John Henry Cardinal Newman – to name but a few, as they say – or the great doctors of the Church in the early centuries who disputed with the succession of heresies that sprang up like cockle in the wheat of the doctrines of Christianity. So, who am I to say that the likes of those brainboxes, as well as the countless millions of the ordinary faithful, from the first disciples who listened to and believed the words of Jesus Christ down to my own father and mother, are all wrong? I know that many people were praying for me during those times of trouble, and that God's grace and mercy helped me to think clearly after the first feelings of anger and revulsion had cooled down. I mentioned in an earlier chapter, when discussing my play, *The Light of the World*, about the blind man in St John's gospel, that incidents like that one convinced me, as a creative writer, that the gospels had not been concocted by creative writers like myself. Any competent writer or storyteller could invent 'miracle' stories, but although I believe in the miraculous cure of that blind man, it is in the behaviour and speech of the persons involved that I sense literal or historic truth to the extent that I say, 'This happened; it was not invented.' And so with many other incidents in the several histories of the life, death and resurrection of Jesus which we call the gospels or the Good News. In my situation, it was also relevant to consider that Jesus never ordered or forced anyone to believe, as is evident in the case of those disciples who left him because they found his prediction that he would give his body to be eaten by his followers to be 'too hard a saying'. He didn't call them back or shout threats after them, he simply asked the others if they also wanted to leave.

While my greatest loss during my time in Liverpool was the wife and children I had left behind in Limerick, solely as a writer I felt desolate without my books. I was pounding out plays, stories and articles on my typewriter but I was doing so in a small room without a single book. I stood looking into the windows of bookshops with a longing as intense as the hunger I felt when I looked into restaurants or the windows of those tantalising confectionery shops. One day I succumbed to temptation and spent money on a book that I should have sent home with the other few pounds. It was a paperback, a French *livre de poche*, but it was a paperback of the gospels. That was the only book I bought while I lived in Liverpool, and I believe it was put in my hands – or my pocket, being a *livre de poche* which I carried everywhere – by the Holy Spirit. Before I opened it, I read the three quotations on the back cover; respectively, they came from a philosopher, Jean-Jacques Rousseau, a novelist, François Mauriac, and a poet, Charles Péguy, and for a man whose library was a single book, the one in his hand, they could not have been more apt. I think they are worth recording here.

Rousseau: *Divin livre, le seul nécessaire à un chrétien et le plus utile de tous à quiconque même ne le serait pas.* (Divine book, the only one necessary for a Christian and the most useful of all even for those who are not.)

Mauriac: *'Voici la plus frémissante des grandes figures de l'Histoire . . . Cet ouvrier charpentier parle et agit en Dieu.* (Here is the most thrilling of the great figures of history . . . This workman carpenter speaks and acts as God.)

Péguy: *'La seule histoire intéressante qui soit jamais arrivée.* (The only interesting story that ever happened.)

It was in that book that I met a woman who convinced me yet once more that the Good News of the salvation of the human race is a true story. Her name was Salome and she was the wife of a man named Zebedee. Their sons were the apostles, James and John. The mother is listed among the women who helped to support Jesus and his disciples but she also caused trouble one day when she decided to put in a good word for her sons so that they would get big jobs in this kingdom she heard the Master talking about. This is how the apostle Matthew records it: 'Then the mother of the sons of Zebedee came up to him, with her sons, and kneeling before him she asked him for something. And he said to her, 'What do you want?' She said to him, 'Command that these two sons of mine may sit, one at your right hand and one at your left, in your kingdom.' But Jesus answered, 'You do not know what you are asking.' . . . And when the ten heard it, they were indignant at the two brothers.'

Whenever I read that story I am brought back to the house in which I grew up. I hear my philosophic father giving sound advice to one or other of us as we prepared to apply for a job or go for an interview and when his wisdom had exhausted itself on the topic, I hear my mother asking him, 'Do you know anybody with a bit of influence?' In Mrs Zebedee, as I called her in the poem I wrote later to thank her, I could see and hear my own mother and all mothers. And I could see in that story about her, and about the anger of the other apostles, one of the human incidents that I certainly would not concoct to put into a book about some holy man if a group of his disciples hired me to help them in spreading his teachings. Stories of miracles, of course, could be cooked up by any amoral writer or by deceived or deceptive disciples; but who would think of starting off the miracles with the holy man reluctantly taking a hint from his mother and turning water into wine so as to save a young married couple from embarrassment at their wedding feast?

Thanks to God's grace and to Mrs Zebedee, I was still a Catholic when I came home to Limerick for what we thought was to be our last Christmas in Ireland, at least for some years. We had decided that I would go back alone after the holidays, see to the installation of the furniture when it arrived and come back at a weekend to bring the family to our new home in what the priests used to describe as 'pagan England'. When I saw an advertisement in the paper one day for a job in a parochial school in Limerick city, I thought Santa Claus was about to bring us the ideal Christmas present. In spite of the fact that I had applied unsuccessfully for every position advertised during the previous nine months, I applied at once. I decided to ensure that the parish priest who was manager of the school would know the full and true story of my dismissal from the school in County Limerick and to assure him that there were many people, including the Capuchins in Dublin and the audiences who had seen the play in Belfast, Dublin and Limerick, who would not agree with the reverend manager in Pallasgrean or with Ernest Blythe and company in the Abbey Theatre, in judging *Romance of an Idiot* to be an immoral play. I made an appointment to see the priest in charge of the parish where we were living, who was none other than the cultured Monsignor Molony, a man with the reputation of being interested in art and archaeology and music, and a man whose path of life had crossed mine in four ways already. I had served Mass for him a few times in St Mary's Convent when he was secretary to the Bishop of Limerick, he had caused my poem on his Limerick Holy Year Exhibition to be published in the local paper, he had officiated at my marriage and during my Bord Fáilte days a few years earlier I had delivered an eccentric professor of music to his house.

That house was only a short walk from our own. He received me graciously and listened to my story. I pointed out that we were on the point of selling our house and moving to a job in England, but that this job could be the miracle that would keep me and my family living in Ireland. I stressed that I was not asking for anything but that my application be considered on its merits; however, because of the fact that my dismissal by the Archbishop of Cashel seemed to have blacklisted me, I was asking him, as my parish priest, merely to tell this other parish priest that he knew me personally and that I was not an immoral writer who might be a danger to the pupils. When I had stated my case, the monsignor asked me no questions. He merely said, 'Excuse me a moment,' and left the room. The moment turned into more than ten minutes. When he returned, he was as laconic as before he left. 'I think, Mr O'Flynn,' he said, 'that you should take that position in England. I can see that a man of your talents would do very well there.' And that was that. The cultured monsignor never told me what he had done when he went out of the room but I assumed that he had not gone to wash his hands, unless perhaps with the same brand of soap used by Pontius Pilate on a day in Jerusalem long ago.

A few days later I got a brief note from the other parish priest telling me, with regret of course, that the position had been filled. I lit a fire in the back garden that evening and burned any books and notebooks that could be dispensed with, including all my academic notes from all the courses I had ever done and my Irish notes from the six-month period I had spent in Dún Chaoin. The older children helped me and thought it great fun. They were looking forward to going on a big ship and going to live in another place where everything would be lovely. Children don't seem to mind how often they are told fairy tales. When we sold the house after Christmas and left Limerick, they were probably disappointed that we never went on that big ship after all. But we got near enough to it. In fact, we travelled only as far as Dún Laoghaire, from where the ship leaves to cross the Irish Sea to Britain.

Apparently, the Holy Spirit had not taken any notice of the black list, if it existed, or of the opinions of the reverend school managers of Ireland. I was reading the paper on the train from Limerick to Dublin, heading back to England as arranged, and having edified my spirit and enlightened my mind with all that was happening in politics, sport, business, society and even religion, in the Island of Saints and Scholars from which I was being exiled as superfluous to the requirements in any of those areas, by force of habit I began to read the *Teachers* column in the small ads. I noticed two advertisements urgently inviting applications for a position in each of two schools in County Dublin. I shrugged them off as more of the same until I was on the bus from Kingsbridge Station into the city where I would get a train to Dún Laoghaire. I had some hours to spare and I was dragging my case down O'Connell Street when I felt as if a voice were telling me to apply for those two jobs.

Not being equipped with my typewriter and stationery, I went into the GPO and bought two letter-cards and wrote what must have been the briefest applications I had ever made for any job. Coming out of the GPO it occurred to me that I must now be in the condition described by coroners as 'while the balance of the mind was disturbed'. What in

God's name, I thought, would the respective managers, whoever they were, think of an application scribbled on a letter-card, with a Limerick address and phone number and posted in Dublin? And, as I was supposed to start teaching in a secondary school in England in a few days' time, what was I to do if one or both of those managers was so desperate to find a teacher that he actually asked me to come for an interview? Problems like this are a source of confusion, even despair, for the human spirit; they present no trouble at all to the Holy Spirit.

I walked out of the GPO and almost, but not quite, bumped into a man who had also come out of the same building but from the top floor where the radio studios of RTÉ were still located. (They stayed until 1975, when they moved to the new building beside the television studios in Donnybrook). He was a fellow writer named Conor Farrington, who earned a crust as an actor with the RTÉ company. I had come to know him, along with the English actress, Meryl Gourley – they met as students in Trinity – whom he had since married, in 1955 when I attended those public lectures on drama in Trinity College given by Arnold Sundgaard from New York. Conor had some family connection with a playwright more famous than either of us was ever to become, John Millington Synge. He was also one of the three successful applicants who had been awarded an exchange scholarship in those years in the Fifties when I collected my three-in-a-row letters of regret after jousting across the interview table with the great mind of the renowned Monsignor Pádraig de Brún of UCG.

Observing my luggage, Conor enquired about my destination and purpose. I told him what I had just done in the historic building where Connolly and Pearse had raised the flag over the Irish Republic which would guarantee 'equal rights and equal opportunities to all her children.' When I explained my dilemma, whether to go on the ship or hang around, 'hoping against hope' as the paradoxical phrase puts it, Conor, not being a parish priest or an archbishop but a plain Dublin Protestant, insisted that I stay with his wife and himself until I got a reply, one way or the other, from those two ads. Their house was a big house that had once been the county home of some rich landowner or business-man but was now in the suburb of Milltown just across the road from the Jesuits' buildings and from the Shamrock Rovers football grounds at the time. When I looked out of my bedroom window that night, across at the lights in the Jesuits' house, I thought of one member of the community there, Seosamh Ó Muirthile, SJ, the learned editor who, only a few months previously, had 'put on his hat' and gone to put in an unavailing good word for me with a parish priest in Phibsboro. He was one of those good priests whose dedicated lives were a counterbalance that helped me to keep the faith, and I felt sure that if I had arrived at their door across the road, he would have have given me bed and board for a few days just as my good friends, Conor and Meryl, were doing.

I phoned my wife to tell her of the alteration in my plans. Unless the girl writes a book herself, only God can tell what further worry I was causing her as she tried to feed the children (a process which, as all mothers will know, often involved not eating enough herself in those dark days). The next morning, the superior of the Christian Brothers School in Dún Laoghaire phoned me at the Farrington house – he had rung my wife on receipt of my letter-card – and asked me to come and see him. When I did, he turned out to be a man I had met before. His name was McKenna and he was one of that legion of patriotic and dedicated religious teachers, nuns and brothers, who gave their lives, day by day and year by year, in the cause of really trying, through free education, to provide 'equal rights and equal opportun-ities' for the children of the common people of Ireland. I told him my story and my situation. His comments on parish priests and archbishops in general and on those responsible for my problems in particular, were those of a man who must have tangled with and suffered from the dictatorial Irish clergy in his own professional capacity. It is a matter of relevant historical fact that the Irish Christian Brothers, founded by the widower merchant from Waterford, Blessed Edmund Ignatius Rice, in 1802, antagonised the Irish hierarchy early on by refusing to allow the bishops to exercise diocesan control over them as they did over other such religious congregations, and even had the audacity to fight and win their case in Rome.

'I interviewed you in Limerick in 1952,' Brother McKenna told me, 'when you applied for a job in Naas where I was in charge at the time, but you had just been offered a job in the training school in Dublin. I wanted you then and I want you now if you'd like to take the job in Dún Laoghaire.' *If I'd like to* . . . I didn't know whether to laugh or to cry. When I phoned my wife with this next alteration in our plans, she cried with shock and relief.

As usual, of course, there was a small snag. The teacher I was replacing was leaving to take up a job as principal of a school in his native parish down the country somewhere but the change would not occur for a few weeks. That delay was the cause of a peculiar aspect of the whole business. I eventually began work in the school in Eblana Avenue, Dún Laoghaire, on 11 February, which happens to be the day dedicated by the Church as the feast day of Our Lady of Lourdes. It was on that date, in 1858, that the fourteen-year-old Bernadette Soubirous first saw Our Lady in the grotto at Massabielle. A few days later, I received a postcard from Lourdes. It was from an old teacher of mine who knew of my troubles. It was dated 11 February. He told me that he was on pilgrimage in Lourdes and had prayed for me at the grotto that day. And who am I to make any comment on such things except what Hamlet said to his friend, Horatio: 'There are more things in heaven and earth, Horatio, than are dreamt of in your philosophy.'

We sold our house in Limerick, rented a house in Mount

Merrion for six months, and then in August 1964 moved into a new semi-detached house in Glenageary, two miles up towards the summit of Killiney Hill from the seaport town of Dún Laoghaire. With our furniture we brought accumulated debts and the emotional scars of what we had gone through in recent years. But I had a job in Ireland, we had a roof over our heads – the same roof is over me now as I write these words – and we had survived. As soon as I could get my Underwood Portable set up, I had to get down to writing the hack-work that would help to diminish the debts, as well as that other stuff called literature that sometimes is a total waste of time, energy and talent, and more often than not fails to put bread on the table. With that dual pressure on me, and perhaps as a reaction against the frustrations of the past few years, I was commencing what would turn out to be the most productive period of my life as a writer.

26

WHY DEV LAUGHED

Before I tell why, there are a few other stories to tell and some matters to be tidied up. While my wife and I were thanking Our Lady of Lourdes for using what my mother would call 'a bit of influence' in getting me a job in Ireland just as we had finally given up hope, there was a decent man, the headmaster of a secondary school near London, who was expecting me to join his staff in a few days' time, with the family following soon after to take up residence in the modern semi-detached provided by the school board as an incentive. And in an international college for girls in Dar Es Salaam there was a German nun who had told me in her letter how she and the other sisters were looking forward to welcoming us in September. I had already been less than truthful with the board of management of the school in England, who believed my story at the interview that I wished to make a career in education in the British system which had more opportunities for advancement than the Irish one in which the Church and religious orders controlled most of the schools. Their only concern at the interview had been that as a Catholic I might not wish to attend the school assembly each morning at which prayers were said, which made me wonder what exactly the average English non-Catholic knew about the Catholic religion. I wondered now, as I wrote a vague explanation about family problems, etc. preventing me from taking up the job, whether my defection would cause them to distrust any other Catholic applying for a job. When I got no reply, I felt responsible for having queered the pitch for any future applicant with a *brogue*, of whatever quality.

With regard to the nun in Dar Es Salaam, current events in Africa provided me with a credible reason for a *volte-face* that might otherwise have seemed both inexplicable and inexcusable in a man who had seemed so eager to bring his wife and children to share his new experiences in a completely different environment. On the island of Zanzibar, just off the coast near Dar Es Salaam, some political unrest had just resulted in a rebellion and there were fears that the trouble would spread to the mainland. The nun replied sympathetically to the letter in which I expressed paternal fears for the safety of our children, although she herself regarded the Zanzibar conflict as unlikely to continue. She wished us God's blessing and stressed that she would be very glad to offer me a position in her school at any time in the future.

One of the first visitors to our new and only partly furnished house near Dún Laoghaire was the man who had made a transatlantic phone call to Liverpool and given me a telling-off and a hundred pounds, none other than Professor Pettet from Boston. He and his wife were on their way to Warsaw, where he had been invited to do a six-month stint, and they stopped off for a few days in Dublin to visit us. He renewed his offer of a year in Brandeis University drama department, after which, he said, I could be given a permanent appointment there or easily find one in some other university in the US. But we were so glad to be settling down once more and for the children to have the prospect of some stability and continuity in their lives that we had no wish to go on our travels again. And my experiences in England had convinced me that the alternative of going to the US on my own, even for part of the year, was not one that I even wished to consider no matter what bag of dollars might be dangled before us as a rapid solution to our financial problems.

The good friend I had made in Salzburg showed me, during that visit, a side of him that I had not seen before and that illustrated the truth of the Irish proverb, *Ní bhíonn saoi gan locht* (There is no sage without fault). They invited us to dinner in one of Dublin's most expensive hotels. Apart from the dinners I had suffered through while entertaining guests of Bord Fáilte, this was not the sort of ambience with which my wife and I had any familiarity; also, the dining-room reminded me of the kind of place at which I had gazed from the street, with feelings of anger and envy, during my hungry nights in Liverpool. Whatever enjoyment we got out of the fancy grub and the pleasant company was finally spoilt when our host questioned the bill, checked each item, argued with the waiter and counted his change, as if he suspected he was being taken for yet another innocent Yank to be codded. Maybe some experiences during previous visits to Dublin had developed this attitude in a man who had proved, and would continue to prove, generous and philanthropic in our regard – I learned later that he had also helped some writers in the US – but it made me think that the rich are the people who like to account strictly for every penny, while the common man will be more concerned with enjoying his grub or his pint than with counting his change.

About a year after Our Lady had countermanded the order of the crozier that hooshed me out of the Island of Saints and Scholars as an immoral writer, I was watching the television one night 'in the bosom of my family' as the time-honoured phrase puts it. I saw the Archbishop of Cashel and I heard him speak eloquently about Catholic social justice. I went straight to my typewriter and wrote him a letter of five pages, reminding him of how much social justice, Catholic or any other kind, he himself had shown to me and my wife and family when he countersigned that letter of dismissal from the parish priest of Pallasgrean. I pointed out to him that in my view of Catholic social justice, he was responsible for the fact that I had been unable to find a job as a teacher in Ireland for nine months. I reminded him that if I went to Confession to him and told him that I had caused someone to suffer financial or other loss, he would not give me absolution unless I made restitution. And so I claimed financial recompense from him for my lost salary. I asked him to make a Christian assessment himself of what he would add on for the suffering he had caused to my wife and children. I got no reply.

I had come home from Liverpool with an item in my luggage that I considered of great potential significance in my life as a writer but that nobody else knew about so far. This was the play I wrote in ten days in my little half-heated upper room. But if I got that first version down on paper in ten days, that was only the end of a process of creation that had begun about ten years before. It began, unknown to me – as Henry James points out, the significant incident which is the seed of the story usually occurs without the creative awareness of the writer – in the house of that courteous and gentle old widow, Mary Martin (Bean de hÓra) about whom I have written in the chapter recording my six-month sojourn in Dún Chaoin on the Dingle peninsula. I was sitting with her one day by the turf fire in her house when some visitors arrived in a car. One of them was a newly-ordained priest who was being brought around by his family to visit all their friends. The blessing of a new priest was highly regarded in Catholic Ireland and when he had blessed the old lady, her middle-aged son and daughter, and me ('the writer from Dublin'), the woman of the house uttered an old Irish benediction on the priest himself. *'Go maire tú, a athair,'* she said, *'i gcóta bán Chríost.'* (Long life to you, Father, in the white coat of Christ.) There is also, of course, a phrase referring to the life of a priest or religious as the *white martyrdom*, as opposed to the brief and brutal *red* martyrdom of suffering death because of loyalty to the faith of Christ. The Irish expression seemed to me to refer especially to the priestly sacrifice of celibacy.

Some years later, when I raised my eyes from reading a book in a train and saw a priest reading a book some distance away in the compartment, I began to think about the unique place and function of a priest in human society. The priest claims to be the middleman between God and the rest of us. If there is a God, therefore, and if we are destined to go from this world to eternity, the priest is the most important person in the tribe; if there is no God and if we are merely rational animals, the priest is either a fool or a knave. Recalling the blessing with which the old woman had recompensed the young priest for his laying on of his consecrated hands, I began to consider that whether God exists or not, whether the priest is a divinely appointed middleman, maybe a saint, or a fool, or even a conman, the sacrifice of celibacy made by a Catholic priest is heroic in human terms. It is also a testimony to his faith in God and in his vocation, and it is evidence to the rest of the tribe that this man, whatever his faults or personal idiosyncrasies, is willing to give up not only the ephemeral physical pleasure associated with procreation but the deeper and more fulfilling experience of love and paternity in order to devote his whole life, day by day, to the spiritual welfare of the common mob. Without that daily 'white martyrdom' of celibacy, it seemed to me that the job of a priest, whether God exists or not, would be a cushy number not requiring much talent, albeit not as materially lucrative as some other more stressful professions and occupations.

From time to time, amid other bits of writing and the strains of the daily grind, I began to build up a story involving not only a priest but priesthood in the sense of that symbolic and inspirational personal sacrifice of celibacy. It was shaping up as a novel in Irish – I was long enough writing in the two languages now to be almost unaware of which one was the literary vehicle for the themes bubbling up in my mind – but by degrees it was being taken over by the two principal characters, a priest and a young woman, and they were talking so vividly in my imagination that they were turning it into a play. I had written some rough versions of chapters of the novel, as well as scenes of the play, in Irish and English, before circumstances exiled me to Liverpool. I thought at that stage that I would never write in Irish again. I wrote the first version of the full play in English in ten days, as I have already recorded. And now that I was back in Ireland and licensed by the muses to write again in my two languages, I finished out the Irish version I had begun some years before. I hope to give a full and true account of the controversies caused by both *The Order of Melchizedek* and *Cóta Bán Chríost*, as well as the consequences for the poor afflicted scribbler who wrote them, in the next volume of this trilogy.

The year 1966 was a significant one for Ireland as a nation and for me as a writer. It was the golden jubilee year of the Easter Rising, and the national commemorations were the last of their kind to be held. A few years later, the outbreak of the new and increasingly savage troubles in Northern Ireland resulted in a reluctance on the part of the Dublin government to do anything that might be seen as pouring oil on the flames; not only were commemorative military parades abolished but even the patriotic ballads we were taught in school were banned on RTÉ. In the next decade, the revisionists began to provide a new interpretation of the history of Ireland which almost made patriotism a fault rather than an essential virtue of the citizen. And with a timing that appeared significant, from publishers in London there came a biography of Padraig Pearse by Ruth Dudley Edwards, and a new book on Roger Casement by Brian Inglis, both of which brought those two national heroes down a peg or two.

The 1966 commemorations extended also to the world of the arts. The government sponsored literary and artistic competitions, and when I opened a letter one day in which I was officially informed that I had won the competition for a short story in Irish and would be presented with a cheque for two hundred pounds by George Colley, Minister for Education, at a a prize-giving ceremony on the day appointed, I knelt on the floor in the kitchen and thanked God as if I had just been given a ticket for heaven. I earned some more debt-clearing lolly when I broadcast the story on RTÉ and a few pounds more again when it was published two years later as the title story of a collection of my short stories in Irish.

In the Oireachtas competitions of that year, I won the prize for a long poem in Irish with an extended version of the poem with which I had won my first literary competition back in 1952 through Mainchín Seoighe and the *Limerick Leader*. I also won the regular competition for a one-act historical tragedy. This play, *Is Fada Anocht*, so impressed the adjudicators that the Oireachtas committee wrote to me and told me that they would request the Abbey Theatre to stage it during the week of the Oireachtas festival. Sadly, and inexplicably, it was rejected by the Abbey.

The long poem, entitled *Éirí Amach na Cásca 1916* was published by Sáirséal agus Dill (it was their one hundredth book) in a very attractive format with a cover by Anne Yeats. I dedicated it to the man who more than any other teacher had guided me to a thorough knowledge of Irish and an appreciation of the central place of our language in our national cultural heritage. He grew up in Limerick as Augustine Malone – his family owned a public house in Patrick Street – and in the fateful year of 1916 he entered the Irish Christian Brothers, so that his personal golden jubilee in the religious life in 1966 coincided with that of the Easter Rising. In his lifelong work for the Irish language he was known as An Bráthar A.S. Ó Maoileoin. I invited him to accompany me when I went to Áras an Uachtaráin to present a copy of the book to President Éamon de Valera, who was ranked with Pearse and Connolly and Terence McSwiney in his pantheon of national heroes.

We spent an hour with Dev and I was amazed at the earnestness with which he spoke to us about the Rising and other matters as if we were the only people with whom he had ever held such a discussion. He asked me to sign the book for him and when I was found to be a writer without a pen he said, *'Tá go leor acu anseo'* (There's plenty of them here), reached out to the fancy pen-holder on his desk and provided me with one. It was during that chat that I told him about the lads from the Yemen who wanted to talk to me about 'de Valera and freedom'. He laughed at that, as I have narrated, but that was a laugh in the privacy of his presidential study. The laugh I want to tell about later was more public, and it is captured for posterity in the *Irish Times* photograph on the cover of this book. During our talk I told Dev about my wife's comment on my prizewinning poem, which was to the effect that I should now write another poem about the women of 1916, not only those who had taken an active part as members of Cumann na mBan but the wives, like de Valera's own wife, who had been as heroic as the men who went out to fight, knowing as they said goodbye that a life of hardship would be the consequence for them and for their children if their husbands did not survive. As we were leaving the room, Dev called me back and said, *'Abair le do bhean go bhfuil an ceart aici mar gheall ar an dán.'* (Tell your wife she's right about the poem.)

The year 1966 was also memorable in the history of theatre in Ireland because of the opening of the new Abbey Theatre on the site of the old one which had burnt down in 1951. For the delayed opening of the small Peacock Theatre downstairs, the board of directors decided to organize a competition for a new play in Irish. Apart from the cash prize on offer (three hundred pounds was a lot of money in 1966) the prestige connected with such an event would be a feather in the cap of any writer. I decided that in addition to the cash and the prestige, the competition would give me an opportunity to show Ernest Blythe and his fellow-directors once and for all that I was a talented playwright – they kept telling me so while rejecting my plays.

I entered not just one but three plays, *Is É Dúirt Polonius* (the play based on my Bord Fáilte experience), *Cóta Bán Chríost* (the Irish version of the play about a priest, which the Abbey had already rejected in English) and an experimental play, *Cad D'imigh ar Fheidhlime?* based on the Irish saga, *Táin Bó Cuailgne*. I also entered *Cóta Bán Chríost* for the annual Oireachtas literary competitions, where a prize of two hundred pounds was on offer for a new play in Irish. When it won that prize – one of the two adjudicators was the Galway playwright and novelist, Walter Macken, who acclaimed the play as a masterpiece and expressed the desire to play the role of the priest himself in an Abbey production – I wrote and told Mr Blythe, expecting that the play would now be ineligible for the Peacock prize. He replied in cordial terms and assured me that winning the Oireachtas prize would not disqualify *Cóta Bán Chríost* from being considered with my other entries. I need not have worried. The verdict of the Abbey on all the new Irish plays entered for the Peacock opening was that none of them merited the prize. I have always regarded this non-result in any literary competition to be immoral. The setting up of any competition, be it a horse race or a beauty contest or a whistling competition, implies that the prize is to be awarded to the best entry in the opinion of the judges, not to an entry which reaches some imaginary and undefinable standard in the minds of those judges.

The Abbey bosses selected two plays to which they awarded what is insultingly termed a 'consolation' prize of seventy pounds and a production contract. One of these was my play about Bord Fáilte, *Is É Dúirt Polonius*, the other a play by Máiréad Ní Ghráda, author of the very successful *An Triail* to which I have referred in a previous chapter.

Neither play, however, was considered good enough to be the first production in the new Peacock. The work to which this honour was awarded was not a new play in Irish but an adaptation of Myles na Gopaleen's only Irish novel, *An Béal Bocht* (later published in English as *The Poor Mouth*), a satire in which he ridiculed the attitude of the natives of the Gaeltacht in expecting subsidies and handouts. I have chronicled my own experience of that attitude while living in Dún Chaoin but in doing so I indicated the historical and social reasons for it. That the board of directors of the Abbey Theatre should consider an adaptation of Myles's depiction of the 'native speakers' of Irish in those unproductive Gaeltacht areas on the western seaboard to be suitable for the prestigious opening of the new Peacock Theatre seemed to me to be a bad omen both for the art of theatre and for the Irish language. The two plays to which the Abbey Board had given the peculiar sum of seventy pounds each, thus saving more than half of the three hundred pound prize, were produced in the Peacock in the following year without much publicity and without earning their respective authors, Máiréad Ní Ghráda and myself, money or prestige.

That decade of the Sixties was the most productive in the century so far as drama in Irish was concerned. Future bilingual historians of theatre in Ireland will probably describe it as the golden age of Irish language drama. In addition to the Peacock and the permanent Irish language theatre in Galway, An Taibhdhearc, plays were put on in the Damer Hall, situated in the basement of the Unitarian Church in St Stephen's Green, by Gael Linn, the Irish language organization which ran a weekly football pool and used the proceeds to promote cultural activities in Irish and industrial ventures in the Gaeltacht areas. At the Damer, plays by Máiréad Ní Ghráda, Eoghan Ó Tuairisc, Diarmaid Ó Súilleabháin, Pádraig Ó Giollagáin, Seán Ó Tuama and myself were directed with great insight and enthusiasm by Noel Ó Briain of RTÉ and Frank Dermody of the Abbey.

Thus it happened that three of my plays in Irish were running at the same time in 1968, with *Is É Dúirt Polonius* in the Peacock, *Cóta Bán Chríost* in Galway and *Aggiornamento* in the Damer Hall. If any playwright in English had scored this artistic hat-trick, critics and commentators in the media would have been hailing him as a second Shakespeare.

I had entered *Aggiornamento*, a comic satire about the effects of the Second Vatican Council on a small town in Ireland, for the annual Oireachtas competition, where, just as in the Peacock competition, the prize was not awarded. The adjudicator, none other than Tomás Mac Anna of the Abbey, dismissed my effort as possibly having the makings of a one-act play (some years later, as artistic director of the Abbey, he rejected an English version of the play). It turned out to be one of the most successful Irish plays ever, filling the Damer Hall for six weeks, which would be the equivalent of an English play filling the Abbey for six months. It was produced with equal success later in An Taibhdhearc in Galway and by the Everyman Theatre in Cork, and I wrote an English version for television which was shown on RTÉ with the film actor, Liam Redmond, in the leading role. And like my other plays in Irish, there is no mention of it or of its author – no more than of those other playwrights and their works – in any book in English about the history of theatre in Ireland.

I wrote two other plays for television in that four-year period from 1964 to 1968, during which I also wrote a novel in Irish in a month, a one-act play in English in a day, short stories, articles and poems, and God only knows how many stories, plays and talks for radio. Looking back in old age at his years of literary fertility, Swift remarked about *A Tale of a Tub*, 'Good God! What a genius I had when I wrote that book.' As I consider those four years between one belt of a crozier and the next – I'm not letting the cat out of the bag fully, but you can hear it screeching – I feel a delayed-action exhaustion at the thought of the creative energy I poured into all that writing, while changing into my other persona every morning to deliver myself and my two eldest sons at the Christian Brothers' primary school in Dún Laoghaire. There I had to switch off my mind from whatever opus I was working on and become what my pupils saw as the man with the piece of chalk in his hand who was teaching them to read and write. And lest it be thought by any cynic that I did not conscientiously earn my wages in the chalk mines in that period, I must record an event that occurred about ten years later.

I happened to be present one night at a boxing tournament in a hall in Dalkey, to which I had been brought by my friend and boyhood schoolmate, Eamonn Gilligan, a staff photographer with the *Irish Independent*, who was taking action shots of the bouts between young boxers from Scotland and Ireland. The spectators were seated on tiered wooden benches and in one of the calms between the stormy sessions of pugilistic activity, I got a tap on the shoulder and turned to find a young man in his twenties grinning at me and saying, 'Howya, Mr Flynn?' I told him I was fine but he knew by my expression that I was at a loss. 'D'you remember me? I'm (*name*) – you were teachin' me in Dunleary.'

'Ah, yes, I remember you now,' as we all say, 'but of course you were only a little fellow of about ten at that time.' And then he points to his companions, 'D'you remember these fellas? They were all in my class too.' There were five or six of them along the bench behind me, all about his own age and all showing signs of having visited some hostelry in Dalkey before coming on to the boxing tournament. And one by one they called out, the tone rising as the distance increased, 'Howya, Mr Flynn! D'you'member me, (*name*)?' And I responded dutifully, 'Ah, hello (*name*), glad to meet you again.' By the time it got to the last of the Mohicans out at the end of the bench, the audience were all enjoying this little interlude as light relief while the ring was empty. And from the last of my batch of Dún Laoghaire past pupils came the encomium that meant more to me than any inspector's report or approval from a reverend manager or even a bishop. Having identified himself, he shouted for all to hear, 'Mr Flynn, you're the best fuckin' teacher we ever had!' It brought a general round of applause – and why not!

Two literary editors at that time helped to give me the fulfilment of acceptance and publication that is of more importance to the creative writer than the financial rewards which can often be far too little for work of genuine literary quality and sometimes grossly too much for the pulp fiction that is churned out like sausages from a machine by its practitioners. Eoghan Ó hAnluain of UCD published some of my new short stories and poems in *Comhar*, the academic literary magazine whose editor in 1951 had not bothered even to recognize the existence of that 'young Limerick writer' who tentatively submitted some of his first efforts. One of the stories, *Oileán Tearmainn*, I developed later as a television play which won the RTÉ prize in the Oireachtas competitions and was entered for the Prix Italia, an unusual honour for a play in Irish. It also won two of the annual radio and television awards sponsored by Jacobs Biscuits. The prizes were presented by a government minister at a banquet hosted by Jacobs and attended by over six hundred guests, not including the author of the dual prizewinning play who was not invited. I had occasion to remark in an article some time later that they didn't even send me a Coconut Cream.

In the government's own Irish language publishing section in the Department of Education, An Gúm, from whose anonymous editors and civil service bureaucrats I had suffered much in former years, a new literary editor, Éamonn Ó hÓgáin, a brilliant scholar of Irish who, like myself, was a Limerickman and therefore not a 'native speaker' of Irish from the moment he was born, surprised me by the enthusiastic interest and appreciation with which he accepted a collection of short stories, *Oineachlann*, two of the three plays which I had entered in the Peacock competition, *Is É Dúirt Polonius* and *Cad D'imigh ar Fheidhlime?* (the third play, *Cóta Bán Chríost*, was published by Sáirséal agus Dill) and also the very successful *Aggiornamento*. Subsequently, all these plays were on the syllabus of Irish language degree courses in several universities and went into further editions. But the bureaucrats of the Department of Education who had control of An Gúm, and with whom I had crossed pens on many occasions, deprived me of any royalties I might have received from the sale of the plays in book form. When I objected that the contracts they gave me made no provision for the payment of royalties, I got a brief reply to the effect that by publishing my plays they were making them available for amateur companies from whom I would receive production fees. While it was true that English plays by writers like John B. Keane, Brian Friel and Hugh Leonard, all contemporaries of mine, were frequently performed by amateur groups, the performance of plays in Irish by any groups associated with the Gaelic League or other Irish organizations was likely to occur as often as a blue moon, a fact of which those bureaucrats were well aware. While I gained the fulfilment of literary creation and that inexplicable feeling of ethnic cultural inheritance from writing those plays in Irish, my total financial reward from performances and publication was probably not much more than a competent busker in Dublin's Grafton Street would earn in a few weeks.

Perhaps because of the success of my Irish plays on stage and on television in that year, I was invited by the Gaelic League's Oireachtas committee to open the Oireachtas Drama Festival in 1968, the venue for which was the Peacock Theatre. That was the night when Dev laughed in public, and it is with this long-promised story that I end this first volume of the story of my life as a writer. I was asked to speak for about half an hour before the production of the first play in the competition (there would be one each night), my topic being drama in Irish in the general context of our national culture, and I was told that the guests of honour would be the President and Bean de Valera. This was the lady who, in the early years of the century and of Sinn Féin, as a young Irish teacher named Sinéad Ní Fhlannagáin, had conducted a Gaelic League evening class in Irish in which Éamon de Valera and Ernest Blythe and others had been her admiring pupils (Blythe tells in his autobiography how all the young men competed to try to see her home and how she diplomatically allowed several at a time to accompany her – 'but however he managed it,' said Blythe, still with a nostalgic touch of envy, 'the Long Fellow got her in the end'). In the event, Bean de Valera was not well enough to attend but the 'Long Fellow' himself, still hale and hearty but now seeing things only 'as through a glass darkly' was there in the box at the side of the intimate Peacock Theatre, while Ernest Blythe sat grinning up at me from the front row, with his fellow-directors beside him.

When I finished speaking, there was an interval while the table and the committee were being cleared off the stage to prepare for the play. I rejoined my wife in the auditorium, but the secretary of the Oireachtas came rushing after me to tell me that 'An tUachtarán' would like to meet me. We went out to the bar where Dev was seated with the honorary president of the Oireachtas for that year, Máirín Ní Mhuiríosa, a lady who had encouraged me to continue writing in Irish when other people seemed set on forcing me to write in English only. While the general mob enjoyed a jar or other refreshment, we three got down to a chat. Éamon de Valera first recalled our meeting two years before at Áras an Uachtaráin and thanked me again for my poem about the Easter Rising of 1916. Then he asked me what I thought of the present state of the Irish language.

Meanwhile the press photographers snapped away, standing or going on one knee as if in homage to the President. Having grown up in County Limerick, Dev was no more a 'native speaker' of Irish than myself or the aforementioned scholarly literary editor in An Gúm, and he was interested to know how I had arrived at the ability to write plays and novels in Irish. When I mentioned that in my early days as a writer I had decided to work my way methodically through Dineen's dictionary but had never gone very far up that Everest of lexicography, Dev said that in his Gaelic League days he had begun to do the very same thing and also had not got very far because of the pressure of politics. We all agreed that Dineen's is an extraordinary conglomeration but I observed that there were many words and phrases in it that would be of use today instead of some of the artificial terms being concocted. It was the era of the miniskirt, and when I gave this as an example, explaining that the ersatz term in current use was *mini-sciorta*, whereas, I said, Dineen has *'sciorta giortach* (a short skirt). It was then that Dev gave a hearty laugh, a moment captured by *The Irish Times* photographer. When my wife and I happened to be in Limerick soon after, her uncle, the late Jack Beegan, who was a staunch supporter of Dev, asked me to explain to him what it was I said that had caused Dev to laugh, 'because that man always looks so serious,' he said, 'I don't think I ever saw a picture of him laughing in public before.' And Jack Beegan enjoyed the story so much that he made me repeat 'that story about Dev and the mini-skirt' when we met again a year later.

And so that decade of the Sixties in the twentieth century – a decade noted in the history of the human race for the apocalyptic war in Vietnam and the building of the Berlin Wall that symbolised the Cold War in Europe, for the Second Vatican Council of the Catholic Church and for the first manned space flights by Yuri Gagarin of Russia followed by John Glenn of the US, a decade noted also for the rise to showbusiness fame of four Liverpool lads called the Beatles and for anarchic student protests in universities throughout the world – proved to be an anomalous period in my life, comprising years of trouble and personal turbulence as well as years of prolific literary creativity, in Irish and English, in all genres of literature. But I was sadly mistaken if I thought that my troubles as a writer were over on that day in February 1964 when I began to teach Class 3C (there were A, B, C, streams at each grade) in the Christian Brothers Primary School in Dún Laoghaire. Every schoolday, from the window of my classroom I could see the ship waiting to leave with another contingent of emigrants to Britain, and its siren seemed to be warning me to watch my step. Above me on Killiney Hill that rises up from the town an eagle guardian of the public morals, John Charles McQuaid, watched over the archdiocese of Dublin. And while I worked in the chalk mines by day to support my family (now increased to six, three of each, by the birth of another daughter) and by night or at weekends chained to the typewriter striving to create literature, the clouds were gathering for another thunderstorm that would threaten our resettled family life.

But now I must put myself modestly on a par with the great Dante Alighieri as he got to the end of *Purgatorio*, the second section of his epic *Divina Commedia*, and addressed the reader as follows:

> *Ma perché piene son tutte le carte*
> *ordite a questa cantica seconda,*
> *non mi lascia piu ir lo fren dell'arte.*

(But because the pages allocated to this second cantica are full, the restraint of art does not allow me to go further.)

To be continued . . .